# Ambushed By Love

# *Ambushed By Love*

God's Triumph in Kenya's Terror

Compiled By

## Dorothy Smoker

CHRISTIAN • LITERATURE • CRUSADE
Fort Washington, Pennsylvania 19034

Christian Literature Crusade

U.S.A.
P.O. Box 1449, Fort Washington, PA 19034

Britain
51 The Dean, Alresford, Hants SO24 9BJ

Australia
P.O. Box 91, Pennant Hills N.S.W. 2120

New Zealand
126 Broadway, Palmerston North

© Copyright Dorothy Smoker, 1993.
First Edtion 1994

Cover Picture: SuperStock Inc

ISBN 0-87508-740-X

APPRECIATIONS

Heartfelt thanks to:

• The East Africa Revival Team, and especially the several hundred brothers and sisters of Kenya's Central Province who were involved. This is their book in every way.

• Dr. David W. Shenk, who encouraged me to consider gathering these testimonies, and when the work began, took it under the wing of the Eastern Mennonite Board of Missions.

• Carol Zimmerman Larsen, recently of "Focus on the Family" staff, for tireless, fine-comb editing and improving of my Swahili-style English.

• Michael and Anne Waterhouse Botwin, for outstanding service in taking most of the photos and for very helpful suggestions in editing.

• Rob and Elizabeth Toms, who bought my house and added money enough to get this project going—what vision!

• Ken Brown and Bob Delancy of Christian Literature Crusade, for excellent advice and editorial wisdom.

• All the dear ones, both in the U.S. and England, who supported this task by prayer and giving. God bless you!

• The Lord, for guidance, protection and health from begining to end.

Dorothy Waterhouse Smoker

"O Nebuchadnezzar, we are not worried about what will happen to us. If we are thrown into the flaming furnace, our God is able to deliver us; and he will deliver us out of your hand, Your Majesty. But if he doesn't, please understand, sir, that even then we will never under any circumstance serve your gods or worship the gold statue you have erected." (Daniel 3:16–18, TLB)

(LATER) The King said, "Praise the God of Shadrach, Meshach, and Abednego! He sent his angel and rescued these men who serve and trust him. . . . There is no other God who can rescue like this." (Daniel 3:28–29, TEV)

# TABLE OF CONTENTS

# FOREWORD

## A WORD ABOUT THE AMBUSH

### The Very Reverend John G. Gatu, Th.M., D.D.

This book is a collection of the stories of some of those Christians who suffered and learned the power of Calvary love by living through the furnace of the years of Mau Mau struggle for well over seven years, 1952 to 1960. They were church members who had responded to the message preached by brethren from Uganda about the need to be born again through the cleansing blood of Jesus Christ. The Ugandans had heard it from some people with transformed lives from Ruanda-Urundi. Now these Kikuyu of Central Kenya knew their sins forgiven by God's mercy, and that they had been given the hope of heaven and a wonderful life now.

Little did anyone know that a movement of peasant people, with no outside support, could resist so long the pressure of their whole tribe and of the British Colonial government as well. As you read, you will notice that many of these telling their stories started out as fierce Mau Mau guerillas in the mountain forests, or as members of the dedicated Mau Mau support army in the cities. One by one they were overwhelmed by the love, joy and fearlessness of those they killed or tried to kill. When these killers met no cursing but only forgiveness and prayers for their good, some were changed and may be said to have been ambushed by love.

For a long time since then, these revival brethren of Central Kenya, though urged to do so, have resisted the publishing of these accounts, fearing it would amount to self-glorification or something like blowing one's own trumpet. They have deeply felt that anything worth talking about should always and foremost give glory to Jesus Christ. We are not offering this book to you now to imply that we of

9

the East African Revival in Central Kenya are some kind of special people, but to give illustrations of God's miracles among ordinary peasants who trusted Him like Daniel's friends of old. They declared, "We are not worried about what will happen to us. If we are thrown into the flaming furnace, our God is able to deliver us; and he will deliver us out of your hand.... But if he doesn't, please, understand, sir, that even then we will never under any circumstance serve your gods or worship the gold statue you have erected" (Daniel 3:16–18, TLB). All praise and honor belong to God, who delivered them and us by His wonderful love at Calvary.

Now about the compiler. For a long time we were hesitant, and it was not until our dear sister Dorothy Smoker volunteered to do it that the brethren felt a little easy and then accepted the idea of producing a book. Dorothy and her beloved late husband, George, were missionaries with the Mennonite Church in what was then Tanganyika. They were among a number of missionaries who received the blessing of the East African Revival personally and identified fully with the brethren in these countries. Their contribution, particularly during the days of the State of Emergency, was in the production of the Swahili paper called "Mjumbe wa Kristo" or "Ambassador for Christ." Through it they gained a more intimate knowledge of the revival fellowship than many other expatriates, particularly during those days. Not only did Dorothy and George hear of God's doings, but they also witnessed it on many occasions when they traveled around Kenya. We of the East African Revival cannot thank her enough for undertaking this work. Although it agrees with her belief in non-participation in military matters, we know that the effort rose out of a deep and dedicated love for the brethren in East Africa and the conviction that such experiences should be shared more widely than on the slopes of Mount Kenya. I know Dorothy would not wish me to say this, but I feel that I must: If it had not been for her willingness to spend her meager savings as a career missionary, the revival brethren could not have undertaken this work, as they did not have the money to do so.

One person who was intimately involved with Dorothy, assisting her in the gathering of these facts, was Sister Naomi Gatere, who did not live to see the fruit of her labors. She, with two other sisters, was called to higher glory through a fatal car accident on July 30, 1993. We thank God for her zeal and commitment to the Lord and her desire that this book be published.

Almost sixty years after its begining, the Revival is alive and well here in East Africa, and it is the hope of all of us that this book will make some contribution and be for the enrichment of those who will read it. We pray that some of you will be ambushed by that love of Calvary as these were, and we shall with you thank and give glory to our Father in heaven.

John G. Gatu

Nairobi, September 8, 1993

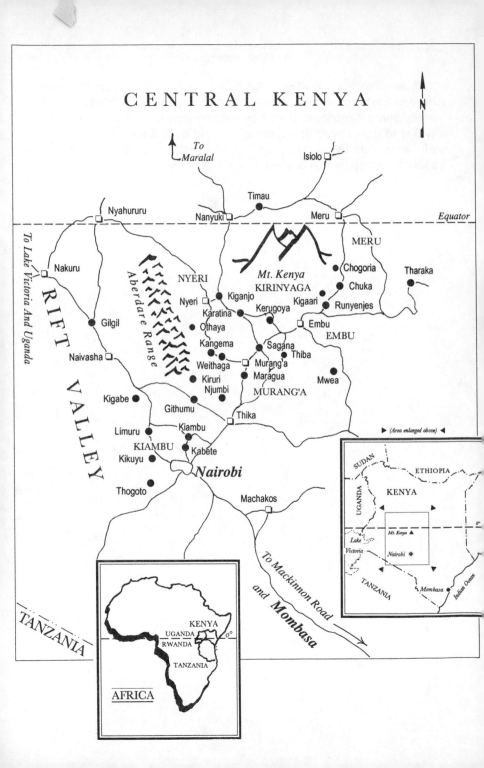

# CHRONOLOGY

1844–46 Missionaries Krapf and Rebmann begin work on the Kenya coast, mostly with freed slaves, under the auspices of the Church of England and the tolerance of the Sultan of Zanzibar.

1887 Imperial British East Africa Company is formed.

1891 Arrival of the first Scottish missionaries.

1895 Britain declares Kenya its Protectorate. The first station of the Africa Inland Mission is started.

1896 Building of the British railway is begun from Mombasa, the port city on the Indian Ocean. Built with 32,000 Indian laborers.

1897 Influx of mission societies into Nairobi and central Kenya.

1901 Railway is completed to Lake Victoria.

1903 First Scriptures in Kikuyu are published.

1904 First influx of white settlers from South Africa.

1914 World War I begins. Kenya is drawn into Britain's fighting in German East Africa, which becomes Tanganyika, now Tanzania.

1918 Global influenza sweeps across Kikuyuland, decimates the population. Much tribal land is temporarily unoccupied.

1920 The British Empire declares this land its "Kenya Colony."

1926 Alliance High School for Boys is begun at Kikuyu by the Alliance of Protestant Missions.

1929 Controversy over female circumcision causes widespread secession from Protestant churches in Kikuyu, Embu, Meru.

| | |
|---|---|
| 1930 | Anglican Divinity School is opened at Limuru. |
| 1937 | First visit of a team from the Ruanda Revival to Nairobi, with a week of meetings at Kabete and visits elsewhere. |
| 1938 | Ruanda Revival speakers at Kenya African Keswick convention. |
| 1942 | Oathing of freedom fighters secretly spreads in Nairobi. |
| 1943 | Kenya Missionary Council becomes Christian Council of Kenya. |
| 1946 | Jomo Kenyatta returns to Kenya from England. |
| 1947 | Kahuhia Revival Convention, first of many, as spiritual revival sweeps across Central Kenya. |
| 1948 | Kangaru Revival Convention; revival reaches Meru and Embu. |
| 1949 | 8,000 attend a revival convention at Kabete. |
| 1950 | 15,000 at revival convention in Thogoto, Kikuyu. |
| 1952 | Eruption of anti-British, anti-Christian violence in Kikuyuland by Mau Mau guerillas. October 20th, a State of Emergency is declared by the Governor of Kenya. Kenyatta and other leaders are jailed. |
| 1953 | First Christian martyrs are killed by the Mau Mau. |
| 1957 | Maseno Revival Convention (Western Kenya), the first All East Africa Revival convention after five years of Emergency. 12,000 in attendance. |
| 1958 | Kahuhia Convention, in Kikuyuland, 6,000 present. |
| 1960 | State of Emergency is declared ended. |
| 1961 | Release of Mzee Jomo Kenyatta, who exhorts Kenyans: "Forget the past and love your neighbor as yourself." |
| 1963 | Kenya's Independence Day, December 12th. Prime Minister Kenyatta says to the British: "You forgive us, and we will forgive you!" |
| 1964 | Vast multinational All East Africa Revival Convention at Mombasa, 20,000 in attendance. |

# LIST OF TERMS

*Words and customs which may need explanation,*
*or help in pronunciation.*

AMBUSHED: to be taken captive by surprise by those lying in wait along the way.

BURLAP: A coarse woven material of jute or hemp.

CHIEF: a native officer appointed by the British to rule over a section of Kenya during colonial times. A Chief was responsible to the British government to maintain law and order, collect taxes, etc. His staff consisted of an Assistant Chief, several Headmen in charge of districts, and soldier-guards.

CORNCRIB, GRANARY OR "GHALA": a huge woven basket on low stilts with removable lid, for storing a half ton or more of the grain harvested by a family. One or more ghalas would normally be found in the yard of a farmhouse. Some sort of ladder would be available for putting in and taking out the corn or millet after lifting the lid.

DATE OF BIRTH: When an interviewee is uncertain of the year of his/her birth, this indicates that the parents and nearby relatives were not literate at the time and did not record things. The year can be estimated, but with some uncertainty.

DEATH AND BURIAL: Inherited tribal laws of the Kikuyu group of tribes forbade touching a human corpse, even of close family members, so there was no burial of the dead. People facing imminent death either walked out into the forest or wilderness or were carried out, to be devoured by predators and scavengers. If someone died suddenly in a house, that house was cursed and untouchable with all that was in it, and strictly avoided. This custom, for the most part, has given way to "Western style" burials in this generation.

THE EMERGENCY: A "State of Emergency" was declared by the

British colonial government in Kenya on October 20, 1952. In American terms, this was a "declaration of war" by Great Britain against the Kikuyu rebels. Wartime regulations were in effect for about five years, but the State of Emergency was not formally declared at an end until 1960.

*FACING MT. KENYA*: The title of the book written by Jomo Kenyatta while he was living in England in the 1940's, which gives a scholarly but readable account of the culture-religion of the Kikuyu nation before the invasion by Europeans. It clarifies the reasons for some of the problems resulting from British colonial policies. This book became the bible of the young, educated leaders of the underground independence movement, and may account for the second aim of the "Mau Mau"—to get rid of Christianity as well as British government.

FEMALE CIRCUMCISION/GENITAL MUTILATION (clitoridectomy): was practiced on all girls by the Kikuyu and many other Bantu tribes. It was performed in tribal ceremonies, traditionally required before a girl's eligibility for marriage. Since there were no precautions for sterilization of instruments, this frequently resulted in maiming or bleeding to death and so doctors and other missionaries forbade it. Many church members defected over this issue in the 1925–1935 period. Two generations later, it has now almost entirely died out in the tribe through education and westernization.

"HARAMBEE!" (Hah-rahm-BAY): a shout signaling the moment (-BAY) for a united push or lift by a number of people on a job. It is used by workmen who need to lift or push a heavy object, i.e., by fishermen moving their boat into the water. This became the rallying cry of Jomo Kenyatta's new government in 1963. He used it as a shout to get all tribes to work together to build the newly independent nation.

HOME GUARDS: Kikuyu tribesmen who, along with natives of other tribes, were drafted by the British to act as policemen, guides, informants and interpreters in their fight against the Mau Mau.

KIKUYU (Key-KOO-yoo): a Negroid people of Kenya having an agricultural economy and speaking a Bantu-family language.

"KINU": a wooden mortar hollowed out of a large hardwood log. The hollowed space is two or three feet deep, with a base to enable it to stand upright to about four feet high. It is used by a woman standing up pounding grain or roots in it for food, using a long hardwood club as an outsized pestle or "mchi."

"MZEE": a special title of honor given to Jomo Kenyatta. It actually means "old person." Older members of a family were traditionally highly honored. "Mzee" gradually became used as an honorific when addressing anyone highly respected. As traditions have faded, it is now used in addressing almost any man whose name you don't know.

PERSONAL NAMES: Those who were born in non-Christian, traditional homes grew up with only tribal names (Mwangi, Wanjiku, etc.) until they were baptized. At baptism they chose, or were given, new foreign names, sometimes from the Bible (Samuel, Geoffrey, Naomi). Those who were born to Christian parents were usually given Western names at birth, as well as a tribal name.

PRONUNCIATION OF NG'A: African words (such as Murang'a and Ng'ang'a) have a soft pronunciation of the *ng'a* syllable, making it sound like "si*ng a* song" in English. The syllable itself has no special meaning; it is simply one of the common syllables of the Kikuyu language.

REMAND: to be put in custody, locked up in jail, pending a trial.

SISTER=WIFE: In tribal custom, a man respected and consulted his sister. But his wife, being purchased property, was treated as a slave and, by many men, frequently beaten. In the revival fellowship group, the position of a wife was lifted to being her husband's partner, helper and equal. Therefore, in order to indicate publicly this change in her position, a husband began speaking of his wife as "my sister." Since this would be meaningless in Western countries, "sister" in the original is here usually translated "wife."

SNOW: In one story, the phrase "as white as snow" is quoted. Snow is known to the people of central Kenya because of the two great snow-capped mountains they can see: Mt. Kenya and Mt. Kilimanjaro. Only a few of the people, however, have actually touched snow.

WOMEN'S MARRIED NAMES: Upon marriage, most Kenyan women will take their husband's family name as theirs. However, in some cases, they keep their original family name and append to it the first name of their husband, in a hyphenated form. For example: When Naomi Wanjiru married William Macharia she became Naomi Wanjiru-William. (See story on page 184.)

# 1

## THE CONFLICT—AND THE AMBUSH

### INTRODUCTION

In England it was called the "Lunatic Express." But British engineers, starting before the turn of the century, kept on building their "crazy" East African railway. It extended from Mombasa, on the east coast of what is now Kenya, to Lake Victoria in the heart of Africa. In spite of savage attacks by lions, and angry people—who at night ripped up the iron tracks laid in the daytime—they persisted. On the way, the railroad builders "discovered" and relayed news of the fertile Kenya highlands, extolled the great Rift Valley with its lakes, and confirmed the "snow-capped mountains on the equator" so recently ridiculed by many of the learned geographers of London.

Before the turn of the century, pioneer missionaries had come into central Kenya exploring the land, opening schools, hospitals and churches. In the lush land all around Mt. Kenya and west to the Aberdare Range, Scottish Presbyterians, Wesleyan Methodists, and the Church of England folk started working in separate areas of this huge Central Province. All of these ground-breakers knew that they were working in an area declared in 1895 to be a British protectorate, bordering the German-controlled Tanganyika to the south.

Mission schools became a quick success because young Kikuyu boys (and girls!) were fascinated with reading and writing. They often managed to get to school even without their parents' permission. They read the Bible, learned catechism, and most of them would join the local church—being especially attracted by the prospect of a new Western name at baptism! Most were longing for higher education, which a few did attain.

Then in 1920 the British Empire declared this protectorate a Crown

Colony of the Empire to be called "Kenya Colony." The Colonial Office advertised Kenya to prospective settlers as having good land and cheap labor. A Governor and administrators were sent from England to establish an administration intended to benefit both the indigenous people and the new settlers. Settler-farmers moved in rapidly to the fine farmland, now within reach of a railroad. They either did not realize or did not care that they were taking over tribal lands which had been passed down by father to son for generations. Some of the land they thought unoccupied was only temporarily empty, due to the devastation of the recent great influenza epidemic. Whatever the excuse, they later discovered that taking tribal land was a dangerous oversight, as also were the poor wages they paid. Both caused indignation and helped fuel the rebellion that would upset the settlers' plans for the future.

As early as 1921, African political protest began with a man named Harry Thuku and his East African Association. After Thuku was deported in 1922, others carried it on secretly. Its name eventually was changed to the Kenya Central Association, and in 1928 a young man named Johnstone Kamau Kenyatta became its leader. He soon realized that the local Colonial officials were not listening to African complaints, and that he would have to go to England to represent his people to the Cabinet and Parliament. There, in 1930, J. K. Kenyatta (as he was known) wrote for the London *Times* an eloquent and impassioned plea for consideration of the African people's dilemma in the colony of Kenya.

By the 1940's there were two very different grass-roots movements sweeping through the tribal areas of Kenya's Central Province. These were: (1) an underground political rebellion against British rule, and (2) a spiritual renewal in the churches. These two powerful forces were destined to clash in the "Mau Mau War" of the 1950's and affect each other considerably.

## THE SECRET REVOLUTION

In 1938 Kenyatta's thesis for an anthropology course at the London School of Economics was published as a book entitled *Facing Mount Kenya.* Peter Koinange, a close friend, had suggested that he needed to choose a better, shorter name than "Johnstone" to put on it. Together they coined the name "Jomo"—because they liked the sound of it, and it was close to the Kikuyu word for "pulling a sword from its scabbard." Kenyatta's book became well known in England

and was devoured by the restless young people living in Nairobi. It clarified for them who they were and the reasons for their resentment of British government policies. It helped to turn their grumbling into a full-blown revolt. This anger was smoldering during World War II, but it burst into flame at the end of it when Kenyan soldiers returned from overseas with new democratic ideas and new fighting skills.

Rebellion spread from Nairobi, the capital city, to all the towns and farmlands around Mount Kenya and the Aberdare Range. The organized political revolt was based in the Kikuyu tribe, but included its two cousin-tribes, the Meru and the Embu. These three tribes together were by far the largest tribal grouping in Kenya, with two to three million people.

In 1946 Jomo Kenyatta returned to Kenya to a hero's welcome. He added his insights to those of a council of trusted leaders whose plans were now well under way for an army to free their land and them from British colonial rule. The plans called for guerilla warfare against the white settlers. They planned to use trusted Kikuyu house servants of the settlers, who had become secretly a part of the rebellion, to kill their masters and steal their guns. There would also be lightning raids at night, followed by a quick return of the fighters to the safe shelter of their bases hidden in the dense mountain forests.

Their aim was to frighten and drive off the white settlers, reclaim tribal land and end British rule. They also had another goal: to get rid of the "new religion" Christianity. These discontented Kenyans suspected that missions had been a part of the colonial scheme for taking the land from the people. Tribal church members were seen as government collaborators, who should be won over or killed just like any other traitor to the freedom cause. Activists began saying everywhere, "Jesus didn't live here before the British came. He came on the first boat that brought these white people to our land. When the white rulers go home, they can take their Jesus with them!"

Kenyatta's book had triggered a revival of the tribal prayers and sacrifices which this educated generation had neglected. The rebels started praying every morning to Ngai, their god who lived on Mt. Kenya. They were making sacrifices to spirit powers, and taking oaths enforced by powerful curses connected with the evil spirit world.

The leaders of the insurrection wanted a totally united people with no traitors and no leaks. They planned to force every man and woman of the Kikuyu, Meru, and Embu tribes to take the traditional oath which they had adapted to this situation. Their oathing ceremony included the killing of a goat, drinking its blood, eating its flesh, and swearing both to support the Freedom Army and to give up Christianity. Anyone breaking the oath by refusing to kill, for instance, would die under its deadly, evil curse. There were further, advanced oaths for warriors and committed partisans. Many in Nairobi had taken the first oath as early as 1942. By threatening death to anyone who refused to take the oath, and by killing the first stubborn ones, they fully expected to coerce all the members of these three tribes to actively support the fight for freedom. They counted on the people's bitter resentment of government policies and of the low wages paid by all whites. It appeared at first that they would be able to persuade or force everyone to take the oath. Indeed, a large majority of church members and most of the Kikuyu in the employ of the British did take the oath secretly. The freedom fighters ("rebels" to the British) were confident they would succeed in achieving full unity because one thing they knew for sure was that every tribal person is terrified of death. Or so they thought.

As violence increased, on October 20, 1952, the Governor of Kenya abruptly announced on the radio that he had arrested Jomo Kenyatta and other known leaders, and he declared a "State of Emergency" in the country. This amounted to a Declaration of War by the British Empire against the Kikuyu-related tribes of the Central Province of Kenya, that is, against the guerillas who were being called "the Mau Mau." ("Mau Mau" is not a Kikuyu word, and its origin is disputed, but it was widely used as a name for the guerilla army.)

## THE SPIRITUAL RENEWAL

The other notable movement of the 1940's was a Christian spiritual awakening, at that time called the "Ruanda Revival." Ruanda (now Rwanda) was a small Belgian-controlled area west of Lake Victoria. The revival there was not only among the local populace but in time became an East Africa-wide renewal. It had already spread from Ruanda into Uganda by teams of Africans—with a few missionaries—all telling how their lives had recently been transformed by the Lord Jesus. Small teams of these enthusiasts came into Kenya from Uganda. One team reached the Nairobi area for a week of meetings in 1937. They were testifying how God had become real to them and changed them. At first only a few listened and responded. Young Obadiah Kariuki was one of these early ones; then dozens and later hundreds were renewed.

By 1940 there were thousands in Central Kenya whose daily lives were so obviously changed by Jesus that this became the exciting news of the day. The awakening spread from person to person through the local "grapevine," without any consultation with the authorities in the church denominations. The unofficial outdoor meetings, announced by word of mouth, caused much excitement and hundreds, sometimes thousands, of people hurried to see what was happening.

People of the communities affected—especially shop owners and those who were keepers of the peace—were delighted because these "revived" people were paying old debts and returning stolen property with apologies. Neighbors were attracted by the new lifestyle they saw in the homes of the revivalists. Wives were elevated to become respected partners in the home, and children were also affected. The joyous singing of families could be heard early every morning, rising through the grass roofs of many homes. No wonder others sought the "new birth" themselves; and when they did, they found themselves welcomed into a loving and supportive family of God—the "fellowship" in their neighborhood.

At first, some leaders of established churches felt by-passed and spoke against the movement, fearing it might be a dangerous cult. They heard that lay people were preaching, saying that baptism and confirmation were not enough to assure one of entrance to heaven. These unauthorized preachers were telling people they needed to come personally to Jesus for forgiveness of their sins and then testify openly to what He had done for them. Some missionaries and church elders were embarrassed to hear "good church members" admit publicly that they had been stealing church money or living in adultery, drunkenness or witchcraft before Jesus saved them. But before long everyone saw that the lives and homes of these people had changed remarkably. They were now living in peace and joy, working well at their jobs and also supporting the church generously. When they became the main Christian bulwark against the Mau Mau threat of takeover, the opposition of the church hierarchy faded away entirely. It was virtually gone by the time the Mau Mau conflict was half through. From then on, most candidates chosen for ordination came from this enthusiastic group, and the first African bishop of the Anglican Church was the same Obadiah Kariuki who had embraced this "revival" lifestyle when he first heard and saw it.

## THE UNBEATABLE FORCE MEETS A STRONGER POWER

The Freedom Army hadn't realized they would meet a roadblock in the close-knit "revival fellowship" which now numbered in the ten thousands, both in farming areas and in cities. The oath administrators had seen so many of the ordinary church people take the oath that they were really surprised by this minority of convinced Christians who fearlessly refused to take it. Even though the fellowship people were generally sympathetic with the Mau Mau goals of seeking national independence and restoration of their land, they could not accept the goat's blood, the curse, the promise to kill, and the banning of Jesus. These made it totally impossible for them to take the oath. Also, because they knew that Jesus had promised them eternal life in heaven with Him, they unanimously reached the decision that it was far better to die than to take the Mau Mau oath. There were probably close to a hundred who were killed simply for their loyalty to Jesus Christ, and these eventually were called "martyrs" by the churches. Those who escaped death were surprised every day to be alive, because they had deliberately chosen Jesus Christ and were ready to die for Him at any time.

Through all the war years, the renewal people—both those who lived and those who died—loved and forgave their enemies, trying earnestly to share with them "the better way." Even the greatest leader of the freedom fight, Jomo Kenyatta, was affected by this amazing love and forgiveness, as Bishop Obadiah Kariuki will tell in his account of visiting his brother-in-law, Kenyatta, in detention.

## THE SURPRISE ON INDEPENDENCE DAY

To the amazement of the freedom fighters, their hero Mzee Jomo Kenyatta, when he was released, apparently had had some change of mind, influenced by Christian love and forgiveness. In one of his first public statements he advised his countrymen, "Forget the past, and love your neighbor as yourself!"

Independence was granted to Kenya by Britain in December 1963. Mzee Kenyatta had been democratically elected to be the first Head of State in the newly independent country. There was to be a radio broadcast of the inaugural address of Kenya's first Prime Minister, soon to be called "President." His ex-freedom fighters were eagerly expecting that with independence they would be allowed to take some revenge on their enemies. So most of the remaining white settlers in Central Province had barricaded themselves in their homes, guns at hand, ready for an attack, while listening to their radios.

Radio waves took the Prime Minister's words around the world. Mzee Jomo Kenyatta spoke first to all the different tribes of Kenya. He challenged them to forget their prejudices and to all work together to build a great new African nation. His watchword was "HARAMBEE!"—"All together, now PULL!" Then Jomo amazed everyone by speaking directly to the "enemy"—those British colonialists who were still in Kenya. He invited any of them who were willing to help in building the new Kenya to stay, adding, "You forgive us, and we will forgive you!"

These eight words prevented a massacre and ended the war. The fearful settlers relaxed, amazed. Some white farmers and business people did stay and help. Others came later. Kenyatta's unity and forgiveness speech established a friendly atmosphere in the newly independent Kenya. It soon became known as a country willing to work peaceably with people of many nations for the common good.

The fight to gain self-rule and reclaim the land had been successful. Christianity, however, was certainly not ushered out of the country as the Mau Mau had planned. It only became stronger, purified through suffering. Near the end of his life, President Kenyatta said to those near him, "You may bury me as a Christian." And they did. This was not the Kenyatta of the early days!

## WHAT THIS BOOK IS

This book is basically oral history: accounts now written for the first time, related by some of the Christian survivors of the Mau Mau uprising. These are true stories of men and women, educated and uneducated, who describe what happened to them and to those near them in the 1950's. It is a record of sincere Christians in danger of death because of their faith, the story of a people who lost their fear of death and could love and forgive their would-be murderers. It is also the story of some of the fiercest fighters who were spiritually ambushed by the love and forgiveness of their enemies.

The faith and joy of these Christians in danger can challenge churches worldwide to relearn the power of the blood of the Lamb over all temptations and over all evil powers. From these Kenyans we may be able to learn the secret of turning bitter enemies into friends and brothers.

Amazingly, this movement with its great conventions and frequent small fellowship meetings is still alive. It is now called the "East

African Revival" and can be found in many places both in East Africa and overseas. It is characterized by the joy of being forgiven by God and by one's peers, the making of restitution, jubilant praise, and the loving affirmation of each other with a fraternal hug. The "fellowship people" have become valued in many communities of East Africa for loving-kindness toward neighbors, for their dependability, and for honesty with money.

So the stories recorded here, though mainly from the 1950's, include also a few out of the 1980's which give a glimpse of their children—the new generation in Kenya—who in the same spirit are both resisting corruption and loving their enemies, following in the footsteps of their fathers and mothers in the faith. These more recent accounts reveal the strength in two modern young families in Kenya who have surprised murderous gangs of thieves by meeting them with Christian love, earnest prayer and fearlessness.

The hope of those who have shared these experiences is that they will inspire their own grandchildren and great-grandchildren. They also want to encourage people in nations around the world who live in difficult and dangerous situations. To these they are saying, "Dare to trust in God through Jesus Christ. He will be with you, and whether you live or die you will come through the fire triumphantly!"

## THE CHURCH OF THE MARTYRS

After Kenya became an independent nation, it was decided that the new Anglican church in Fort Hall (now Murang'a Town) should be dedicated to the memory of the recent martyrs who had died for their stedfast faith in the Lord Jesus Christ. It became known as the Church of the Martyrs. The wrought-iron gate shows a rifle and a spear opposite each other, representing the colonial forces against the traditional Kikuyu sprear. (Jomo Kenyatta was called by Kenyans "Burning Spear.") Between the spear and the rifle rises the cross of Christ and a hovering dove of peace, symbolizing the spiritual power given to the martyrs and their fellows to love their enemies and change some of them into friends. (See picture section.)

On the main door of the sanctuary there is a brass plaque with the names of more than forty martyrs from the large Murang'a District who were known and counted at that time. We now know there were probably that many more in other districts around Mount Kenya, though we don't know all their names.

Inside the sanctuary, one whole wall is given over to a now famous mural painted by a young African artist. It depicts, African style, scenes of the life of Christ—from His birth to His resurrection. Underneath the panels is related the story of the Good News coming to Kenya, then an account of the fighters, the martyrs, and the exultant resurrection and victory of Jesus' people.

†     †     †

FIRST BISHOP AND FIRST PRESIDENT
Obadiah Kariuki and his brother-in-law Jomo Kenyatta

When I (Obadiah) was born in 1902 or 1903, I was named "Kariuki" for my grandfather and I observed all the traditional Kikuyu rituals for growing up, such as circumcision rites. My father's youngest brother, Thiong'o, however, had been baptized, together with his sister Nyambaara, at the Anglican Mission School. They had taken the names of Joseph and Mary. When my Uncle Joseph came and made a polite, formal request to my father to take me to live with him and go to school at Kabete, my father granted this request!

About this time, my family was evicted from their ancestral land at Kanjuu by the Colonial government. The land thus taken was sold to a newly arrived European settler-farmer, and we were made beggars. So British colonialism struck my family a very hard blow. We had no land to call our own and no other means of livelihood. If that were not enough, on that land the graves of all our forefathers were lost to us, including that of our dear grandfather Kariuki for whom I was named. My father moved to Ndumbu-ini where he died shortly after, and before long my mother died in childbirth and I was orphaned.

My uncle Joseph Thiong'o, my guardian, was a dedicated Christian and became the outstanding gentleman in our family. Through his own perseverance and hard work he became a wealthy man by the standards of those days. Looking back, I realize that I was very fortunate indeed to have him as my uncle. Through him God guided my footsteps toward Christian service.

He enrolled me in the mission school at Kabete when I was about 12 years old. Schools attracted me because of my burning desire to learn how to write the new, alien alphabet. My uncle had earlier astounded me by writing something on a piece of paper and later reading what he had written! I realized that this sort of "witchcraft" could only be understood by those who had gone to school, so I gladly went and learned that and much more. After a while I was able to earn my school fees by working a few hours every day in the nearby home of our compassionate headmaster Rev. Harry Leakey. He was the one who baptized me in 1922 and then sent me to the noted CMS Buxton School at Mombasa where I got religious training to become a mission school teacher.

After graduation, I spent a year at my old school as Canon Leakey's deputy. Then in 1925 I was given charge of the school at Kiambaa for two years, receiving solid support from Chief Koinange and his council of elders. I was 24 years old when I was nominated by Canon Leakey to be among the first students at the recently opened Alliance High School in Kikuyu. This was an overwhelming thrill for me. After the two years of high school, I married the daughter of Chief Koinange, Lillian Wairimu, and taught school until the year we went to St. Paul's Theological College in Limuru. By then we had four children, and it was a struggle to keep food on the table.

During the year at theological college, our Principal, Canon Butcher, showed us some magazine reports of the Ruanda Revival and challenged us also to seek the empowering of the Holy Spirit. Although I prayed ardently for God's power, I just got exhausted and hungry. My problem became clear to me in the next day's lesson from Isaiah 6:5–8, which tells how God's angel first brought a burning coal to cleanse the young prophet's unclean lips. Then when Isaiah heard God's call for a messenger he could say, "Here am I, send me!" I hurried out to my secret place in the bushes for meditation. I prayed with all my might for this kind of cleansing. I confessed my sins as He showed them to me. When I begged for God's forgiveness, I felt something escaping from my body and was pervaded by a spirit of joy and a sense of comfort. I could pick up my books and go home knowing that in His forgiveness I had found the power and glory of the Holy Spirit, and was ready to answer His call. All my life I have never gone back on the reality of what happened that day. Even when I was resented and ridiculed for it by my colleagues, I knew in my heart that God's power was available to me when I honestly dealt with my sins and received His forgiveness.

We, the theological students, were all given a year of field experience. I was sent to be interim pastor at Kabete and headmaster of the primary school there. Rev. Howard Church joined the staff at Kabete that year, and his brother from Ruanda, Dr. Joe Church, with a team of seven from Ruanda and Uganda, visited him. They shared their "revival" experience of walking in the light of Jesus Christ. Other Kenyans joined me in confessing their sins, being forgiven and becoming new witnesses of Christ. Many received Him into their lives for the first time. Simeon Nsibambi stayed at our house during those meetings, and through him my wife experienced the wonderful light of Christ.

Some of our church leaders opposed this "new teaching." When the revival message spread through the Kabete area, almost the whole council of elders felt the church was threatened by the "Followers of Ruanda." Some sneeringly dubbed them "Obadiah's Group." We were summoned before church courts and our meetings were banned from church buildings. We felt no resentment and enjoyed our fellowship under the trees.

The group became known for honesty and self-respect because the power of the Holy Spirit enabled us to publicly return any possessions or properties gotten illegally or contrary to Christian ethics. On the other hand, there were also some backsliders. But in spite of setbacks and opposition, the movement continued to grow across the whole of Kenya and East Africa.

There were two great revival conventions in 1949 and 1950. As they were going on, Kenya was undergoing political convulsions under the leadership of my brother-in-law Jomo Kenyatta. (We had married girls from the same family.) In 1952, the State of Emergency was declared. This resulted in a shift of public attention from the revival movement, as hostility and bloodshed came on the land from all quarters.

Personally, when I heard in the early fifties that the Mau Mau had started fighting for our rights as Kenyans, my sympathies were with them because of the suffering my family had gone through at the hands of colonialists. I did not see anything wrong with fighting for freedom in one's own country. What most of us in the church at that time objected to was the violence, coercion, and finally the forced oathing to make people join the Mau Mau movement. Our political leaders could not conceive of any way other than oathing to secure allegiance to their independence movement. But they made it impossible for many Christians to join the movement because such oathing called for a spiritual commitment which Christians could give only to Jesus Christ. The lack of Christian support in the movement was unfortunate. It was sad that the freedom movement early on sent young toughs to harass us in churches, overthrowing tables and pulpits and manhandling members at revival meetings as early as 1950.

By then I had become an ordained priest, had served in two pastorates and been a tutor for six years at the new St. Paul's Theological College. From St. Stephen's Church, Nairobi, at the end of 1951, I was posted as Rural Dean to Fort Hall (Murang'a Town).

I was ministering there when our Kikuyu people were killing each other for refusing to participate in forced oathing. The situation got too difficult for the missionaries who had been running the churches and pastorates before the Mau Mau disturbances. So they said it was up to us Africans to defend the faith with courage, even with our lives. It was a trying time. More blood was shed in Murang'a and Nyeri Districts than in any other region involved in the fighting.

Unfortunately, we were caught between two dangers: on the one hand, no Kikuyu, not even a revival brother, was above suspicion in the eyes of the colonial authorities during this period. But at the same time, anyone staunchly professing the Christian faith could suffer death at the hands of the Mau Mau freedom fighters.

So acute was the danger from these two opposite directions that our revival brethren stopped regular public meetings. Many took refuge in the comparative security of Weithaga mission station, while others moved into Murang'a Town where the armed government forces were stationed. At Weithaga, our group decided to carry on with reading the Bible and praying together that the Holy Spirit would visit us and give us strength. Together we asked God to protect not only believers but all people, so that peace would return to our country.

A colonial official came and informed us that he had some young people whom he would like to see praying with our group. The administration, he said, would reciprocate by providing us with fifteen armed men, because we were in great danger from Mau Mau terrorists and it was his duty to protect all people. I told him that we were willing to join in prayer with anyone as long as we were allowed to conduct our meetings as we saw fit. I said we did not need the type of protection that guns can give. My attitude was exceedingly annoying to the official. His proposal had not been made because he thought his men needed prayer or because he was suddenly interested in protecting us. We found out he actually suspected us of not being sincere in our professed worship of Christ. He thought our meetings were a way of disguising and sheltering

Mau Mau followers. Thus he wanted to bring in his own people to spy on our activities.

In those days, wherever I happened to be, especially at Sunday services, I urged my people to pray for those who had gone into the forests around us to fight. They were our own flesh and blood and were undergoing untold suffering. We prayed that the bombs might miss their targets and that the children might come home alive. This called for real courage on my part, for there were always informers in our congregations.

During the Mau Mau revolt, many people were being killed. They were mostly the forest fighters or the informers, most of whom were killed by one side or the other. During 1953 and 1954 I had to perform Christian burials almost every morning. In the end, I found I did not fear death anymore.

I often needed to travel at night, in the car which had been given me by the Mission, to visit those who were wounded and suffering. I had no driver's license, so one night I asked my European colleague to drive the car for me because I felt compelled to go and find out if a rumor was true that one of my congregation had been killed in the bush. He objected, "But you may be ambushed on the way, either by Mau Mau or by these crazy English youngsters *they* have sent out!" My reply was that there was so much killing going on that I was completely unconcerned for my life. I repied, "I know I shall die one day; so if I die, let it be in the service of God's people. But I simply have to go and find out if the rumor is true." Eventually my colleague came with me and we drove through the back country and found the body of our parishioner. We immediately organized a Christian burial service and afterward returned home without a scratch, having completed our duty as Christian clergy. Through this sort of daring, we were able to unite our flock under the cross of Christ, and for this I can only give thanks to God for His grace.

Eventually, as a result of our uncompromising stand, we were harassed neither by the Mau Mau nor the administration. Both sides came to realize that we were not hypocrites but were, in fact, true worshipers of Christ. For myself, I am deeply convinced that Christians, especially those who faced death rather than take the oath, contributed to the return of peace to this country. Their blood, as much as any other, nourished the tree of freedom. Many Christians were detained and died in detention camps, but today we are a free people in the eyes of God and the world because we were not afraid to shed our blood to bring about change.

In the midst of all this spiritual isolation, tension and social muddle, I appealed to the colonial government for permission to visit Jomo Kenyatta in detention at Maralal. My action was not based on the fact that I had now become the bishop in Kikuyuland, but because he was my brother-in-law and had been a long-time friend. I asked myself, "If politicians from different parties have gone to see him, why not a representative of the church?" I was surprised not only to be given permission but also transportation from Nairobi to Lokitaung. As a result, Kenyatta and I met again after seven years of separation.

I was allowed to stay with him for almost an hour. We discussed various aspects of life in Kikuyuland. He was anxious to know what was going on among his people. I tried to relate the events that had occurred since his detention as well as I could remember them. Before I left, he said he was extremely happy to talk with someone who was a close friend and relative. He also expressed his need for a Bible. Luckily enough, I had taken one with me. I was excited by his humble request, and I presented my Bible to him. Later he told me he read it from beginning to end! I found out from him that the prisoners were awakened about five o'clock in the morning and forced to work in a quarry until eleven a.m., being subjected to inhuman treatment by the warders. From eleven o'clock on, in the intolerable heat of the desert day, he said, they had nothing to do, and he enjoyed reading his Bible.

After this visit, I went, with two other church officials, to see the Governor of Kenya, Sir Patrick Renison. I urged him seriously to consider freeing Jomo Kenyatta from detention. I told him I was sure that such a step would not result in chaos but lead to peace and stability. This was a real risk, and it took all the courage of my Christian conviction. Our meeting took place in 1958.

After that, I organized a rally at Murang'a to which people of all denominations and religions were invited to pray for the return of peace and unity to our country. A large number came despite the barriers and restrictions on travel. I told the people who gathered, "This is a big day for the church of God. It is a day to pray for the release of Jomo Kenyatta." For years Kenyatta's name had become sinister to white settlers, and others had been known to lose their lives for simply mentioning it. To many therefore it sounded immoral for an African bishop to stand in a pulpit and pray for

Kenyatta! But I had taken courage from him during my visit, and my love for him had been regenerated at our meeting. I was convinced that his release would only benefit the country and the Christian community. I was encouraged and gratified that rain fell as we were making our petition to God—I felt a sign had been given that our prayers were heard. We now are witnesses that my predictions were right.

Jomo Kenyatta was released in 1961, and in 1963 Kenya was granted independence! I was not surprised that when he came to organize his government, the new head of state stressed the message of love and forgiveness. As he put it in a Kikuyu proverb, "We shall not give to a hyena twice," meaning that we should not demean ourselves to the level of our oppressors by becoming oppressors in our turn.

(Excerpts, by permission, have been taken from Bishop Kariuki's autobiography: *A Bishop Facing Mount Kenya*, Uzima Press, Nairobi, 1985.)

Comments by the Very Reverend John G. Gatu, Th.M, D.D., former Moderator of the General Assembly of the Prebyterian Church of East Africa: The Right Rev. Bishop Obadiah Kariuki was among the first Kenyans to be affected by the preaching of the revival message. At first there were many people who doubted that a priest in the Anglican Church could be "a real brother in the Lord." Bwana Obadiah, as he was fondly known, was able to do exactly that. In the early days, both in Uganda and Kenya, revival brethren were put out of the Church or excommunicated because their testimonies were not considered to be in keeping with the tradition of the Church.

Bwana Obadiah and Canon Elijah Gachanja remained faithful to both the Church and the Revival Movement and therefore became stalwarts in the revival fellowship in those early days. During the State of Emergency, 1952–1956, as Rural Dean stationed at Weithaga, Bwana Obadiah was a great source of strength and encouragement to the many who had to leave their homes and dwell at the mission. These were not Anglicans only, but also those of other denominations.

When, in 1955, the Anglican Church of Kenya decided to have suffragan bishops, Bwana Obadiah Kariuki and Festo Olang' were the first to be so consecrated at Namirembe Cathedral, Kampala, Uganda. This was also a landmark in the East African Revival because both of these were strong members of the Revival Movement and therefore this meant an indirect recognition of the effect of the revival within the Church.

Even those of us who were not of the Anglican persuasion felt so spiritually uplifted by this as to consider them "our bishops too," something which a Presbyterian would normally find difficult. We all owe him a great debt for the way he helped many of us in the ordained ministry, without any of the denominational prejudice which was very common in those days. Praise be to God!

# 2

# ENEMIES WHO BECAME FRIENDS

*"But God's mercy is so abundant, and his love for us is so great, that while we were spiritually dead in our disobedience he brought us to life with Christ. It is by God's grace that you have been saved."*

Ephesians 2:4–5 (TEV)

*"You have heard that it was said, 'Love your friends, hate your enemies.' But now I tell you: love your enemies and pray for those who persecute you, so that you may become the sons of your Father in heaven."*

Matthew 5:43–44 (TEV)

*"Never take revenge, my friends . . . . Instead, as the scripture says: 'If your enemy is hungry, feed him; if he is thirsty, give him a drink; for by doing this you will make him burn with shame.' Do not let evil defeat you; instead, conquer evil with good."*

Romans 12:19–21 (TEV)

### INTRODUCTION

During the large 1958 Revival Convention at Kahuhia in the foothills of the Aberdare Mountains a man stood up in the crowd and said, "I was one of those who murdered Andrew Kanguru, and when I went back to the forest I couldn't sleep, thinking how he loved us and prayed for us before he died."

(It seems that the day after the murder of Andrew, this freedom fighter, with others of the gang, hid in the forest across from the churchyard where Andrew was to be buried. They wanted to see if they had accomplished their purpose of scaring the "saved ones" into joining the fight. There they watched the joyously triumphant crowd who had gathered to celebrate Andrew's "coronation" in heaven! And how they sang! The Mau Mau fighters were stunned and said to each other, "Well, we didn't accomplish much, did we?")

At the convention this ex-Mau Mau continued, "I couldn't fight, so I was captured and put in a detention camp. There God found me and Jesus changed my life. Now I've been released and I've come to see if Andrew's wife is still alive. If she happens to be here, I'd like to ask her to forgive me." She was there, and she went to him lovingly and said "Brother, we forgave you that night!"

• • •

About this same time, in Kirinyaga District south of Mt. Kenya a man named Nathaniel Kamuye, though a church member, had joined the fighters and become leader of an undercover gang who were operating to clear out the the "traitors" from the villages. These spies were still living in their homes outside the forest, so they wore masks in order not to be recognized when they seized people and administered the oath.

In June 1954, Kamuye's gang brought in a young fellow named Gathiomi who, though the rest of his family had been cooperative, was stubbornly resisting taking the oath. The fighters treated Gathiomi cruelly, chopping him with knives, beating him with clubs, hanging him by a rope and then dropping him down hard, threatening him with a slow, painful death—but he continued to resist. He would only gasp, "I forgive you, but I can't drink the blood of your goat because I have taken the blood of Jesus Christ." Kamuye couldn't believe that a boy of 19 or 20 who hadn't yet been baptized could resist with such determination. Finally, promising to take the blame, he persuaded the gang to let the boy go home if he was still alive and able to walk. So they agreed. To their great suprise he was able to slowly walk home, *and he did not report the mistreatment to the police!* In every way he showed them he had forgiven them, as he had said.

Kamuye, that Mau Mau leader, is now Pastor Nathaniel, who still points to Daniel Gathiomi as the one who first showed him the power and forgiveness of God in Jesus. (See the picture of them together in the center pages.)

• • •

In the Kiambu District, not very far from Nairobi City, there was a fierce and dedicated Mau Mau fighter named Kibe, a man full of hate to whom murder came easy. But he, too, was ambushed by love while he was still captain of his gang in the forest.

Late one night, Kibe's determined band of Mau Mau fighters went to break into a house and kill all who were in it. While circling the house, they heard the people inside praying earnestly to God for "those dear people in the forest whom He loves." These believers were asking God to supply the Mau Mau fighters' needs, and to protect them so He would have time to reveal Himself to them and save them from being lost. Amazingly, these Christians were pleading for the lives of these men so they could go to heaven when they died! This was too much for the fighters who were outside listening. They could not attack and kill those who would pray so earnestly for them. So Kibe's gang slipped quietly back into the forest, very puzzled and shamefaced.

Next, Kibe's men were ordered to kill "a troublesome Christian" named Simon. When they went to his house, he opened his door to them and fed them a fine meal of hot sweet potatoes and prayed God's blessing on them. They had been famished and ate almost without realizing what they were doing. In the end, all the would-be killers ran away and hid in the forest. To Kibe, alone in a forest hideout, God revealed Himself and forgave him. Right there this Mau Mau captain became a believer in Christ.

You may read their stories as they themselves told them. It is interesting to note that Simon and Kibe had been boyhood playmates, both living with their parents on the Karen Blixen coffee farm near Nairobi. Karen's story is featured in a book by Isak Dinesen and in a film called "Out of Africa."

There are other testimonies by hardcore forest fighters or activists who turned to the very Jesus they had sworn in the Mau Mau oath to banish from the country. Each of these found life abundant in Him. Two or three of these ex-Mau Mau fighters became, and still are, outstanding evangelists in East Africa.

## A SWEET POTATO SURPRISE
### Paul Kibe, Kiambu

As a child, I didn't want to go to school because I didn't want to have to listen to Christian teaching. My parents were working on the white settler's farm in the area that is now called Karen, a suburb of Nairobi. I hated the testimonies of African neighbors called "saved people," and I hated the white people. I wanted our land to be free from their rule. Though I didn't go to school, I learned to read at home with the help of some people who knew how.

In 1946 I took the oath to drive the English out of our country. I continued in secret politics until 1952 when the Emergency was declared. Then I immediately went into the nearest forest to join the guerilla fighters. I fought with them for three years without a break, finding it easy to sneak out at night to steal goats and cattle and bring them into the forest for our food. I became leader of my band of Mau Mau. We had guns, pistols and long knives. I taught my colleagues my hatred of white people, the colonial government and those "saved ones" in our tribe whom we called traitors. I didn't know that God had other plans for me.

One night we were quietly surrounding a house of stubborn Christians, intending to break in and kill everyone. As we got near the house, we heard voices coming from a group inside, mostly women, praying for all of us whom they loved who were out in the forest! They were earnestly asking God to protect us so we would have a chance to get to know Him. We were superstitious enough to be afraid of the power in there, so one by one we quietly left and went back into the forest. Even though I hated people like this, there was a small voice inside me telling me that what they believe is true. Slowly it dawned on me that if I should ever turn to Him, He would forgive all my sins and give me eternal life. How I hated that voice! I determined not to listen to it and refused to think about it.

The enemy British were bringing in big guns and airplanes. They had cut us off from all access to food supplies outside the forest, and in our lowland forest there were almost no wild animals left to hunt. So we were beginning to face great hunger, eating mainly leaves and grass, but as we grew thin our hatred and determination only increased.

Our next assignment was to kill and rob a young Christian farmer, Simon Ng'ang'a. No one knew we had been childhood playmates on the coffee farm. When I was chosen to be the one to strike him first, I took a stronger oath, with a terrifying curse on it, to strengthen me to kill this traitor.

That night we slipped out of the forest and started pounding on his door. I shouted. He recognized my voice and called to me to wait a minute, he would come to the door as soon as he lit the lantern. He opened the door with a big smile, holding up his lantern. We were all met with the wonderful aroma of hot cooked sweet potatoes! We were angry, but very hungry.

"Come in, friends!" he welcomed us loudly. "Come sit at the table and have a meal with me." He brought a huge tray of hot sweet potatoes and made a lot of sweet, milky tea, a meal I hadn't seen for years. We sat down.

"First, let us give thanks!" He raised his hands and prayed, thanking the Lord for the food and for "these dear ones You have brought to enjoy it with me." He asked Jesus to bless us and protect us and save us by His blood unto eternal life. He really poured out his heart for us. All three of us ate a big meal, then not one of us could kill him.

We each ran off into the forest in a different direction, trying to get as far as possible from the others. I was imagining what the gang would do to me if either of the others reported my cowardice. I remained in hiding for three days, dreading the power of the black curse of evil spirits which I had come under when I took the last oath to kill Simon. Besides that, I began to feel the much greater power of the terrible judgment of God on me for all my sins of murdering, stealing, serving evil spirits, and much more. Finally I told God I was willing to die for my sins if only my spirit could be healed, set free and joined to His Spirit. He showed me clearly that Jesus had already suffered and died for my sins and paid the full price to set me free.

On the 23rd of April, 1955, I gave up the struggle and asked Jesus to forgive me. He forgave all my sins and washed my heart clean. I knew I was saved. I deserted from the Mau Mau and walked out of the forest with no weapons, lifting up a branch of a tree in each hand. The government had promised amnesty to any fighters who surrendered in this way, and had spread leaflets in the forests telling us this.

I hadn't bathed or cut my hair for three years, but I didn't remember how filthy I was when I went straight to the District Officer. I told him, "I have left the army of the Mau Mau and have been a very bad man, but God has turned my spirit around. I can no longer kill people, because Jesus won't let me. From now on I will be telling people about Jesus, because He has forgiven me my many bad sins."

The District Officer said, "All right, you go report to the Chief and the Headman, and we'll keep watching you for a while."

I went into town and found some of the fellowship people, and told them, "I have been a bad man, a murderer and under the control of evil powers, but the Lord Jesus has forgiven me and set me free. I am happy and can love those I once hated, because I have Him." Some must have thought I was lying or joking, seeing me so filthy and with my hair twisted into dreadlocks. But they received me and took me to bathe, got me clean clothes and cut my hair. They received me lovingly and soon I realized that I was as clean inside as out. Ever since, I have been preaching Jesus, and I love Him today.

## A TOP AGENT DEFECTS
Phillip Kibotho, Kiambu

I was born in 1914 in Murang'a, but in 1917 we moved to Kiambu. I didn't know my father, who died when I was a baby. When I was six years old I began herding the family goats for my mother. When I was older, my mother's brother took me home with him to go to school. My mother was not happy about it. I stayed only three months, having learned nothing, and preferring to dance and sing the Kikuyu songs at home with my friends.

When I was fourteen, I was herding and working part time in the kitchen of a white family who lived in the Aberdare forest. In 1929, while I was herding, I went to listen to a Sunday service in a nearby church. There someone read Revelation 9:1–11 about the great locusts who ate up the people who did not have the mark of God on their foreheads. I remembered the chance I had had to go to school and learn to read, and I thought with horror that if I had stayed in school I wouldn't be eaten by those locusts! So I determined to learn to read, even though I had to do it in the evenings. I found some boys who were going to school and asked them to show me the first letters. I scratched them with a stick on my leg, and quickly learned A–E–I–O–U and KA–KE–KI–KO–KU, etc. In three months I could read the Kikuyu Bible.

In 1930 I went to work for an Asian in Nairobi for six shillings a month. In the city I bought a hymn book and marched on Sunday with the Salvation Army. I preferred the first church I had visited, the Africa Inland Mission Church, because they baptized under the water. In 1933 I returned home and went to the Africa Inland Church where I was taught and baptized that year.

Back in Nairobi with my aunt, my father's senior wife, I saw her son had written on a small blackboard: 2 x 2 = 4. My head began to spin. I could read books but had not heard of arithmetic. I was ashamed, but felt that once I understood how it worked, I could figure it out. I studied numbers diligently during the time I was working in 1934 and 1935. From then on, I taught reading, writing and arithmetic to other laborers on white men's farms, for which I charged no fees. I married my wife in 1940 in an Africa Inland Church where I was sometimes the preacher. Shortly after my marriage we moved to another white settler's farm where I was promoted rapidly. I had already learned to speak and understand English, and now I learned Italian from a war prisoner on assignment there. So I could translate for the farmer and the workmen-prisoners he had taken on. I was also my employer's hunter for meat, and their cook. Finally I was farm manager and accounts clerk while the owner was gone, at the high wage of twenty shillings (almost $3) per month!

In 1942, feeling I had learned it all, I thought, "If we Kikuyu could all agree together, we could drive the white people right out of our country." When I suggested this to others, they said I was crazy. I explained, "It was good that they came and taught us their wisdom, but now we have learned it and don't really need them. They could go home. If someone lights a lantern for you after dark, that is good. But in the morning you don't need it and you turn it out." My friends told me not to say such things, but I thought them. I went on attending the Africa Inland Church and became a trusted elder there.

In February 1948 I went to visit a friend in Naivasha and he took me to see an oathing ceremony. I immediately took the Mau Mau oath to join with others in driving the white man out of our country, as I had dreamed. First I burned my identity card and then decided not to go back to the white farmer. I was afraid that with all this fresh hatred I felt for whites, I might kill him some night. Then I began figuring out how to give every Kikuyu the oath, and was also making plans for the fighting we would need to do. In 1950 I began administering the oath in Nairobi, and established a supply base to support the forest fighters. I was ready to respond to every request from the Freedom Army and its War Council, and could send out to them whatever supplies they asked for. I could also receive and give shelter and provisions to those who came out of the forest. I had managed to steal rubber stamps from every government department and had the forms for sending Mau Mau in a "legitimate way" to the hospital for treatment. I became the primary contact man in Nairobi for the Mau Mau generals.

Although I had never liked deception, I still went to church every Sunday morning at ten, and devoted the rest of the day and week to Mau Mau work. My preaching occasionally helped to disguise my work for the freedom cause.

Eventually I heard that British soldiers were searching for me. As their hunt grew closer, I asked the War Council for permission to join the fighters in the forest. They needed me in Nairobi, but finally gave permission. The day I was saying goodbye to my team members in Nairobi, I was arrested and put in jail.

The years that followed were full of court trials, and I could usually confuse or threaten the witnesses against me. I had times of hard labor and other times of special treatment. There were frequent beatings by white officers and then favors from African guards to whom I secretly gave the oath. One night in a cell by myself, I made two prayers: "God help me not to get other fighters in trouble. And keep me from worrying about my family." (I had four children at that time.)

Once when I was moved from one jail to another, I met a man who was saved. His testimony and his peace made a deep impression on me. Both of these were new to me, and I couldn't forget him. Later when I was in a camp in the Northern Frontier, I clearly heard God's Spirit saying to me, "Be saved!" But Satan answered, "You can't. You would be killed!" I was distressed. I previously had threatened to kill fellow prisoners by "accident" if they became disloyal. It would be easy to do, and now I faced that possibility myself.

A true Mau Mau always prayed at dawn facing Mt. Kenya, in the names of the traditional father and mother of the tribe. I went on praying with them, but quietly prayed in Jesus' name. I felt I ought to stand up and confess my sins and declare my faith in Jesus, but it was just too dangerous. I was too well known. I was troubled. When I tried to sleep at night, a parade of my many sins would pass in front of me, and the question came, "How can I be rid of these without confessing them openly?" Finally, after I had been moved to the huge Manyani Detention Camp, I decided it would be worth being killed in order to be free of this inner condemnation.

It was July 31, 1955, and preachers had been standing outside the wire fence trying to preach, but no one listened. I asked permission to stand out there and speak with the microphone. The authorities agreed. The prisoners all gathered quickly to hear what I would say. I didn't say much about the oath, but I told about my life, my sins, and how Jesus had come to me to forgive and save me. I confessed that I had been afraid to say this openly for fear of being killed, but now I was not afraid any more.

When I went back into the camp, the other Mau Mau prisoners

were all quiet and avoided me. I found out that they thought I had lost my mind and were sure that very soon I would be sent to the hospital for the insane. They were also afraid I might become violent at night, and so kept their distance. They were more convinced of my insanity when I began to preach to the British officers and the Kenyan guards. I was content to stay in detention because I felt sure the Lord was going to return soon and I would go to Him, so it didn't matter where I was. I was more eager to see Him than to go home and see my family. I had wonderful peace and knew I was a free man despite being locked up.

After a year or so I was given privileges to conduct services in other camps and even outside in the community. At that time I was in a camp near Murang'a Town, and when I went out on Sundays I got to know Heshbon Mwangi and the other brethren of the fellowship meetings. I had never heard of fellowship meetings before, but the Lord had been teaching me many things and we discovered that we were one in spirit.

I was released in 1957. I had much restitution to make, and forgiveness to ask of many. I went wherever the Lord prompted me to go. I also went back to preach in the detention camps. Since my conversion my eyes have been on Jesus alone. When the way gets hard, the thing that has enabled me to keep going is being quick to repent and to apologize. My peace is steady because I keep on being cleansed by Jesus' blood. I went back to the white farmers from whom I had stolen things and to whom I had lied, and asked forgiveness. I couldn't find an Italian I had cheated, but wherever I could, I asked forgiveness of those to whom I had given the Mau Mau oath and of those who had been my partners in sin.

I testify to Christians, "If you get saved without repenting and making things right, you will grow colder every day and will eventually give it up." God has taught me that when I meet a real problem not always to pray that He take the difficulty away, but to be willing to walk with Him through it. He is a truly wonderful Saviour!

### FROM ACTIVIST TO MODERATOR
John Gatu, Kiambu, Nairobi

My father and mother were among the first converts of the Gospel Missionary Society (Baptist). I went to school in Kambui and was baptized in the Baptist tradition. I was what you might call a good boy. In 1941, however, when I went into the army I started enjoying

myself like any young man. I drank and smoked and did many other
bad things. I was in the East Africa Signal Corp serving in Kenya,
Somalia, and Ethiopia. As a result of my drunkenness, my rifle was
stolen when I was in Addis Ababa, and I was sentenced to prison for
56 days. Two days after I arrived in jail, however, the guards discovered that I could speak some English, so I was asked to become
official interpreter. As a result, I was able to stay in the sergeant's
mess and was treated like an officer! I lost my Christian faith completely in the army, but I still carried a Bible in the bottom of my kit
bag.

I was appointed to represent Kenya in the Victory Parade for
World War II in London in June 1946, and there I first met Mzee Jomo
Kenyatta. This was quite an experience for me, as I had heard much
about him.

After I left the army in 1948, I tried quite a few new things. I had
some further training and tried making films and also journalism.
This was a time when the Spirit of God was working very much in
Kenya. In 1949 I was in Nairobi working for the Colonial Film Unit,
but I was getting tired of Nairobi life, and heard there was a job of
clerk available at the mission office near our family home in Kambui.
I thought if I could get that job I would be very happy. I had worked
in a legal office and taught myself typing in the army. So when I
applied, I got the job, and started working there in February 1950.
This took me into an area where the Revival Movement was very hot.
There were people preaching in marketplaces and on buses.

I was much more attracted, however, to the underground revolution
spreading through the tribe. People were saying, "This Jesus is a
white man, and didn't live here before the English came. He came on
the ship that brought the first white man to Mombasa!"

Here I was a clerk in a mission office where a lot of Christian
things were happening. But the fact was that I had met Jomo Kenyatta
and I was also, on the side, working for a newspaper which was
very political. We reported many of Kenyatta's speeches. I became
radically involved in the underground movement. I took the Mau
Mau oath, and after a short time I started giving it to other people.

My conscience was disturbing me. My Christian upbringing was
still very much in me. I went to church with my wife, Rahab, on
Sunday mornings. But after the service I would disappear for the rest
of the day so I could go to administer oaths. I felt I had all the reasons
why we should fight the white man, and why I didn't believe in this

Christianity. I explained it as the white man's way of disguising himself so he could steal our land. I tried to prove that the coming of missionaries was a preparation for colonialization and wrote some articles on this for newspapers. I was living a double life.

One morning—it was the 21st of October, 1950—I awoke after a very bad night worrying about many things. I opened my Bible. Just like that my eyes fell on the Epistle of James chapter 1, verses 22 and 23, where it states that we must be doers and not just hearers. It goes on to say that if you are a hearer only you are like someone who looks at himself in a mirror, then walks away and forgets all about it. I had never known anything to grip me like those words did. They described just the kind of life I was living. I would go to some of these conventions and I would inwardly laugh at people who were standing up and giving their testimonies and weeping for their sins, and I thought "For heaven's sake, what are they weeping for?" It came to me very clearly that the words of James described me. I would hear the Word of God and forget it. I didn't know the person I was in God's eyes.

I went to church that morning and I can't remember what the preacher said because the words of James were ringing in my heart in a way I could not resist. At the end of the service I stood up and said I wanted to say something. They all thought I was giving an announcement from the mission station. But just before I got up I had realized that this is none other than the Holy Spirit speaking to me personally, and I had just said to Him, "Lord, I accept that this is You speaking to me. Forgive me all my sins, and accept me from this day onwards." So when I stood up I said, "I want to tell you that something has just happened to me, something very unusual." And I told them the whole story and how I came to read those words and commit my life to Jesus Christ. And I asked them to pray for me and help me ever to live for Him. There were such praises to God in that church! I got a warm welcome by the believers.

My old friends said, "Oh, John is just trying to keep his job with the mission." Others said, "Give him three months!" But the Lord went on helping me, and suddenly I felt an urge to involve myself in Sunday School. I organized a class, and by December we had several groups ready to meet young people of another church in a Scripture memory contest. We did very well with repeating verses. When we came back from the Sunday School Rally, an elderly gentleman told me he had said, "Wouldn't it be a wonderful thing if this young man

John were to be interested in the ministry of the church!" Before long, it became very clear to me that the Lord was calling me to the full-time ministry of the church.

The Lord gave me good training in the local Theological College, where my family lived with me most of the time during the Mau Mau fighting. Occasionally we were in danger. One night, we and the children all had to climb up into a tree to avoid being in the middle of an attack, but God kept us safe.

After a brief time in a parish, I was made Deputy General Secretary of the Presbyterian Church. I was sent for further training to Scotland, later to Pittsburgh for administrative skills, and later to Princeton for a world view. Between these times I was made General Secretary, and finally Moderator of the Presbyterian Church in East Africa. At the same time I was Chairman of the All Africa Council of Churches and worked for national reconciliation in Nigeria and Sudan.

During all my life since the Lord saved me, it has been in the revival fellowship that I keep being personally challenged and refueled for spiritual growth. Our honest sharing in small groups is the one thing above all else the Lord has used to keep me going and restore me to seeing Jesus Christ as the center of my life. The minute I start to deviate from the center and try to build something on the side, I have needed the brethren to help me to come back to Him. They have always done it. For this I praise God.

## THE SECRET REVOLUTION GROWS
### Zekaria Mutunga, Meru and Nairobi

I was brought up in a traditional Meru home and attended a Catholic school where I learned church ritual but was not baptized. As a young married man I went to Nairobi in January 1948. At first I had work tending a white man's garden. Then I joined a crew of builders, first as an apprentice, then a builder. There I got involved in the fast-spreading, secret freedom movement later called Mau Mau. All over the city and in African suburbs there were clandestine night meetings to discuss how to get rid of British rule and reclaim our hereditary land. All of us who had taken the secret oath had membership cards and our names were written in the books kept at our headquarters. (These books were later seized by the police!)

In August of 1948 there was a general strike by all African workers for higher wages. At that time ordinary laborers were getting merely

12 shillings a month (about $1.50), with up to 100 shillings (about $12) being paid for clerical work or teaching. A Senior Chief (government-appointed official in charge of a county) was getting only 16 shillings ($2) a month! My crew went on strike with all the other African workmen. Chief Peter Koinange sent out his agents on bicycles to all the white settlers' farms in his county, with orders to cut off an ear of any Kikuyu worker who had refused to strike! Harassed British administrators called a large meeting and asked why we had gone on strike. We replied, "We want higher wages!" (Actually we wanted much more than that!)

Within a few days Eliud Mathu, our first African Member of Parliament, informed us that Jomo Kenyatta had gone to negotiate with the white leaders and that they had agreed to raise the minimum wage to 100 shillings a month, so we went back to work. But we were still seething inside at the huge difference between our wage and that of any white person doing the same thing. That year my building crew was working on a wing of the King George Hospital in Nairobi.

I remember a large night meeting in 1951 in Kaloleni, a "black" section of Nairobi. Both Eliud Mathu and Jomo Kenyatta were there. We were gathering money, and with each man giving only a five pence coin, we filled six burlap bags full! These were put into Kenyatta's car. I remember Jomo saying, "We people of Africa move slowly, but we have a wild beast in our midst to deal with. I will seize and hold his tongue and you grab his legs and scratch as hard as you can!" He left the meeting early. When the police came, the meeting stopped. Many ran away when we were warned they were coming.

"Who called this meeting?" the police demanded. We answered, "Eliud Mathu, our Member of Parliament." He was still there and they asked him, "Did you alone call this meeting?" "Yes," he answered with a smile. We always protected Kenyatta.

The government saw more and more indications of unrest, but there were many more they didn't see. Early in 1952 we already had five hundred ex-army soldiers with their guns in the forest under Peter Kimathi, ready for guerilla action.

The British Provincial Commissioner of Central Province called a meeting of all Senior Chiefs to convene at Kiambu on October 8th. At one p.m. that day we heard on the radio the announcement of the death of one of the Chiefs. The fighters from the forest had been lying in wait for the "traitor Chiefs" along the road. That morning Senior Chief Waruhiu of Kiambu was on his way to the meeting in his car when the fighters stopped him at gunpoint. The guerillas asked, "Are you Senior Chief Waruhiu?" He answered, "I am." Immediately he was shot, with two of his aides.

Before the government declared the "Emergency" that month by an announcement on the radio, they were able to say, "Your leaders have been imprisoned! Jomo Kenyatta and his associates are on their way to a high security jail in the far north" (Lodwar).

We were furious! From that hour on, it was all-out war. British officials were reluctantly beginning to realize that the issue was not only wages but that this was a rebellion against their colonial rule. However, the wartime regulations applied only to our three related tribes: the Kikuyu, the Meru, and the Embu. Anyone found with a Mau Mau "membership card" was arrested.

I had been picked up the same day Chief Waruhiu died and sent with others to Nanyuki. We were beaten and told to admit that we had taken the Mau Mau oath. They had us fill in a form and sent us home. Fifteen days later we were arrested again and given a much worse beating for "conspiring against the government." From then on I suffered many things in detention camps until the end of the fighting.

Up till 1968 I didn't really know God at all. By then I was back in my home village in Meru District. There one day I heard a blind man, Justus Mwangi, preaching about Jesus. He had been a hard-core fighter, who was able to do many things for the Mau Mau in the forest because he was blind and had special privileges. But Jesus had changed him and I saw a light of Heaven on him. Through his testimony I also became a new man in Christ. Praise God!

### A MAU MAU LEADER
### Daniel Muthomi Theuri, Nyeri

In my childhood I herded sheep, and I also helped with cultivating, wood-cutting, and carrying water from the river. I wore charms against evil spirits as other children did. When I was 12 to 15 years old, I followed other teenagers to the settlers' farms where we first worked on coffee plantations. Then I went to a farm where I would be paid for herding cattle. It was there I began to wish I knew how to read and write. So when I was sixteen I went home and enrolled in school. There I was also taught Christian doctrine and I was baptized in 1945.

When I left school in 1949, I went north to Nanyuki and got

employment in the Water Department. Those were the days when the Mau Mau rebellion was in the making and we were all preparing ourselves for war. Many of us discarded our church connections and took two oaths so that we were reckoned to be soldiers in the guerilla army, even though we were continuing in our government jobs. We kept alert to places where people kept their guns. We stole them and delivered them to our fellow soldiers in the forest. The British were our enemies and we began to set fire to their crops and hamstring their livestock at night. Of course this upset the white farmers and made them restless, which is what we wanted.

Late in 1952 the Emergency was declared by the colonial government. Many young men my age joined the forest fighters at that time, but it seemed wise to our generals that some of us with government jobs should stay outside to support those who went into battle. The Englishmen I worked with in the daytime had no idea that I turned into a Mau Mau guerilla after dark. Those of us working in or around military camps stole guns, and at night we took them into the forest.

In 1953, I became more aware of how dangerous my life was becoming and I decided that I should take a wife who might bear me a son to carry on my name. So I eloped with a girl of the tribe, and took her to Nanyuki where I asked the government for housing for the two of us. The next year I was transferred to Nyeri, and the following year to Fort Hall, which is Murang'a now. Since my co-workers trusted me and didn't know I was a leader of the Mau Mau, for a while they gave me the job of screening other Kikuyu. For three months I told the British officers which people were Mau Mau and which were not! Then I went back to my work in the Water Department.

In 1970, after our country was free, I took up my lapsed membership in the Presbyterian Church, and I enjoyed working with the people of God. I was chairman of the committee when we built a large new church building and I have served as a deacon. All these years I enjoyed meeting with the fellowship of the saved people, especially after I was retired from the Kenya Water Department in January 1983. But it was wasn't until January of 1990 in a convention of the brethren that the Lord was able to speak to me personally. There He showed me my sins and brought me to the cross for forgiveness and healing. Now I know the Lord Jesus as the Saviour of my whole life.

## A TEENAGE TERRORIST
### Joseph Kariuki Karanja, Murang'a

When I was born in 1934, my family was living in the Rift Valley in the Uasin Gishu area near Eldoret. My parents weren't Christians and I learned farm work and herded my father's goats. I went to school for one year when I was fifteen, then dropped out because I preferred farming and was caught up in the secret rebellion against our white rulers. I took the Mau Mau oath when I was seventeen, but then when I was at home with my mother I was very sick with relapsing malaria almost a whole year, because we didn't have good medications then. Finally in 1952 when I could work again, I became an agent of the Mau Mau as well.

After a while I left work and went to Nairobi and stayed with my two elder brothers for one week. In the second week I was picked up by the police and moved to the area where my father was born: Njumbi in Murang'a District (high in the Aberdare foothills). We were put into a barbed-wire enclosure at Gitugi. We fought with the police for two hours, so we were beaten mercilessly. Then they sent in trained dogs to attack us, who ripped up our shirts and shorts—so no one could have run away wearing so few rags. Then they crammed us, between 60 and 100 men, into a room 20 by 20 feet for a week! The second week orders came to the British soldiers that Operation Anvil was starting, and that these holding camps would no longer be used. We were beaten again and then released, but they promised to follow us with guns.

My brother had discovered a cousin of ours who had told him where his mother, our aunt, lived. We found our aunt and she let us stay with her and her children—this was in March 1953. By the end of the month, the British were attacking because people had been murdered in this area and they wanted to wipe out those fighters responsible.

Late in May, together with my brother and cousin, I entered the forest to fight with the Freedom Army, and we set up a forest hideout from which we dashed out at night to attack government camps. We were very mobile, moving all around the mountain range and north to the Nyeri area, under the command of General Dedan Kimathi, who was first-in-command of the Army. His second was Mbaria Kaniu, in charge of the Murang'a area together with General Mathenge Mirugi. But the fighters were in many groups, and we led our own.

In October I had some trouble. One night we were sneaking out of the forest to go to our aunt's house, when enemy soldiers spotted us and I was shot. It was only a flesh wound, and I got treatment for a few days at a first-aid clinic we had in the forest. I hadn't recovered from the wound when I came down with pneumonia, because the weather had turned very cold and food was scarce because the enemy had surrounded the forest. It had become much harder to go out and bring in food from the countryside. I had a high fever when enemy troops came upon us and killed some. But, with another fighter, I was able to hide in the forest; we were lying in a thick tall-grass cover. He left, but I lay there for three days too weak to move, a long way from anyone. I was eating grass and found some grasses are a bit sweet. Then I managed to walk to where there was a house and a "ghala" (a huge woven basket for storage of grain, on a frame to lift it off the ground). I was too sick to open the ghala, but lay down under a tree nearby, hoping that someone who came for grain would see me there. I lay there for three days and no one came. Then I awoke and prayed to God. Let me say that the Mau Mau prayed to God a lot. Every morning we prayed facing Mt. Kenya with arms upraised; whenever we moved camp or started on a journey we prayed. When I was sick, I prayed and then could fall asleep. After I prayed, a spirit came onto me and said, "You better get up and go home; then God can do something for you." I decided that I would get up and somehow manage to go to my aunt's house. When it was dark I went to the edge of the forest, where I found some ripe fruit I could eat.

The next evening I stumbled slowly to my girl-cousin's house. I greeted them and they asked if I wanted food. I said I needed some thin gruel. I hadn't eaten for so long, I thought I couldn't manage more, but after I drank the gruel I was ready to try other food. And then I fell asleep. Early in the morning they begged me to find some other hiding place, because they knew that if I was discovered there their house would be burned with all they possessed, and I would be killed. They were grieving much to have to beg me to leave, but they said, "You can go to your aunt's home. She can give you shelter."

I said, "All right," and knew it didn't matter what I did; either way my life would be very short. I left and went a few miles, saw a town, but didn't go into it. I crossed a river, went further and came to my aunt's home. We greeted each other and she said, "You sit down." I stayed with them about a week, but I realized they were arguing about what to do, because I was sick and it was hard to ask me to leave.

Finally I decided to go and turn myself in to the government, so I went walking slowly and leaning heavily on a cane. They had pity on me because I was so thin and sickly, and told me to rest another week. Then I begged the Home Guard if possible to send me to a hospital to get well and get my thoughts straightened out; then I could come back and help them. They found a way to send me by a vehicle to the Murang'a Hospital where I was under treatment for six weeks. I was released on December 4, 1953, and then was alternating between government jobs and detention, always restless, unsettled and quick to fight—until May of 1955 when I went home to my aunt.

All this time I knew God had been speaking to my spirit, showing me my restlessness, and my rebellious, hateful attitude toward everyone. Then during the months I lived with my aunt, I started going to church for the first time. There I got to know and love an evangelist named Stephen Gathaia. He was the first person I had known that I could talk to about anything personal. I informed him I didn't want to be a Christian. I had known many Christians in the forest among the Mau Mau and I didn't want to be like them at all, Christians in name only. "How did you come to be different?" I asked. He gave me his testimony how Jesus had saved him, and told me that no man could save me. What I needed to do was to pray to God to shine His light into me and show me the Way. Every single day, Stephen came to see me after work and spent some time teaching me the Word of God. This went on till the 30th of October when I was in great distress because God was showing me clearly all my sins against Him, which were very many and dark—there was nothing evil I hadn't done. Then I invited Jesus to come in and take over my life, and He did!

That was just the beginning of all His Spirit showed me: there were things I needed to make right with people I had sinned against. I apologized to all my aunt's family for my ugly spirit and filth, and I promised to return a five shilling note I had taken from my cousin, which made him glad. It wasn't easy to earn five shillings in those days, but as soon as I did, I returned it. There were many other things to return. When I went into the forest, I had helped myself to someone's good suitcase. I returned it. The hardest thing for me to deal with was a blanket I had stolen from a detention camp I had hated. The Spirit kept reminding me, and I got moved in February 1956 to work quite near that camp, which still had prisoners in it.

Finally I broke down and repented of my hardness. The next day after work I went to that camp with the blanket rolled up. I told the guard at the entrance I needed to see the person in charge and told him what I wanted to do. He let me in and I went to the office of the commandant. I told him God had changed my life, and that He had told me to stop being a thief and to return this blanket I had stolen from this camp. I gave him the blanket and said I was prepared to accept whatever punishment he saw I should be given—I only wanted to have a free spirit. He was quiet for a while, then said he accepted it—and there was only one thing I must do. He told his soldiers to blow the whistle to call the prisoners together for an announcement. Then he said I must tell them what I did and why I was bringing it back. I felt rebellious, but I repented and I told them all that I had been and what Jesus had done for me. I told them about the blanket I had stolen here in this camp and that I had brought it back, and now God had given me this chance to speak to fellow prisoners because He could do the same for them. When I finished they were quiet, and the commandant said I could come back any time and talk to his prisoners.

God did many other things for me, and I began to meet the fellowship folk. When I had a chance to talk to those who had been staying on the Weithaga Mission compound, they sang and praised God and said, "We have been praying daily that God would save the fighters in the forest, and He is doing it!"

Before long God gave me a job in the Land Adjudication Office, measuring out parcels of land for the people who needed it. It was wonderful to keep on learning to know the brethren, such as Heshbon and many more. In 1961 I married a sister in the Lord, Leah Wanjiku, and God has given us five children. The government trusted me completely to be fair to everyone, so I was sent to different areas of Kenya where there was land to be divided. Everywhere my wife and I met the brethren and entered into fellowship with them. In the end we were in Nairobi and active in our Anglican church, and in the fellowship there. Recently I retired, and we are back in Murang'a where I am Lay Reader in our church. Jesus is Good, so whether the times are good or bad, we are in Him and that is good.

A BLIND SOLDIER
Justus Mwangi, Kirinyaga

My parents were not Christians. They drank a lot of beer and I

learned to do the same and many other things. We were living in the
city of Nairobi. My parents did encourage me to go to school, and I
went for a while but then gave it up.

Blindness came to me in 1949 when I was working as a truck driver's
helper, loading and unloading. After I lost my sight, I went to the School
for the Blind in Thika where I studied for a short time. There I caused so
much trouble that I was expelled and sent home in 1952.

In November of that year I took the Mau Mau oath and became
one of the freedom fighters. Even though I could not see, I was as
fierce as any. I smoked tobacco and marijuana to keep me from
feeling pain if I should be shot by a gun. I was a guerilla, and I took
the advanced oaths and went on to become a very dirty person in
body and mind.

In 1954 I was helping the Mau Mau by bringing them government
passes to travel through closed areas. I could get these in Nairobi or
from the District Officers upcountry. I would go to them boldly,
taking another blind person or two with me and someone to lead us,
and ask for passes to go to get food upcountry or clothing in Nairobi,
whichever the Mau Mau needed. Sometimes I got the passes from
the Police Special Branch. The government issued these, stamped
"Blind Completely" and specially colored to show it was only for the
blind. These I gave to the Mau Mau, and they used them to go to
Nairobi or back to the forest. I was very clever at this and much
praised. For a while I lived in one of the special government villages
and was known and respected for my cleverness. There was a law in
the villages that everyone must be back inside by 4 p.m. Even though
I often came back at 6 p.m., I was never questioned because everyone
respected me. Later, when contact with the Mau Mau was impossible, I
went back to live at home in Nairobi.

One night in 1956, God spoke to me and showed me all my sins
that would surely take me to hell fire. Of course I didn't want to think
about this. I loved the praise and respect I got for being clever,
especially the praise by the Mau Mau before the time when they
were being defeated. Even then I was stubborn and loved being
honored. But God told me I must leave the guerillas, and my evil life.
I feared getting saved because I didn't want people to know how
wicked I had been. But God kept coming along beside me and giving
me little pushes until finally I began to weep with many tears. It was
then that I turned to Him and cried out to be saved. I repented of my
many sins, and He cleansed me in His blood. The saved brethren

received me joyously.

I was still an unmarried man and while I lived alone I continued praising Jesus and praying for His help. I wanted to learn more. I already knew how to make leather out of hides, and so I began to work in a tannery. But I wondered how I could live alone. The revival brethren were praying with me because we didn't know where I could find a wife. We prayed until 1975 when the Lord gave me a sister in Christ and we were married. Through prayer and much waiting on the Lord He has blessed me in many ways. He has given us three children, and I never stop praising His grace and power. Every chance I get, I share my testimony and preach the Word of God.

My work now is in helping other blind people. The tannery gives opportunity for work to four blind people, and I am the manager and supervisor of this community of work. Before I was saved I had stolen a great deal from other tanners and made myself rich. I did this by selling leather for 50,000 shillings ($7,000+) and writing down 30,000 shillings ($4,000+) for the record. Thus I could keep the balance for myself. But Jesus made me a free and new man. He has taken away the lust for money. I am now a dependable and honest employee, and we live well loving Jesus.

## SHAKEN BY COURAGE
### Nathaniel Kamunye, Kirinyaga

In 1954 I was diligently administering the Mau Mau oath. I was leader of the guerillas in our town who were called the "kamata gati"; that means we were under the command of the forest fighters, but living at home and acting for them in our community.

In June of that year, I was with my troop of "kamata gati" when we seized a young fellow whom I knew. His father and brothers were with us, having gladly taken the oath, so I was surprised at this young fellow for standing against us, because I knew he was still in primary school and hadn't yet been baptized. He was amazingly loyal to his Jesus and I couldn't imagine why! My job that day was to be recorder and judge, so I wasn't giving the oath.

I observed this boy, Gathiomi, as he was severely beaten and wounded. Despite the beating, he would not agree to drink the blood and take the oath. My fellow Mau Mau fighters tried various tortures, but finally it seemed to those administering the oath that there was nothing to do but kill him. The threat was made and he was given some time to consider this. They all tried hard to persuade him, but he seemed to prefer to die rather than take the oath. All of us, as Mau Mau, had sworn that even if our mother or father refused the oath, we would kill them. Yet here was this kid, Gathiomi, who hadn't even joined the church, but was ready to die for Jesus! I had been baptized when I was a child and I was presumed to be a faithful Christian, but here I was a leader in the Mau Mau!

When Gathiomi was brought before me for judgment, I took off my disguise so he would recognize me and I could talk to him seriously. He didn't preach to me. Instead, he calmly said he was choosing to die rather than take the oath in the blood of a goat because he had taken the blood of Jesus to save him. This displeased me, but I only pitied him and tried to explain to him what death would mean for a young unmarried fellow. He said, "Yes, all of us die. Death can come in many ways, but I will just be with Jesus, and that's fine." I realized he had no fear of death at all, and I had never known anyone before who had lost his fear of death. I certainly hadn't. Death terrified me.

When the other Mau Mau asked me toward morning where they should throw his body, I stood up for him. I said, "He is refusing simply because he knows Jesus, and not because he is against us. If we who have beaten him had known Jesus like that, we would have had something to stand for too. We have eaten his chickens and wounded him and want to kill him, but I for one don't see any reason to do that simply because he knows Jesus." The rest grumbled, saying it would be bad to let him go because our job was to kill all who refused the oath. Nevertheless, when I said they could put all the blame on me, they agreed.

When I saw he was still alive, we took him out of the burlap bag in which he had been tied up most of the night, and I told him he was released to go home if he was able to walk. To our surprise, after a little help, he was able to walk away even though he was wobbly. We then hurried deeper into the forest to hide, feeling sure he would report us and we would be pursued by government forces. When we settled down, I said to my men, "That boy had God with him, or he would have died."

We got word from our scouts the next day that when he got home, he just changed his clothes and went back to his school. He hadn't gone to report us to the police, or said anything to incriminate us. Evidently he didn't even hold a grudge, but just went on with his faith. All my fellow fighters had to admit then that they were amazed at him.

Even though I had been touched by Gathiomi's fearlessness, I continued in rebellion toward God through my time in a detention camp. After I was released, I found a good job in Nairobi where every evening I was carousing with friends. Then one day in 1962 I bought a magazine on the street and read in it some verses from the Bible: "You say, 'I am rich and well off; I have all I need'. . . but . . . you are poor, naked and blind. . . . Listen! I stand at the door and knock; if anyone hears my voice and opens the door, I will come into his house and eat with him" (Revelation 3:17 and 20). That evening I drank heavily and tried not to think about God. But around midnight, I cried out to God and began a new life.

I moved to Tanzania and the next year I went to Bible School and then to Theological College. In 1966 I became a pastor in Kasulu Town. I returned to Kenya in 1973 and found work at St. John's Church in Pumwani—a crowded section of Nairobi. I have always felt a debt to brother Gathiomi because he first touched my heart for God, even though at that time I wasn't ready to repent of my sins. Maybe I was something like Saul of Tarsus, who was touched by Stephen's testimony but wasn't ready to be changed until he saw Jesus for himself on the road to Damascus.

Daniel Gathiomi and I like to testify together how Jesus brought us both into faith in Him. Because of that faith we haven't been shaken even when we are under heavy attack by Satan. I am grateful to the Lord for this privilege of preaching Jesus now, though I was so far from Him at first. (See the photo of them together in the center section and read Daniel Gathiomi's account in Chapter 3.)

## FOURTEEN YEARS IN THE FOREST!
### Lawrence Kimotho, Mwea, Kirinyaga

I grew up in a traditional Kikuyu home where there was beer-drinking and fighting. I learned young to drink local beer and fight. The one bright spot in my youth was my older half-brother, a son of my father, who was an earnest Christian. He taught me to read, took me to church, and let me read his Kikuyu Bible. I watched his lifestyle with wonder until the time when he moved away because of his job with the Department of Agriculture.

I was married, had four children, and was working in Nairobi as an automobile mechanic when Jomo Kenyatta returned from England.

Kenyatta was talking both secretly and openly about working toward independence for our country. I was swept wholeheartedly into the excitement of the secret revolution and promptly took the Mau Mau oath. After that I was no good at my job, and went back home to Kirinyaga District on the southern foothills of our sacred, snow-capped mountain, named by our tribe "Kirinyaga." For the rest of that year I went about with a group which was administering the oath. We brought adults in groups into a building or forest area, slaughtered a goat, and explained to them that everyone must swear loyalty to the revolution or be killed. We came upon a number in these roundups who resisted the movement. I don't remember them all, but I can't forget a man named Erasto Katindi of Kabare who died "for Jesus." So also did the daughter of our Subchief Siera and her two grown daughters. All three chose death over the Mau Mau oath. I was amazed at these people.

In January 1953, I left my family and went into the forest on Mt. Kenya to join the freedom fighters. I stayed in the forest for fourteen years! For a while I fought with the soldiers of our troop. Then two of us were sent out for scout and guard duty to a remote, unprotected section of our great mountain forest. The different companies of the Freedom Army were so mobile that sometimes when we tried to make contact or report to leaders in other sectors, we found the places deserted where we expected them. At first we had a rifle, but when our ammunition was gone we had only hand weapons and ingenuity for protection and food. During all those years we had no contact with farms or villages, and we depended only on the forest for food. We ate game animals, wild honey, and sometimes found wild fruit.

After two or three years, an announcement reached us by leaflets dropped from aircraft stating that the war was over and no action would be taken against those who laid down their arms, came out of the forest, and turned themselves in to the British authorities. But soon we heard that this was not true and that many of those going out of the forest were killed or imprisoned. From then on we paid no attention to government fliers dropped by airplanes. This is why we knew nothing of what was happening in the country outside our forest. We heard a rumor that the country was being granted independence in 1963, but thought it was another trick.

My partner Edward Kamina and I stayed faithfully on guard. He called me "Kiptanoi." When our clothes wore out, we made ourselves suits and caps of gazelle, antelope and baboon skins, and sandals of buffalo hide. (See center section for a photo of him in his forest suit.)

There were many streams from the rain and melting snow, so we always had water; however sometimes we would go for five days at a time without food. We learned to dig great pits on the elephant or buffalo trails. When one of these big animals fell in, we stayed near that area and had food for many days, drying and preserving what we could.

I know now that God was speaking to me and drawing me to Him ever since my childhood when my brother told me about Him, when I read some of the Bible and heard what was said at church. Then in the forest I saw indications that supernatural spirits could communicate with us. For instance, there were a few prophets among us who told our company of fighters where to expect the enemy the next day, and usually they were right. Then during one battle, men were being killed all around me. Suddenly a bullet hit and went clear through me. I expected to die, as there was no medical assistance. When instead I recovered and became strong again, I was in awe, and was convinced that God had some purpose for me and would keep me alive.

I started reading the Bible leaflets that Christians occasionally dropped over the forest by plane. We treasured these and they became God's words to us. So it was no wonder that when we finally came out of the forest, I came with a testimony, and was looking for God's people.

What finally convinced both of us in 1967 that the freedom fight was over was that someone came looking for us and showed us the new Kenyan coins and currency with the picture of our president, Jomo Kenyatta, on them! At last we knew for sure that our war was won and we could go home to our families. My children who were little when I left were all teenagers! We had two more children after I returned. I farm rice and other crops in this Mwea area where there is now irrigation, using water from the mountain on which I lived for so long. I am praising God with all my heart, and I love the fellowship of brothers and sisters who also rejoice in Him.

## CHANGED BY A VOICE
### Paul Mwangi Njonjo, Nyeri

I grew up in a traditional Kikuyu home and became a farmer without ever entering a church or school. So I had the same lifestyle, religion and vices of my parents. When the Mau Mau oath came along, of course I took it and asked what I could do for the freedom fighters. I was inducted into the forest army and served there for six years and two months, with all the hardships and dangers of living in the wild. I learned how to repair guns and even to make them from steel tubes salvaged from bicycles and other things. It also became clear that I had some unusual ability to foretell or predict what the enemy soldiers were going to do, so I was honored as a prophet.

After the war I went back to farming and planted a field of coffee trees for cash, as well as cultivating my food crops. I was working in the coffee farm one day when I heard a Voice which clearly said, "Mwangi, you must be saved!" I was very startled and confused. That is all it said. I had never been in a church, so I had no idea as to what to do or what this was all about. I laid down my tools and started off down the road to find some "saved person" to ask. As usual, I pulled out a cigarette paper and started to roll up my tobacco, Kikuyu style. Something stopped me, and as I was crossing a river I threw the tobacco into it, then went on my way to find someone who was saved.

Finally I found one woman, and I told her about this strange Voice and what it said, and told her, "I've come to ask you how you managed to get saved." She answered, "You go home now and on Sunday you come to church." On my way home I knew something good had happened in my spirit. I went by way of my field and took my work tools home. Then I gathered up all the supplies of tobacco I had in the house. In handling it, I coughed like a youngster who is touching it for the first time! I got rid of it all and have never touched it again.

Early on Sunday I went to my brother and borrowed his jacket coat so I could go to church. I went in and listened to all they said and saw what they did. At the end, a Voice told me to stand up and tell them what had happened to me. I stood up. Silence. Finally someone asked, "What do you want?" I replied, "I want to say something about Jesus Christ. I want Him to be my Saviour." All over the room people stood up, and to my surprise, many came over and greeted or hugged me lovingly. I had never seen or imagined anything like this. This went on and on until everyone there had personally welcomed me. Then I sat down.

Ever since that day these people have taught me and showed me God's way. Now I tell everyone that this Jesus will save absolutely anyone at all. I know that for sure. I am not lying when I say that

Jesus is in me. I became a new person. My life has been completely changed. Every day I thank Him for bringing me out of my darkness into His light.

## A SECRET AGENT TURNS
### Alvan Njue Gatema, Embu

I grew up in a non-Christian home here in Kigaari and this is still my home area. I wanted to learn to read and write but I did not want to become a Christian. So I went to school reluctantly in 1934. Our pastor was Rev. Johana Muturi, and perhaps to please him I enrolled in his class. There I learned so much about Christian things that for a while I was a half-hearted member of the Anglican Church.

When I grew up, however, I left all that. I married a non-Christian girl, and we had six children. Thus when the Mau Mau rebellion came along, I was glad to take their oath to fight the British and get rid of Christianity. I had to do all that very secretly because I was working for the local County Council. I despised the government, but I needed the job. I was able to do a number of things to help the guerillas. I bought them cigarettes, and gave them my jacket and other things which I could send to them by people who were not in government service. I kept this up until it was impossible to get anything through the military blockade around the forest.

To my disgust, my wife got saved in 1957, and I fought against this bitterly. I threatened that if those "religious nuts" told her not to bring me my beer and cigarettes, I would drive her off and she could go and live with them—with David Karigi and the others. But since she was quiet and a very good worker, I didn't send her away, I just married another wife who *would* do all that she was told to do. I had this second wife for two years, until 1961.

At that time I was Market Supervisor for the County Council, and under me was a man named Joel Mwigaruri. He became a messenger from God to me. He didn't preach, he just dropped a few words now and then, and I saw his life, which amazed me. He never took bribes from the merchants, as I did constantly.

One day in February 1961 I read a disturbing story from the Bible about a rich fool who was told he would die that night. It upset me and I was terrified. That night the Lord Jesus came to me and showed me all the ropes that had tied me up. He pointed out my sins as He saw them, including all the bribes I had taken, and I had to agree with Him—and I asked Him to set me free. Then He loosed me, and made me a different person.

The next morning I jumped on my motorcycle and hurried over to Joel's house to tell him I had been saved. After that I went to all the farmers and merchants I had cheated, and told them, "I won't be demanding money from you any more, or liquor or any other kind of bribe, because Jesus has set me free!" They were all delighted, though some had doubts because they knew I was a loose-living drunkard. But Jesus had truly delivered me.

Then the Lord spoke to me that it was not His will for a man to have two wives—in this I had broken His Law. I hurried home from Kirinyaga where I was working then and made arrangements to return my second wife to her family. I rented a car and took her, her child, and all her belongings back to her parents and explained to them that she was no longer my wife. I confessed that I had done wrong to take her, and I asked their forgiveness. After I left, they accused me in the law court of ruining their daughter. I made no defense but explained why I couldn't take her back. I paid the fine in goats that they demanded.

My wife is now my "sister in the Lord" and our home is full of His peace. I have learned that the way to guard the joy we have is to be willing quickly to repent of anything God shows me is wrong, and then make it right if I can.

When we remembered that we had never had a Christian wedding, we decided to have one. I asked Brother Joel to stand with me as my "father," although he is younger than I, and my wife and I were remarried as Christians. God is blessing us to this day and we live with Him.

## IN TWO PRISONS
### Justus Thiruaine, Meru

I was a very bad man. So it was no wonder that in 1952 I took the Mau Mau oath, joined the guerilla fighters in the forest, and began to administer the oath to everyone by force. We were especially tough on those who said they were "saved." We felt sure we could make them give up their testimony and come into the forest to fight with us.

In 1962 we had to develop a new oath we called "Repair," because so many of those coming out of the forest were betraying the Mau Mau cause by telling the details of the first oath. We felt they needed to be taught a lesson and brought back into the fight. So with my gang I watched for those who had defected, and wherever we found them, in the city or country, we attacked them and slashed them with our long knives, telling them to get into the war again. By the time our country got its independence in 1963, we had cut many of these—not killing them, but letting them feel our hate. When we could, we also stole a cow from these betrayers and had a feast in the forest. By then I was really becoming a criminal capable of anything.

Finally in June of 1965 I was arrested by our Kenya police and brought to court for breaking the leg of a citizen. I hadn't actually done it myself, but my men had done it under my orders. I was sentenced to four years in jail. I accused the judge of not being fair because I hadn't done it myself. For that, he added four more years to my sentence and ten stripes of the whip. I was furious and threatened the judge, saying, "When I get free of these chains, I'll kill you!" The judge said, "Man, you had better pray hard to God! If you go into jail like this, you could contract tuberculosis and die there." I was astounded that a fellow African would tell me to go to God and to pray to Him.

When I was being admitted into the Kamiti prison I was brought to the governor of the prison and he read my record. Then he said, "You are a very bad man." He listed my crimes and also advised me strongly to seek God, saying I was in danger of contracting a disease and dying in the prison.

One day when we were taken for a meal, I saw a man there reading his Bible. I went over to pester him and taunted, "So what are you reading?"

He answered, "The reason you are disturbed about this is because you are in two prisons."

"What do you mean—two prisons?"

He answered, "Your body is in prison and your soul is in prison too. Do you know how to read?"

"Yes."

"All right," he said, "Here, read this."

He directed me to 1 Timothy 6:7–9, and I read, "What did we bring into the world? Nothing! What can we take out of the world? Nothing! . . . [and] those who want to get rich fall into temptation and are caught in the trap of many foolish and harmful desires" (TEV). At that moment God invaded my mind and I had to admit these words were true. Inwardly I cried to the Lord, "Please save me!" I asked the man, "Where can I go to church?"

In the second prison service I attended someone read from Luke 4, verse 18: "The Spirit of the Lord is upon me. . . . He has sent me to proclaim liberty to the captives." Right then I realized that I was set free, for God had helped me. I asked the preacher, "What shall I do to get baptized?"

They told me, "It can be arranged if you have truly received Christ's offer." I had, and they baptized me without delay, giving me the new name "Justus." Then I asked, "What have I been baptized to do?" I have been learning that ever since.

My prison sentence was shortened to five years, as I had become a trusted evangelist in the jail. As the time approached, I began thinking about my wife. I prayed, "Lord, when You choose to release me from this place, could You do something about the wife I left at home? If she is going to resist You and work against me in my new walk with You, could You please arrange that she has died before I get there? But if she is going to accept You and go with me, then give us fellowship together."

When I reached home, my wife was there and I told her that I had been saved. She replied, "Which church do you want us to go to?"

"Methodist," I replied. We went together, and the Lord saved her and we have been praising God together ever since.

It wasn't easy, but I went to those whom I had injured by cutting and asked their forgiveness; also to those whose property I had stolen, and gave them my testimony. Some of them said, "This man has gone crazy. Being locked up in prison so long can do that!" But I knew I wasn't insane, God had changed me.

A real problem we had was that while I had been in jail the land had been portioned out to people and we had not been counted in. So I prayed, "Lord, I don't want to fight over land. Please, if it is Your will for us to have a small farm, You give it to us." And the Lord did it. He gave us fifteen acres! He has helped in every way. I can testify that the Lord both saves and keeps, because that is the way it is.

## A RUFFIAN REFORMED
### Jason Njara Njogu, Kirinyaga

My parents believed in the power of the medicine man. So as a young boy, I was often treated by the shaman. In my youth, I learned to sing Kikuyu songs, was a heavy beer-drinker, and lusted for girls. I had made nine of them pregnant before the tenth, whom I married. A name I called myself was "Come-here!" because I reckoned that all women and girls were mine for the taking.

My mother loved me very much, but one day when I was drunk and drugged with marijuana I struck my mother, knocked her down and cursed her loudly. Then I was so frightened at my violent actions that I ran away from home, thinking only of committing suicide. After three months my mother came looking for me and brought me home.

In 1952 I joined the Mau Maus, took the oath and became a guerilla fighter. My assignment was to be a guide or scout to bring raw recruits from Nairobi safely through the forest to Nyeri District or wherever else they were needed. I knew the shortcuts, often leading them to the Embu area. Life in the forest was difficult. After living there for a few days I would go home and be on call.

One night when I came home I beat my wife terribly, and poured a whole bucket of water over her and her bed so she couldn't sleep there. I told her if she didn't like it, she could go home to her father.

The Lord is good, and God laid hold of me in the 5th month of 1957 on the 25th day. He met me on the road. I certainly was not going to church to hear about God! At that time, I called Jesus a "Hindu" or a "white man," as I greatly despised both white men and Asians. I called them criminals who came to cheat Kikuyus and steal our farms. I hated anyone who got baptized and then took a hateful white man's name. This is the kind of person I was when God met me. The word I heard on the road was from a blind preacher named Justus Mwangi, and the man with him. They came to our village and told us what God had done for them, changing them completely. This gripped me. I was especially struck by the verse that "the wages of sin is death" and another one in Revelation 20:15, that only those whose names are written in the Book of Life will go to heaven. I was really frightened and knew very well that my name was not written there. Suddenly, I saw all my sins, including my curses and hitting my mother. I confessed all of them and begged the Lord to save me. He did forgive me and washed me in His blood!

To this day I am still praising God, and I love Him. I am raising cotton here in Mwea and thanking Jesus who is the Saviour of my life.

## CAN A CRIMINAL REVERSE?
### Stephen Muhengere, Othaya, Nyeri

Growing up I tried to be like my father—stealing, quarreling, fighting, and doing anything else the devil told me to do. When I got big enough, in 1946, I went to a settler's farm near Nakuru and got work, for a monthly wage of 8 shillings ($1.15). After three months I went into Nakuru Town and got work from an Asian doing building, for 28 shillings a month ($3.80). In 1948 I went to Nairobi and got work in a soda bottling plant for 48 shillings (almost $7.00) a month. I stayed there until 1952 when I took the Mau Mau oath. I gladly joined the fight to get our freedom from the white men and their religion. Soon I began to oversee the work of giving people the oath. I was at home in Nyeri when Jomo Kenyatta was arrested and the Emergency was declared. The war heated up, so I hurried back to Nairobi. I found the greatest need the army had just then was for those who would supply food for the fighters in the forest. I was put in charge of a squad assigned to getting provisions. We robbed people. We broke into shops where we stole everything we could carry, and then sold the stuff we didn't need. We worked hard and provided a lot of food, so I was promoted to the rank of Sergeant Major.

But in the British offensive of 1955, called "Operation Anvil," we were arrested in Nairobi, and were sent first to Langata Camp and then to the huge detention camp at Mackinnon Road. There we suffered terribly. We were beaten and were given very little food— for a while, just thin gruel. We were forced to bathe in a ditch which dropped down to 30 feet deep in the center, so all who could not swim drowned. There was one blanket for four men, and our coats were taken away, so in the cold season we shivered night and day. When we were forced to break stones, our mush was mixed with diesel instead of cooking oil.

Three friends and I escaped. One was killed and I was wounded. Eventually we were recaptured, stood trial, and were returned to Nairobi to serve our nine-month prison labor sentence. After a brief visit home, we were put into the Manyani Camp where I was held for six more months, then taken to Mwea to work on the government irrigation scheme for raising rice.

Finally I could go home, though there was no joy in it. I had no friends. I had married and we were raising a pig. When we sold it for 200 shillings ($28), I could finally buy some clothes. In my home I was miserable, and in desperation I finally decided to give up Mau Mau and try going to church. I went one Sunday just as a spectator. I don't know what they said, I only remember one song: "Have you been hiding sin?/One day all sins will be revealed/And you will find that sin brings death/It will take you straight to hell!" I couldn't get it out of my mind, and that made me decide to follow Jesus

Christ. Then I could see all the terrible things I had done, and many were truly satanic. I was like the man Jesus met who lived among the tombs, cutting himself. I cried, "Lord, I'm a sinner and I want to be forgiven." And He did forgive me and receive me as His child. All I can say is that God is very good, because I had no hope at all in the world until I found Jesus. Since that day, Jesus has been my Saviour.

The people I used to hang around with couldn't believe I could change, but now they are amazed at the difference in me. When we were drinking together, I used my money as if I had lost my senses. Now I use what I have carefully, for the family. There are still some trials, as my wife has not yet been saved, but I have great hope that some day she will. The Lord be praised!

## A SCHOOLBOY MAU MAU
### Peterson Wambugu, Nyeri

In 1952 I was a primary schoolboy, brought up in a Christian home. After the Emergency was declared, my father became a captain in the Home Guard organized by the government. I slept with him in their camp. But my uncle, whom I loved, and many others I knew, were in the forest with the Mau Mau fighters, and I liked to go into the forest to visit them. From them I learned to hate the white people and their rule over us and agreed with the aims of the freedom fighters. I was glad to take the oath when I got the chance, because then I knew I was one of them.

Sometimes when I went to my aunt's home for a meal I found my guerilla friends there, and could give them whatever information I had heard among the Home Guards concerning their movements and plans for attack. That way they could prepare an ambush or move to another area. They were grateful that I was their spy and they encouraged me to bring them cigarettes and other things from the supply store available only to the Home Guard. Because my father was a captain, no one ever challenged me or asked where I was taking the supplies. Later I took the second oath when I was a sixth grader in school.

In 1954 I finished eighth grade, and because I was tall I was hired in 1956 as a local policeman and my contact with the freedom fighters ended. By this time the British were gaining the upper hand over the Mau Mau and many thousands were in detention camps. The next year I joined the Kenya Police, and went to their training college. After graduation I was sent back to my home area, and was stationed at Mukoraini.

Even though I had been brought up by Christians, I was living a very fast and loose life, and easily fell into the policemen's habits of demanding bribes and beating those people who hesitated.

But in 1959 my life changed. It was then that I heard the Good News of salvation preached in power by Silas Muchina and others in the area where I was stationed. Through them I was drawn to Jesus Christ. I spread out all my sins, from my childhood on, before Him, and His forgiveness at the cross thrilled me. He completely changed my life. I began to tell my police friends and the officers about Him when they asked me what had made the difference in me. I was soon promoted to be a corporal.

Ever since that time I have been active in the church and helping all the brothers and sisters with whom my Christian wife and I fellowship. Our children are now grown and on their own. I retired in 1988 with a higher rank than before. We are farming and serving the Lord.

## SATAN'S SOLDIER
### Samuel Muhindu Munuhe, Nyeri

I grew up in the traditional Kikuyu way in Mukuruini Village. My parents let me go to school when I was 12 years old and I stayed through third grade, when I dropped out for the circumcision rites.

During World War II when we were fighting the Italians, I worked up north in Marsabit for the army for six months. Then I went to Nairobi and got work in the railways, maintaining the iron parts of trains. Finally, I turned to carpentry and building and got married in 1947. Our first child was born in 1951, which seemed a long time to wait.

In January 1952 I took the Mau Mau oath and left work in order to go with five others to our home area to give everyone the fighters' oath. When we met with the people we had ordered to come, we showed them a long knife, a rope, a hoe and a shovel, and promised to use them to kill and bury any who refused to take the oath. In our area no one refused it, not even church members. We gave the oath to everyone, young and old.

I was arrested in September, and was kept in the local jail for a month. In October the Emergency was declared, and for three months I was put on hard labor in Narok in Masai land. Then I was shifted for four months to the Embakazi Airfield outside of Nairobi (now the

Jomo Kenyatta International Airport). There I was assigned the job of carrying huge loads of gravel in a large iron basin on my head. The war was heating up, and the soldiers in charge of us were so angry about it that they beat us mercilessly. Some prisoners were killed.

Next I was sent to the huge detention camp at Manyani, and put into the special enclosure for the hard-core Mau Mau. There the one aim of the guards was to break our spirits. We were frequently beaten and food was scarce. We were threatened and cajoled by the white officers, but we were totally unwilling to renounce the Mau Mau oath. At times food was withheld for an entire week. Some died from the beatings, and some from typhoid fever. When preachers came we saw them as animals, and if any prisoner turned to their teaching or renounced the oath he had to be removed quickly from our compound or we would see that he was killed. I was finally released in November 1957.

At home I found my wife and child as I left them, and after that we had another child every year. I was a notable drunkard and was addicted to marijuana, fighting and chasing other women constantly. I didn't beat my wife, however, or swear at her. When she got saved, I stared at her, saying fiercely, "Look me in the eye! Don't imagine I will ever follow you in this, because I never will!"

I went on more than ever in drunkenness and marijuana. One time I was so befuddled I thought the trees were enemies blocking my way, so I pulled out my knife and attacked one of them, stabbing it and giving it a mighty blow with my club, shouting, "Take that! You'll see that I am a mighty man! If you are so strong, follow me!" Then I attacked another tree, shouting, "You can't escape me, you'll see!"

I was still a carpenter and builder when I could do it, but I spent my evenings and days off in debauchery until February 1967. One night I was very drunk. When I went to bed, I was suddenly bent double and I couldn't raise myself. This startled me sober. I took all my clothes and all my wife's clothes that were in reach and stuffed them under my head, but still I couldn't raise it up. Then I heard a gentle voice saying, "Muhindu, you will die. And when you are dead, what do you think people will say killed you?"

Then slowly I was able to lift myself up, and I answered, "I know. Yes, I am a great sinner. Can You forgive me?" I began to shake like a leaf and I woke up my wife. She cried, "What's the matter? Are you sick? Are you in great pain?"

I said, "I think the Lord is saving me." Then she thought I had lost

my mind. "Help me pray!" I cried. "I don't know how. He doesn't
hear what I say."

She sat up and I tried to pray, then she prayed. We went on like
this. Finally I said, "Tomorrow I'll go and give a testimony in the
prayer meeting." When I went into the church, the devil came into
me and I got such a terrible headache I had to get up and go home.
But then it was gone without aspirin. It's no wonder, of course, that
Satan was angry, because for many years I had been one of his
strongest soldiers!

Finally on Sunday I went to the place where the chuch was meeting in our neighborhood, and I didn't wait for anything. I stood up
immediately. "What do you want?" someone asked. I told them
what had happened to me and that God had saved me. A neighbor of
ours spoke out and said, "I doubt it—how could a brutal savage and
drunkard like he is continue even a month as a Christian man? You'll
see what happens."

I went to a church elder, and he asked me, "Are you saying that
you won't be going to the beer drinks?"

"I won't be going. I have been saved."

I went to my father and said, "I am completely changed." I told
my mother and my sisters and brothers and all the tribal elders. One
of them said, "If this fellow really is saved, he won't be brewing or
distilling our liquor anymore. Who will I get to do it?"

When God changed me, there were many who saw for the first
time that God really is the mighty Saviour they had heard He was.
Now there was no doubt about it, and they came to Him too. I found
that He keeps on changing me more and more as I go on.

I have rejoiced in Jesus since that time, all the rest of my life. I am
still a carpenter, and recently I put a roof on brother Solomon's new
home. The Lord has brought me through some difficult times, even
when my dear wife was taken to heaven. I am waiting for His
coming. Any time He comes will be fine with me.

A YOUTHFUL SPY
Stephen Kehia, Nyeri

Although my parents were not Christians, I found out that I was
born in 1938. I was able to go to school when I was nine years old. But
though I sat in religion classes, I avoided baptism and the church.

When I was fourteen, I was excited about the freedom fighters
who were in our nearby mountain forest beginning guerilla warfare

from their base there. I took the Mau Mau oath and became a scout who could be sent on errands. I was also able to be an informant for them because my father was an Assistant Chief. I heard many discussions in our home which provided clues to my captain in the forest on the plans of the government and the movement of troops. Since I was still considered a child, nobody noticed how often I ran into the forest or asked me what I was carrying. In this way I could be useful to the fighters, and my work for them continued until the British army sealed off the forest to all contact with the outside.

In 1958, when I was twenty, I was hired as a guard in a detention camp. Two years later, when the detention camps were closed down, I was moved to a jail where a number of "incorrigible" Mau Maus were still in custody. By this time I had become such a drunkard that my wages as guard lasted only a few days, and during these drunken sprees I was absent from work, for which I was repeatedly under discipline. Then when I had no money and found inmates who offered to buy drinks for me, I would take them with me to the bar where we drank together. One day I was seen by the chief warden in the bar with a "criminal" from the prison, and I was dismissed in disgrace. My life as a drunkard went on, however, until 1966. By then, even my father was so disgusted with me that his words cut me deeply, and I began to see myself as others saw me.

I had carefully stayed away from any contact with Christians, but when a drinking buddy suggested we go to see what happens in the meetings of the fellowship at Chamwenge so we could make fun of them, I agreed.

The thought had passed through my mind that if their Jesus could cure my drinking, it might be worth considering if I didn't have to become a fanatic. At Chamwenge I met a relative who asked me if he could read me some verses from 1 John, and I let him do it. He read the first chapter, and one sentence gripped me: "If we say that we have no sin, we are deceiving ourselves." That was true of me and my resistance died. I cried to Jesus and He saved me. He also broke the chains of my bondages to strong drink and adulteries. My life changed. There were many of whom I had to ask forgiveness, but Jesus helped me do it. His joy has filled my life and strengthened me. Now I love all those I hated, even white people! I am praising God every day!

## A MAU MAU TEACHER
### Henry Kuruga, Kirinyaga

Because my father had no use for Christianity and because I was the shepherd of his sheep, he didn't want me to go to school. But I went anyway in 1944, with the help of my uncle who stood up for me. I took the Primary Examination in 1944, and by 1953 I was finishing teacher training. I took the Mau Mau oath at that time.

I started teaching in 1954 at Kangaru. By that time I was a heavy drinker and woman chaser, swearing at and reviling people, and therefore fighting viciously. I was proud of being "a civilian Mau Mau fighter." In 1957, when I had made a schoolgirl pregnant, I lost my job and was out of a job for a year. This was fine with me, because I had plenty of time to go right on in my sins.

To my great surprise, the Lord touched my spirit in 1958 when I heard a verse from John 14: "Jesus said,'I am the Way, the Truth and the Life. No one can go to heaven except by coming to Me.'" This jarred me deeply. I couldn't stop myself from pouring out to Him all my dirty sins. To my amazement He forgave me, made me clean, and folded me to Himself! I couldn't keep quiet for the joy of it and told all my friends. They thought I had suddenly become stupid, because this sort of talk is only for women and uneducated men.

I said, "Well, if this salvation is stupid I'm happy to be stupid. When I was 'smart,' as you call it, I was always attacking people and getting girls in trouble, or beating them for rebuking me, but God is amazing! He has touched my heart, turned me around, and made me a new man. All I can do is thank Him."

Although I have gone through trials in my life and made mistakes, I keep on seeing the astonishing things God can do. I live only by daily trusting His free grace. I know I don't have the strength in myself to keep on loving and serving Him. He is my day-by-day Saviour.

## A THIEF PAYS BACK
### Justin Kamao Mwangi, Murang'a

I was born in 1934. Surprisingly, I was sent to school. Though my parents were following tribal traditions, they knew the value of an education for the children. When I was in eighth grade and 18 years old, the people giving the Mau Mau oath came to our area, and I went with some others of our class to take it. I didn't have high enough grades in the final examinations to go on to high school, but I was given a certificate which helped me get training for work in a medical clinic. It also helped me that I was related to the Assistant Chief, Jimna Kimori, who helped me get work in the Murang'a District Hospital. I worked there for a year while living in all sorts of sin, especially stealing, and I was always getting in trouble with my supervisor. Finally I decided this wasn't the place for me, so I thought teaching might be better. Through the kind intercession of John Kanguru, missionary Cyril Hooper accepted me into the teacher training course at Kahuhia, but during the whole two years I secretly kept on my stealing and loose living. Then I started teaching in a mission school.

At the beginning of my second year, 1956, my father died— leaving me, the eldest, to care for my four brothers and two sisters. Almost immediately after that, a girl in the school reported to her father that I had made her pregnant and the father demanded that I marry her and pay the fine and dowry. I had to do that, and nearly went crazy with all the new responsibilities I didn't want. I was teaching at Kangema, and my relative, the Subchief, managed to get me appointed Headmaster, which increased my salary. At that point I nearly ruined the school: I stole for my own needs the money collected by parents for a new building. I was full of anger all the time, and left my wife to chase schoolgirls.

Then in September of 1959, the Lord Jesus intercepted my downward rush. I was trying to teach the story of Noah and the ark to the students and had to tell them that God had decided to bring the flood on the earth because of the terrible sinfulness of the people. God spoke to me and clearly told me that this was my last chance. He said, "Jesus is the ark, and you have been refusing to go in. Go in now or be drowned!" I accepted what I already knew, that I was one of those sinners who deserved to be destroyed, and cried to Jesus to save me. Then because He is unbelievably merciful, the Lord saved me and washed all my terrible sins away!

I went back to school the next day an entirely different person. Suddenly I was the guardian of all the things I had been pilfering. I had to discipline those who were doing what I had been doing myself. I called together the parents and teachers to tell them what had happened to me, and to confess how I had been stealing; and I asked their forgiveness and patience while I repaid, as quickly as I could, all I had stolen. The parents were happy to hear this and in time God helped me to give back every penny. My wife was also saved soon after that. Our nine children are grown and helped me celebrate my honorable retirement from teaching at the end of 1988. This was saddened because my wife had been killed in a car accident earlier that year, but the family of God in the fellowship held me, both weeping and rejoicing with me.

## FROM HATE TO LOVE
### George Gichuki, Nyeri

When I was eight years old my parents started going to church. They became Christians, so I was able to go to school. I attended high school at Kikuyu Langata, and in 1945 I was baptized in the Presbyterian Church. My teacher training course was at Machakos Town of the Kamba tribe. After that I was posted to a school near home in Othaya, Nyeri.

People in my area were taking the Mau Mau oath in 1952 before the fighting actually began. I took the first oath then and learned many of their secrets. Many other church members, and even some people with a testimony of being saved, took the oath in order not to be killed.

Later I took the second oath, called Grade 2, which inducted a person into the army. They said my work for now was to go on teaching, giving them part of my salary, and later they would call me to fight in the forest. It was purely by chance that I wasn't called to join the guerillas. I wanted to go, for I hated the white settlers. I could see their farms and businesses were large and prosperous, but the Africans working for them were grossly underpaid. The more we talked about it, the more bitter I became.

I hated other people as well. I was a drunkard, and had married because I caused pregnancy in a schoolgirl. I would leave her at home and visit other women and girls, so our home was a place completely ruined by Satan.

In 1956 there were special meetings in Othaya Town. Hiram Mundia of Nyeri and Tiras Kariuki of Kiambu were preaching, and I attended. Through these messages my spirit was stirred. One day I realized that I had no peace. I was full of hatred for my wife and there were many more things that displeased Almighty God. I was ruined by hatred and adulteries and had no rest of spirit at all. Suddenly I realized there was help available. I learned it through words written by Paul in one of his letters. He says something like this: "Those who follow the flesh can never please the Holy Spirit, but those who are led by the Spirit will be victorious." On December 2nd that year, in the morning, I received Jesus and opened every room in my heart to Him. He came in and filled me with joy and happiness. My life turned around and I became a new person. My drinking and smoking stopped, and my adulteries ceased. Joy filled me and has continued until now. Later my wife was saved too, and we love our children. I love the Lord who helps me, and I trust that I will live with Him to the end of my life. Praise Him!

## LOST SHEEP COME HOME
Gideon & Florence Muraia Thuo, Murang'a

Gideon: Both of us were born on the same white settler's farm in the Rift Valley, near Nakuru, to non-Christian parents. My father was a polygamist. He was also presiding officer in the local African court and had seen the advantages of learning to read and write, so he was willing for me to go to school. But there was no school nearby. Fortunately, he was also a friend of the Rev. Elijah Gachanja who visited us occasionally and taught us children about God—and he took me to his home in Nakuru so I could go to school. There I took on a veneer of Christianity, which included being baptized and confirmed. I was able to go on to the Kagumo School, then entered the Technical School at Kabete in 1948. In 1949 when I went home to my parents, I found my childhood neighbor and playmate, Florence, there. She had also managed to get some education and a baptism name, and we were married in tribal style.

Florence: When Gideon went back to the school at Kabete, he left me pregnant on this sisal farm with no job. Working on sisal, the wage was two shillings (about 15 cents) a month. The only way I saw to support myself was to brew beer, using the bug-damaged grain which was not salable in the market. Laborers who were willing to buy beer, however, boycotted mine because I hadn't taken the Mau Mau oath. So I took one, then two and three, and carried on a brisk business.

Gideon: When I visited Florence, I heard about the Mau Mau secret rebellion to get rid of our white rulers. I gladly took their oath then, and in 1952 at Kabete I learned to give the oath to other students. When I became an instructor in the Technical School I had a house, and my wife and child came to Kabete to live with me. I was quite active in Mau Mau, even giving the oath to young children because they could easily carry ammunition and other things to the fighters without being noticed. In 1954, when the war in the Aberdare Mountains was intense, I was moved to Naivasha and began to fix and make guns for the guerillas. I was never arrested for it because I was also working for the government.

When it seemed the Mau Mau were being defeated, toward the end of 1955, the government offered amnesty to all who would confess their participation in the "rebel" movement. My wife and I both felt it was time for us to come clean. So we went and surrendered and were forgiven. But after that, a fighter coming out of the forest named me as being his supplier of ammunition, so I was arrested and sent to Embakazi Camp. I was fortunate that I had mentioned ammunition in my confession and had paid the fine of six hundred shillings. But our stories did not match in every point, so they kept me in detention in the station camp for three weeks. Then I was released to go back to my work of instructing students in the Technical School.

At that time I began to hear the voice of the Lord speaking to me. I marveled that while others had been killed and tortured, I had escaped. We began to attend church again. I realized I might have sinned in taking the oath, but excused that because we were afraid to die. We had a church wedding and the children were baptized, and people began to know us as Christians. After that we were transferred to the Technical School at Thika.

Florence: After we moved to Thika, our fourth child was born, but before he was a year old he got sick and died. It was then I began to hear the voice of the Holy Spirit showing me my sins. I read Jesus' words that it is those who become as little children who inherit the Kingdom of God, and I looked at my life. It seemed that I must have been born in sin. I had begun to steal and lie when I was very young. I stole sugar and tea and bread from my stepmother—things she wouldn't share with us. I hated her for the way she treated us, and hated the white people who made me carry heavy loads and cultivate with a heavy hoe. Suddenly I was seeing these as sins and they were heavy to me.

Our pastor in Thika was Sospeter Magua, and he visited us when our baby was sick and buried him when he died. He could sense that I was troubled and had great fears. He told me gently, "You have something, my dear, that you need to talk about with the Lord Jesus. Why don't you tell Him what is worrying you." Finally I bowed, and God showed me, as if on a TV screen, all my sins from my childhood until now. Then I was able to pour them all out as I was seeing them. Jesus took me in His arms and I knew He had washed them all away and accepted me unconditionally.

That was on a Saturday night. The next morning in church I was embarrassed and scared, thinking I ought to say something, but was frozen to my seat. Then someone read Luke 12:8–9, where Jesus said that if anyone is ashamed to speak for Him to people, He will be ashamed of that one in heaven! So I stood up and told everyone that Jesus had saved me and what He had saved me from. My husband looked surprised, but all the fellowship folk were rejoicing. I didn't go right home after church, but stayed and praised God with those in the fellowship meeting. There everyone hugged me and assured me that I was born again into a whole new life, with a new family of brothers and sisters. They have been close to me all the rest of my life.

Gideon: The Lord saved me in 1959 when I was a church elder, lay reader and teacher in the church. At the same time I was also full of hate, planning how to get rid of these Britishers who ruled over us. The day I was saved, I fearfully went to Mr. Spencer, the principal of our Technical School, and said, "Please forgive me. I had been wondering how we might arrange to kill you, but now the Lord has saved me, and I love you."

He answered, "If God has forgiven you, I also forgive you." I was very grateful for this, as I had expected at least to be put in jail. I praise the Lord very much for giving me this gift of life which I didn't deserve.

In 1963, after our national independence, I was sent to England to study in Leeds University, and was strengthened and blessed to meet the English fellowship brethren. Mrs. Beecher was the first to hear about me and contact me. Through her I met many, as well as the brethren visiting from Africa, including Festo Kivengere. I returned home with a diploma in 1967, praising the Lord. For a long time I worked in prisons, teaching inmates technical skills and how to know Jesus. I retired in 1986 and I am still praising God for loving and forgiving me. I truly love Him.

## MAU MAU SPIES
Reports by Gideon Irambu, Meru, and Martha Solomon, Nyeri

At the time of the Emergency, Jonah Matii, who is now a brother in the Lord, was a spy for the Mau Mau. During the day he worked in an army camp of the Home Guard, but at night he reported to the

Governing Council of the Freedom Army. He informed them what he had observed or heard of army plans. He would take them the goats stolen for them in daytime by young goatherds he knew. In addition, he also gave the Home Guard leaders false information about the location and movements of the Mau Mau.

The most successful transporters of food and other things into the forest to the freedom fighters were old women—grannies. For years they had been accustomed to carrying heavy loads on their bent backs by a strap around their foreheads. No one challenged them and they were very clever in disguising their loads. Some of them came on a regular weekly or biweekly basis. The Mau Mau generals called them their "Special Branch" and honored them for selflessness. They always brought news and sometimes informed on traitors. No soldier on either side ever molested them.

There were Mau Mau spies who pretended to be in fellowship with Christians in order to report on them. These spies knew all our customs of greeting, singing and sharing, and they could give believable testimonies. Therefore we usually trusted them. Even when we were suspicious, we did nothing about it, because we put our trust in God and were quite prepared to go to heaven whenever He chose. These spies gave the Mau Mau information on the travels of our preaching teams that went about to evangelize and to encourage brethren in outlying places. The purpose of spying was to enable the fighters to ambush the Christians. But after the early days of fighting, the Mau Mau seldom did that, having learned respect for the power of our God.

# 3

# SOME NARROWLY ESCAPED DEATH

*"Through faith they fought whole countries and won. . . . They shut the mouths of lions, put out fierce fires, escaped being killed by the sword. They were weak, but became strong. . . . Through faith women received their dead relatives raised back to life."*

Hebrews 11:33–35 (TEV)

*"Then I heard a loud voice in heaven saying, 'Now God's salvation has come! Now God has shown his power as King! Now his Messiah has shown his authority! For the one who stood before our God and accused our brothers day and night has been thrown out of heaven. Our brothers won the victory over him by the blood of the Lamb and by the truth which they proclaimed; and they were willing to give up their lives and die.'"*

Revelation 12:10–11 (TEV)

*"He is our God! We have put our trust in him, and he has rescued us. He is the Lord! We have put our trust in him, and now we are happy and joyful because he has saved us."*

Isaiah 25:9 (TEV)

## INTRODUCTION

The Emergency declared by Great Britain on October 20, 1952, began an all-out war on the Kikuyu guerillas who had already begun attacking white settlers and their own tribal "traitors."

The revival people knew very well that by refusing the oath they were facing death. They identified with the story of Shadrack, Meshack and Abednego (Daniel 3:17–18, TLB), men who said, "God is able to deliver us; and he will deliver us out of your hand, Your

Majesty. But if he doesn't, please understand, sir, that even then we will never under any circumstance serve your gods. . . ."

The revival people met in local and area meetings to seek the will of the Lord for them during this dangerous time. Agreement was rapidly reached that they were to love their enemies on both sides of the fighting, do good in any way possible to those who hated them, and accept going to heaven with joy rather than deny Jesus. Gradually another conviction grew among them: that their only weapons would be love, prayer, and the Bible.

In this chapter you will read the accounts of those who were raised up from the brink of death, or barely missed the fatal blow. All of them knew that the power that kept them alive was God, who is always original. Sometimes He used angels or even the enemies themselves! One of these enemies was Kamuye (now the Rev. Nathaniel), whose testimony appears in the preceding chapter. He saw the power of God in young Gathiomi (now Daniel) who relates his story here. Another was the fierce Kibe (Paul) whose plans were upset by Simon, who tells us here how he happened to have hot sweet potatoes that night.

✝     ✝     ✝

### IN A LION'S DEN
#### Daniel Gathiomi Mbugi, Kiboro, Kirinyaga

My father was a witch doctor–medium, so I could not go to school until I was in my middle teens. When I was 19 years old I was still in primary school. The year was 1953 and my life was really committed to Jesus Christ. I was teaching Sunday School and was sometimes asked to preach in church. Mau Mau oathing had started. One Sunday I taught my class about Peter denying the Lord, and I was indignant about what he did. I told my class that I would never betray Jesus by taking the Mau Mau oath, even though my father and brothers had taken it.

One afternoon after school there were men wearing masks waiting for me at my father's house. They seized me, dragged me outside, cut me with knives and beat me with clubs. I was in great pain when they dragged me on the ground to a house about a half mile away. Standing in two lines they made me pass between them, each one cutting or hitting me as I went. I put my hands up to protect my face, but by the time I got through the line I knew they wouldn't stop until I was dead.

I was asked, "Now will you take the oath?" and I said, "No, I won't." Then I was knocked down again and cut all over with two-edged knives. After a while they said, "Get up!" I got up slowly and they asked, "Are you ready to take the oath now?" I refused, saying I would be glad to go to heaven because Jesus was there. They began to hit my head with their clubs and whips. When I still refused, they stuffed me into a granary where corn was stored, and put two men there to guard me. The others were in the house eating my chickens which they had stolen.

After some time, because I seemed unconscious, they stuffed me into a burlap bag and tied it shut. It seemed to be their plan that I should die there. However, while they were doing this, God showed me how to hold my arms up in front of my face so that there would be a little room in the sack for me to move and breathe. They dragged me in the sack along the ground into a grove of banana trees and left a guard to watch me.

After a long time I was taken out of the bag and into their "court-room." Someone in charge had taken his mask off, and asked, "Do you know me?" I said yes. It was Nathaniel Kamuye, a neighbor. He asked, "What's the matter with you? All the rest of us who are church people have taken the oath. Why won't you?"

I said, "I have taken the blood of Jesus, the Lamb of God, and I can't take another oath and another blood after that. So now go ahead and kill me." He explained how terrible death would be for me, but I still said, "No."

When the judge came in he asked, "Are you the fellow who is refusing to take the oath?"

"Yes," I said.

"Are you ready to die?" he questioned.

"Yes," I replied. They tied a rope around my neck, threw one end over a rafter in the roof and pulled me up to the top so that I was being strangled. Just before I died, they let go and I dropped hard to the floor. They asked again, "Now will you take the oath?"

Faintly I said, "No" and then passed out. They stuffed me back into the burlap bag and dropped me into a dry pit to die. God was still with me.

The pit I was in had once been used for mixing mud for plastering a house, but now grass had grown in it. I was unconscious when they threw me in. Just before daylight the next morning, someone poured water over me and I woke up in great pain. There were two men pulling me out; one was Nathaniel Kamuye, the other was Joel Mwaneke. They asked me if I could walk and saw that I couldn't. Then each one took an arm and they helped me like a baby who is being taught to walk. I was very weak. I had blood all over my head and clothes, and blood was still oozing from the wounds on my legs. These two walked me along about ten steps. Then God strengthened me and they saw that I was standing on my own. I began to take small steps by myself and was able slowly to walk home, which fortunately was not very far. When I reached the small river, I walked right into it and tried to clean myself a bit in the water. The bloodstains faded a bit, though my clothes were still dirty. I walked on home where I took off my dirty school uniform, put on other clothes, and washed my face and head. Then I walked to school even though I was late.

The teacher asked, "What in the world has happened to you?"

I replied, "Well, I was attacked by a fierce swarm of bees." Maybe they guessed the truth, but I couldn't tell them because I knew what would happen then. The attack would have been reported to the British soldiers and the houses in the village of those responsible would have been burned down. If they came back, the Mau Mau involved would have been seized, locked up and beaten terribly. I lied in order to spare them. I had asked the Lord to forgive them, and I didn't want to hurt them. I had been teaching my Sunday School children to forgive and do good to their enemies.

That first day back at school I didn't sit in class, I only asked them to give me some medicine for pain. They gave me some, and I laid down on the grass in the shade of a tree until the end of the school day. By the time I reached home that day, I had lost all fear. And the next day I studied in my classes as usual.

While I was gone, my father had been told that I had been killed by the Mau Mau. So when he saw me alive he was very astonished and believed that I had been raised from the dead, which, in a way, I had. After that, my father believed in God, burned his paraphernalia of witchcraft, and later was willing to be baptized. My older brother was saved after that too, and a younger brother was saved later. It was my younger brother who used to say that I had been considered the "useless filth" of the family because I refused to take the oath, but that actually I was God's fertilizer, thrown into His compost pit, which later made new life grow in them all!

It truly was a miracle of God that brought me back to life and got me home again with forgiveness in my heart. Even the Mau Mau gang, after learning that I had not accused them, spread my story all through the forest among the other freedom fighters. All who heard it said, "Let no one ever touch that boy again or try to get him to take the oath!"

I was baptized in 1958, and took the name "Daniel" because I felt I had been in a lions' den and escaped.

(Actually, the attacks on the "Jesus people" lessened as the Mau Mau realized that these were not the sort of enemies who would do anything against them or their cause. *Compiler.*)

## HOT SWEET POTATOES
### Simon Ng'ang'a, Kiambu

My parents were workers on the Karen Blixen farm on the edge of Nairobi City, and I had to herd my father's goats, so I didn't have much chance to go to school. By 1936, both my parents had died, and we children were left alone. I felt a great emptiness inside. Nevertheless, I did manage to go to school enough to learn to read the Kikuyu Bible, and I was baptized in 1937. I tried to share the Good News with others, but I was troubled because I had an uncontrollable temper and I still hated the white people who had taken our land and left us naked. I had no idea what a Christian should do with persistent sins.

Then I heard there would be a big meeting at Kabete where God's Word would be preached by some visiting speakers, so I walked there and joined the crowd. A man read some words of the prophet Isaiah: "Though your sins are like scarlet, they shall be as white as snow" (1:18, NIV). He said God is calling us—yes, even church members—to come to Him, to admit our sins and have them all washed away. He said that was what he had done. So now he was forgiven, free, and full of joy—which they all obviously were. Also it seemed to me that the speakers knew all about my private life. How could they know about my despising others, the unclean thoughts and deeds I had, even my fighting? They seemed to know everything! I didn't respond then, but I went home with all of these things on my mind, and with my heart longing for the peace those people had.

Finally in March of 1946, at ten o'clock one morning while I was breaking stones as my job on a white man's farm, I came to Jesus!

The owner was there and I told him right away: "I have just been saved from my fighting and hatred!"

He was puzzled and asked me, "Are you telling me that my people here are bad?"

I said, "No, that's not it. I am the one who is a sinner and needed to be saved."

When I told my fellow workers, they didn't understand at all and asked, "Are you trying to be a white man, or what?"

"No, indeed," I answered. "It's just that my sins needed to be cleansed—my fornications and fighting."

Walking away, they said, "But everyone is like that. This man is hard to understand!"

One thing that had gripped me at Kabete is that anyone of any tribe, even a white man, could admit his own sins and have the same joy. The visitors who had spoken there were of distant tribes, and there were even a few white people who admitted that they needed to come to God for cleansing. They were no different! And since then I have found out that even Americans are the same. But anyone who refuses is left behind.

That year I went on a journey to Kahumbo in Murang'a to see John Kangoro, because I needed fellowship. I knew no one in my district who had been saved. John and I loved each other very much. I was encouraged, and when I went home I told everyone I could about the peace of belonging to the Lord Jesus. Two other young men in this village were saved, Simon Nyithondu and Paul Wakaba. That was the beginning of the fellowship here, and God kept adding more.

In 1952 the whole area began to erupt with Mau Mau talk and everyone was taking the oath. They were saying to me, "What's the matter? You won't join us in this fight? So what will you do when we are dividing up the white man's farms? You will be left out!"

"Well," I said, "I'll leave that up to my Father God."

We three saved ones were beaten up badly with clubs while men yelled at us, "Lovers of white men! You refuse to take our oath!"

I answered, "I have already taken an oath in the blood of Jesus."

"He's mad!" they screamed. The three of us kept on walking with Jesus stedfastly, though we were constantly threatened with death. One Mau Mau fighter named Jakundu Kariri told me I would soon be dead, and I said I would be happy about it if that was God's choice for me. We didn't know that that man was so soon to be killed, but he was.

I was farming alone then on my parents' land. One day in 1954, I had harvested the sweet potatoes. Then, to provide food for several days, I had steamed a lot of them in a huge clay pot lined with banana leaves and covered tightly. That night there were guerilla fighters pounding on my front door. I recognized the voice of the one calling my name. It was Kibe, whom I had known as a child. His parents and mine were working on the same farm, so we boys had been like brothers. I supposed they had come to see what I would say about the oath, so naturally I lit the lantern and opened the door. All I could see was that these men were thin and very hungry. So I quickly invited them to a good meal. I made a lot of sweet, milky tea to go with the sweet potatoes. Then I set this before them and I said, "Now, let us pray!" I prayed, "Dear Father God, please help these dear men to know You. They are fighting in order to get good land to cultivate. Please show them they can't be successful in growing things without You!"

While they were eating, I said, "There is nothing wrong about trying to get farm land. The only thing wrong is trying to cultivate it when you are naked."

"What do you mean—naked?"

"A man who doesn't have God with him is naked. Don't you see, all the land is God's, and He is the one who gives us the strength and blesses the crops? How will you manage alone without God's help?"

They listened and ate all they could. The remainder they took with them when they left. I did hear one say under his breath, "This man doesn't need to be killed. When our country gets its independence, he will pray for us."

About two weeks later, I went as usual to the the outdoor public court in our village. And there was Kibe, all cleaned up now and looking peaceful! He said in front of everyone in his confession, ". . . so that night we went to the house of Simon"—he pointed at me— "because we had been ordered to kill him, and I went with a burning desire to kill him." I was shocked, bowed my head and wept as he told what God had done for him. True, I knew they were Mau Mau fighters that night, but I had loved them and felt sorry for them because they were so hungry. Certainly the hand of the Lord was on us all that night! This made me bolder and stronger to keep on preaching about Jesus.

However, this wasn't the end of danger for me. One day I went to the marketplace at Dagoretti, and one of my brothers was there. When he saw me, he pointed me out to the government soldiers, saying, "That fellow has surely taken the Mau Mau oath." So I was arrested and the soldiers stripped off my clothes and shoes and threw me into a deep pit. I was comforted by remembering how Joseph was seized by his brothers and thrown into a well. After a while they poured water on me. But soon I was rescued by a Home Guard who knew me and told these soldiers that I would never take the oath. I was taken out of the pit and given back my clothes.

Then I went into the church and gave my testimony to those who were there. I said, "My dear brethren, God is wonderfully good. His hand is over us and He will deliver us from all evil." The glory of God was among us from that time until now and many have been saved.

When I began to feel a desire to get married, I talked it over with the brethren, telling them, "I want a home where God is in control." They suggested I get acquainted with Damaris Woki at Kabete. I did, and we both felt God's guidance to be married. After the wedding, we moved to the farm we are on now. I'm glad I'm not a rich man. Riches are all right, but a rich man tends to worry about his property. All I have to do is keep my eyes on my Father God and I am the richest man there is, and no one can take it from me. God gave us seven children, and some have died without knowing God. This has given us grief. But in Christ we have a big family of brothers and sisters of all tribes and countries. I have many children in the Lord who love Him, and we praise God together.

## NO FRONT TEETH?
### Heshbon & Elisheba Mwangi, Murang'a

Heshbon: I was born in 1915, the son of a medicine man. My father taught me a great deal of his craft and showed me the plants and trees he used in making medicines, hoping I would some day help him. Most of my early years were spent as a herd-boy, caring for our cattle and sheep.

In 1930, when I was 15 years old, a friend invited me to go with him to church on Sunday. This was entirely new and exciting to me. On Monday I went to learn to read. I was old to start learning and to know God, but once I started I never stopped. My father was disappointed because he knew then that I wouldn't follow his vocation.

When I finished Standard 6, I began to teach school and married Elisheba.

Elisheba: I don't know when I was born, because my parents were not Christians, but we lived in Mugoiri. My parents had many children, but only two of us, girls, survived, so we had lots of work of all kinds to do at home. I remember watching a neighbor woman receive a letter from her husband. She had to ask someone else to read it to her. I determined then to learn to read my own letters and to read the Bible. I had to wait until I was well into my teens and of marriageable age to be brave enough to go to school against my parents' wishes. My first teacher was Heshbon Mwangi.

I began to go to church and to the Bible classes until I was baptized. Then I was ready, and Heshbon and I were married.

Heshbon: We generally believed in Christianity, but knew nothing of salvation. In 1939 I was dismissed from teaching for sexually molesting the girls. In 1940 I was reinstated, but could not teach Bible because I was a bad person.

The first testimony I heard of real salvation was from John Mwangi Kangoro, who told me what God had done for him. He and a few others had been saved some years earlier when a revival team from Uganda & Ruanda came to preach at Kabete. Listening to John, I realized with astonishment that there is a power that can enable a person to overcome sin and have his life entirely changed. I was outwardly trying to please church people, while secretly breaking many of God's commandments. That Sunday, the challenge came from Hebrews 11:24–26, which tells of the choice made by Moses. The challenge was "Are you willing to come out of the kingdom of Satan into the kingdom of Christ in faith and be saved from all your sins?" I made my decision that day and definitely received Jesus into my heart. He began to rule everything and to deal with my sins. I paid all my debts that I could remember and found out what joy there is in Jesus' forgiveness!

Some others began to see the light of the new birth at this same time, but my wife was skeptical and stayed aloof from all of this.

Elisheba: In 1941 my husband got to know a man named John Kangoro and through him something happened to change his whole personality. He became much gentler at home and we had no more trouble living together. There were others who were changed like he was, and they used to come and meet together in our home. I served them gladly, seeing that there was true love among them. I secretly began to long to be like them, gentle and loving—especially like John's wife, Hagar.

Heshbon: John Kangoro and I were both teaching in schools and we never stopped telling the students and teachers what Jesus can do. This was drawing some teachers, but when the children went home and told their families that Jesus had saved them from the evil things they had done secretly, their parents were enraged. Some were church members and were involved in worse things themselves. They accused us of bringing in a new religion and ruining their children. They hated me so much that in June of 1942, when I was returning from a meeting, the fathers of my schoolchildren were waiting for me in the village on the road. Hoping to discourage me from teaching, they knocked me down and beat me until I was unconscious. Finally, I could feel that one foot was cold. I began to pray, "Dear God, if this is Your time to take me home, please take my spirit now. But if not, please give me enough strength to get up from here and go." I was flat on my back on the road, shivering with the cold, because they had taken my coat and shoes. Most of the men were still standing there. I looked around at each of them, then I slowly got up and limped away. That day prepared me for the Mau Mau days ahead.

The next morning, although my body was swollen, I went as usual through the village to the school to teach. The parents were still angry and would come at night and steal our sugar cane and ripening pineapples. I could rejoice and be glad because the Lord was at work saving the school children. For five years I was not paid a salary as a teacher, so my family couldn't have tea or sugar or anything else from a store—so we drank water instead and ate what we could raise, and were happy in the Lord. The great thing was that in 1947 Elisheba, my wife, was saved, and from that day on we have been a team together for Jesus. The Lord has given us eight children.

Elisheba: One September the Holy Spirit showed me all my sins, and I began to repent and ask forgiveness of my husband for all the cruel things I had done to him. I had to apologize to others too. Then I realized that I was "saved" just as he and his friends were, and I became their "sister." From that time we have stood together for God and fought against Satan side by side.

Heshbon: One day in 1952 when the Mau Mau were forcing their oath, I arrived home from a preaching trip and found that my wife and children thought everyone in town had taken the oath except us. I called the family together to pray. I prayed, "Father, Almighty God, we are in trouble, and I am bringing each one of us and our home to You because we want to live here in this place under Your protection. You know the boundary of tall trees all around our yard—please put Your angel guard around us so no one intending to harm us may come through those trees. This way we will know that if one does come, he comes by Your permission and for Your own purpose."

Elisheba: The Mau Mau people were going from home to home and dragging people out to the place where they were giving their oath. Here I was, often home alone during the day, but no one came for me. The Lord certainly put His wings over our house and garden!

Heshbon: One Mau Mau did come. It was during the night of October 25, 1952, about 11 p.m., that a Mau Mau fighter came, leaving his gang on the road. He pounded on our front door with a panga (machete), and I called out, "Who's there?"

He answered, "Mister Jack!"

And I shouted, "Don't pound any more, Mister Jack, I'm coming to open the door for you." At that, he ran back to his friends on the road. I followed him but they had gone on, so I went back home.

Elisheba: The night Jack came to the door, we didn't sleep. Nothing more happened to us that night. However, next morning when Heshbon went to the school, the Mau Mau followed him.

Heshbon: In the morning I went to school as usual on my bicycle, passing several little groups of Mau Mau on the road. Some were talking to my fellow teachers, and they all followed me up to the school. They seized me and hit me so hard with the trunk of a small tree that they knocked out all my front teeth, both upper and lower. I was also slashed in many places with knives and with a whip. All the schoolchildren ran away and spread the word that their teacher had been killed. The fighters carried me to my office (I was the Headmaster) and said, "Show us where the money is!"

I said, "There isn't any Mau Mau money here or anything else of the Mau Mau. I won't take your oath—and if you finish me off that's all right, but I will never take it." Then they dragged me out and dumped me in some grass near the road where they beat me some more, stamping on me with their boots and hacking at my head and shoulders with their big knives, leaving me bleeding and unconscious.

After a while, when I could open my eyes, I saw some of my teachers looking at me with hostility. So I whispered, "I forgive you!" and they left.

Slowly I got up, took my bicycle and tried to get to a dispensary. I couldn't ride; I just fell off. So I pushed it two miles down into the valley and two steep miles up the other side to the dispensary, but I got no help. Slowly I struggled back to the school. Totally exhausted, I found brother Neville Langford-Smith and Rev. Elijah Gachanja there looking for my body. "You're alive!" they gasped, and we all wept for joy.

They took me first to the Murang'a Hospital, then to Neville's home in the Weithaga Mission area where I was received lovingly and put to bed.

Elisheba: That afternoon, one of the students came and told me that missionary Langford-Smith had come in a car and carried Heshbon away. I anxiously wondered if I ought to try to get to the hospital. But then I began to praise God, and my spirit grew quiet and confident again. I was at peace when brother Langford-Smith came to take me to Weithaga to help in nursing Heshbon. I found him very weak and all his teeth were knocked out. I stayed there a couple of days and then came home to help the children with the work. After a few days, I returned to care for Heshbon again. I was pregnant, but was able to keep up this pace while it was needed. The war was getting hotter. Some days, while looking for transport, I was afraid of the government soldiers, and sometimes of the Mau Mau; but the Lord was always with me and protected me and the children. Finally, the next year it became too dangerous, and we were all moved to Weithaga Mission, where we lived for five years. Many other families of the brethren camped there too, and we had truly wonderful fellowship together during that time.

Heshbon: After I was nursed back to some strength again, I returned to finish teaching the school year of 1952. After that I resigned from teaching because I felt a call to be free for preaching and encouraging. Many of our brothers and sisters suffered during those years and many were killed. We were called on day and night to search for the wounded and dying. Also, there were many very large detention camps where we ministered, taking the Good News of salvation, along with Bibles and other Christian books.

After a time, some kind friends helped me get new teeth and I went on serving the church with various titles: Rector, Archdeacon, Vicar General, and now Canon of the Diocese. I praise the Lord for His great kindness to us all our lives. It surrounds and protects and enables us—Amazing Grace!

## WHO DARES GOD?
### Ezekiel Njiru, Embu
#### (By his son, his wife and a neighbor)

Ezekiel was a man of God, an evangelist, who refused to take the oath of the freedom fighters. When enemies burned down a church which he had helped to build at Kithiopi, he kept on preaching in marketplaces and everywhere else people gathered.

In 1952 the freedom fighters began administering their oath to everyone in that section of Embu, but they left Ezekiel alone for a whole year. However, on the morning of January 1, 1953, while he was out milking his cow, some fighters came for him. Not finding Ezekiel in the house, they beat his wife, Rebekah, and two of them took her, with her young daughter, out to Kirimiri in the forest where people were taking the Mau Mau oath. The other fighters seized Ezekiel and beat him. He prayed, "My God, if this is Your time for me to come to You, Your will be done." They tied a rope around his neck and dragged him face down along the ground, through the Ena River to the clearing in the forest, over a mile away. About 600 men, women and children were there. Some freedom fighters were slaughtering goats to provide the blood for those who were administering the oath to people. Several men were digging a grave. When the guerillas saw Ezekiel they celebrated his capture and taunted him, "Ha! Ha! Ha!" and jeeringly sang a blasphemous version of the "revival chorus." As they mercilessly beat and slashed him, he prayed for them.

Kimbo Kali, the general, shouted, "Even your God can't save you now out of our hands! You will never see another sunrise! See, these men are digging your grave! We will force you to take the oath, and then bury you!"

Ezekiel replied, "Though I die, I will never take it. I have taken the oath of Jesus Christ and I am satisfied with His blood! He will save me from your hands or take me to heaven." At that, the leader pierced straight through his throat with a thin, sharp knife to stop his talking. Even though this caused him to lose consciousness, miraculously no blood spurted!

An assistant said to the general, "There are only seven waiting now to take the oath. We will finish and then bury this man." Ezekiel's wife and daughter stood there watching.

While they were still giving the oath to the last ones, a runner came, out of breath, and shouted, "Soldiers in uniform! On the road! Coming this way!"

The general shouted, "LALA!" (the command to disappear)—and the Mau Mau all melted away into the dense forest, leaving only Ezekiel on the ground, his wife, his little daughter, and a man named Njeru who was still digging the grave. Rebekah begged Njeru to help her carry her limp husband out to the road. Between them they carried and dragged him out. On the road they looked for the soldiers. But there were none there!

They continued dragging him down to the river. As they went— Ezekiel later told his son—he heard the Lord speaking to him, saying, "Son, I am restoring your strength now so that you can walk away!" At the river he was refreshed and got up. Njeru had run away.

Ezekiel said to his wife, "You go home now and take care of the children. I am going to town." As he started down the road to Runyenjes, he met a group of fighters dressed in antelope skins. Once again he was beaten and then let go. So he left the road and took a less known path from there. When he reached town, he found Joel Nyaga, a leader of the Christians. When Joel saw him he was startled and barely recognized him because he was so covered with mud and blood from head to foot. People were astonished that he had escaped alive from the Mau Mau in the forest. From then on until the end of the war, he and his family lived in a camp where Christians lived communally for protection and fellowship. As a faithful witness, Ezekiel continued to testify to Jesus until the time of his death in 1980.

## ASSUMED DEAD
### Erasto Kamwana, Embu
### (Over 90, and now with the Lord)

I was born into a non-Christian family of the Embu tribe probably about 1901. Two of my brothers were killed in the First World War. As soon as I could read the Bible fairly well, I was made a teacher of others. I married my wife and we had ten children, though not all lived to grow up.

In 1952, my wife and I were both saved when we heard the Good News and the Lord Jesus entered our lives. At that time, some of the other teachers had taken the Mau Mau oath, but we hadn't heard about it yet.

As usual, one day I rose and went out to work on our land before dawn. I noticed a group of men fording the river and coming up our hill. They looked friendly enough and greeted me nicely, so I had no idea that they were Mau Mau who had come to make me take their oath. When they told me what they wanted, I replied that I really couldn't do that because I had been saved by Jesus and I had taken His blood to set me free. They began to beat me furiously with their clubs and slash me with their knives, so that blood spurted out. I cried out, "Lord, receive me! Take me in!" Then I fell on my back unconscious. They thought I was dead, so as was their custom, they cut off my private parts and stuffed them into my mouth. Then they left.

My son came out to the field and found me there and carried me to the hospital. They say that when the doctor saw me, he put his hand over his mouth in astonishment that I could still be alive. While they were working on me, I was praying out loud, "Lord, take care of us; please protect us."

All of 1953 I was swollen and in great pain. In fact, the scars and the pain have been with me to some extent throughout the rest of my life. It is still painful for me to sit on a chair. But God is good. My wife and I are still together and living at home alone. And the Lord Jesus is still showing me those things I need to take to His cross for cleansing. His forgiveness is wonderful. We are not very well, but we are happy and loving Jesus.

## LEFT TO DROWN
### Abinjah Wacheke, Kigumo, Murang'a

One day I had to go to my husband to tell him that I was now a Christian and walking in Jesus' way. He was furious. He had by then married a second wife in the usual polygamist way. Both he and his other wife then treated me as a slave.

Later, when the Mau Mau oathing reached our area, they told me I would be killed because I was a "saved one" and had refused to take the oath. My husband and his second wife locked me with my smallest child out of the house. It was rainy season, so we slept under the storage granary with a blanket.

The day came when my little girl and I were returning from a fellowship meeting, not knowing it was the day set for me to be killed. A number of Mau Mau fighters came and seized me and dragged me away. I recognized one of them, but I didn't know the rest. I said, "Take me, but don't kill my child!" They threw me down on the ground and began to beat me severely. My little girl ran away crying. I cried out, "Jesus! Save me!" Then they dragged me along the ground and I heard them talking about throwing me into a pit after they killed me. Just then they saw some government soldiers coming, so they quickly changed to another path, dragging me straight down to the river. There they saw some people in the distance and didn't want to be recognized. So they hurriedly cut my head, neck and arms with their knives, tied my hands behind me and threw me into the river face down. Then they ran away, sure that I would drown.

In the water I was crying out, "Lord, am I to die here in the river?" I tried to move myself down the river, but because my hands were tied I couldn't swim. I struggled hard to crawl on my knees, cutting them on the rocks. When I reached a sandy bottom I managed to stand up, but then saw that I was at the bottom of a steep cliff. Several times I tried to climb the cliff with my hands tied, and fell. Finally I fell back to the edge of the water and cried out, "Have I been saved from the river to die on the land? Dear Lord, if my time has come, receive my spirit." As I became quiet, the Lord showed me a narrow path on which I could climb.

When I reached the top, I could see no one around and no houses. I walked and walked and walked until finally I came to a house. I listened and could hear some women inside praying. I managed to call "Hodi?" ("Anyone home?") in a very weak voice. One of them heard me and peeked through the door and cried, "Oooh, it is our sister!" They opened the door and brought me in. Suddenly I could feel all the pain of the wounds, which miraculously I had not yet felt. But it didn't matter because then I was safe, loved and cared for.

I praise God for bringing me through all those dangerous years, helped by my Christian brothers and sisters. I now have my own little farm and grow fruit and vegetables to sell. My children help me, too.

## A NIGHT IN THE MANURE
### Penina Wanjiru & Meshak Kamau, Kiruri, Murang'a

I was saved by Jesus in 1948 in Nairobi. I first heard about salvation from Bishop Yohana Omari of Tanganyika and others in a revival convention. I took the word home in my heart. Gradually, I began to see my sins, and I cried, "Lord, please wash my sins away and save me!" Right then the Lord saved me and gave me life everlasting with Him. From then on I was shepherded in the fellowship by Elijah

Gachanja, Obadiah Kariuki, Sospeter Magua and all the people of God who love Jesus and are waiting for His coming.

One night in 1953 the Mau Mau attacked Kiruri, high on the slopes of the Aberdare Mountains, where we were living. The first thing I heard was someone calling my husband's name three times: "Meshak Kamau!"

We were together in bed. He got up and answered, "Who are you?" We both got dressed. My husband picked up our corn-cutter knife from the room where the children were sleeping and we waited.

The attackers continued banging on the front door, and because the house had mud-brick walls, both the door and the wall started falling down. I had already gone to another room and had managed to crawl out of a window. When I got outside, I started screaming. The attackers ran to where I was and several of them seized me, shining their bright flashlights in my face.

While the attackers were busy with me, my husband had a chance to slip out the front door and run for help. On the path he met two Mau Mau lookouts armed with knives and clubs. Immediately, he struck one of them down. However, in the scuffle he also fell down, losing his corn-cutter. Seeing his escape was cut off, he came back to check on what was happening to me. I had been knocked down on the ground and my attackers were sitting on me, though I was three months pregnant.

When my husband saw he could not help me, he again ran for help. He ran to a neighbor's house but found a number of attacking Mau Mau there also. Several were at the entrance of the house and others were near the corncrib, so he also started screaming. One fighter turned on him and cut off his coat. But he managed to run away in a different direction toward the Kainyi police station which was about three kilometers away.

The leader of the attackers at our house left one guard sitting on me while they looted our house. Though I had a lot of pain and my arms were stretched out, they warned me not to scream. I was in a panic, but when they asked me what they should do with me, I said, "You can do whatever you like." After a while I asked the guard, "What are you waiting for? Why don't you kill me?" He didn't answer, and soon the others called him to leave me and come to where they were.

When he was gone I struggled to my feet and stumbled to the cowshed to hide. I stood behind a large tree in the cattle pen. The

Mau Mau came to look for me, but didn't see me. This attack was on a Friday night. As I was standing there wearily, I remembered the words we had read in the Bible on the previous Wednesday when we gathered in our fellowship meeting with Andrew Kanguru and the others. Someone had read Zechariah 2:8 in which God said, "Whoever touches you touches the center (or iris) of My eye." He explained that this means no one can harm us unless he has been given permission from Above. Thinking about this, I finally sat down behind that tree in the cow manure. While they were looking everywhere for me, I reminded God that I was the iris of His eye and I was trusting Him to protect me and my family. Amazingly, the fighters did not see me. So they went somewhere else. I stayed there all night, shivering in my cotton dress until I was sick.

The next day I tried to find out what had happened during the previous night. Our children were frightened but safe, so I went to inquire about Andrew Kanguru, a special brother in Christ, and found that he had been murdered. The attackers had started with him, and then had gone to the home of Rev. Samuel Muhoro, and finally they had come to our house and others for loot. I asked the neighbors where my husband had gone and they told me that he left and then returned with some police. Then he had left again. They gave me a place to rest until he returned.

My sickness dragged on for about a year. But God kept us safe from the guerilas, and we told others about His salvation. We were not threatened again and lived to bring up our seven children. Praise Him!

### A CHILD IN DANGER
Jidraph Kimura, Murang'a

When the shooting began in 1953 I was eleven years old and in a boarding school at Gituru, about two miles from Githumu, close to the southern end of the Aberdare forest. We lived in fear. Part of our school compound had become a British garrison, so the freedom fighters were often shooting at the soldiers, who were shooting back. In daytime we couldn't walk outside the schoolyard for fear of attack, and at night we couldn't go out of the building at all.

Of course, during vacations when I was at home it was worse— there with my mother in the countryside near Ndakaini. We were Christians, and my mother had not taken the oath. Neither had my father, mainly because he was a government agriculture officer and serving in the Home Guard. For that reason he wasn't at home much. We were called "collaborators with the enemy" by most of the people, so we couldn't sleep in our house at night. We went out after supper to find a place to sleep in the bush country. Of course we heard of the night raids to the north of us and the murder of Christians there.

One night in June 1953, we were enjoying our evening meal at about 8 p.m. when we heard shooting nearby. Mother said, "Oh there must be a skirmish out there. Take care!" We went to the window and saw the flames and smoke of a huge fire. Everyone who lived around us was shouting and running away. We ran too, taking only a few things—I took my school suitcase with my school uniforms and a few books. We threw these into our field of tall corn and hurried far away across the mountain to our aunt's house. Her house was safer because there was no road there, only a path. My mother had the baby on her back, my sister carried our three-year-old brother, and then I followed. That night the whole of Ndakaini Village, including the school, the shops and our house, was burnt to the ground. The school and shops had tin roofs, but they were destroyed as well as all of our grass-roofed houses.

The next morning, we came back to see, and every house in the whole area was gone—all 86 houses—even though they were not close together but scattered about, each on its own small farm. Furthermore, we found every movable thing had been taken, with all our livestock, including my few sheep that father had given me. Only the chickens were left in their small coops—so they became our food for a while. Everything we owned was gone except the clothes we were wearing. We walked to the military post where my father was stationed and found that the post also had been sacked. The men were congregated here and there outside. After the attack, we were all wandering about looking for a place to stay and something to eat. Some soldiers found us and took us to a nearby army post.

Our next danger was from the large contingent of young British soldiers who were brought in the next morning as protectors. Some two days later a group of us, mostly women and children, were outside the army post sitting in the shade of a big tree. We were nearly massacred by these new young soldiers who were practicing with a machine gun about 500 yards away. They must have thought we were terrorists. A young soldier with a bren gun was taking aim at us. My aunt was with us and she was very smart. Jumping up she shouted, "Look! they want to shoot us, let's raise our hands in surrender!" So we did and were saved.

All those years of fighting were terrible, although it was actually easier for us in the boarding school than for those in the countryside. Mother didn't have a place to live, and the family had to move from place to place. I can remember that during my vacations, mother would cook food outdoors on our land near the food crops, and we would eat before dark, sitting on the ground. Then we would slip into the bush, each with a blanket, finding his own place to sleep. It was war, and the airplanes were bombing very close to us now.

Although my father felt he had to fight in the Home Guard, he (with many others) was sympathetic with the reason for the freedom fighting. Even so, he hated their killing. But then, when the government forces went out there were terrible atrocities committed too. That is why we who were caught in the middle suffered so much. I remember once I was beaten by a Chief because he felt my father was on the wrong side. My back was raw and hurting for a long time.

I didn't actually know personally any of those who were killed for gallantly standing for the Lord Jesus, and who when threatened kept on testifying. But I and many other young people with Christian convictions today are a product of their witness and martyrdom. The organized church in our area almost disappeared during the war, but the fire that was slowly burning in my heart and in many others burst out in 1960, 1962, and into 1964 when Christ became real to me.

I was a young man of 21, and as I look back, I realize the Lord was always working in me. At that time, 1964, I was working in the Rift Valley, and wasn't even going to church. I was just a young man who wanted to enjoy life. I thank God I wasn't yet confronted with everything sinful. We didn't have a problem with drugs then. Still, I was drinking now and then, smoking heavily, and assuming that it was normal for young Africans to have girlfriends here and there. I thought that was the life! But strangely, I continued feeling guilty about my sins and wondering, "How can I change?"

On September 16, when I was with some other young men and we were visiting a neighbor's house, something that was said made me seriously ask myself, "How can I follow the good ways?" Right then the Holy Spirit answered in my mind, "What you need is salvation!"

"But what is that?" Then inwardly I found myself saying, "Lord, I do believe in You and want to follow You." I was smoking as usual, and as I was snuffing out my cigarette, I said to my friends, "Something has happened. I am different now. The Lord has just come into my heart and there is no room for anything else. Come along to my house and I'll give you all the cigarettes I have there. From now on I'll have nothing to do with the life we have been leading. I am a new person."

I started reading the Bible, and looking for a church where I could worship and belong. There was no church of my previous denomination, so I went to the Anglican church in Kinangop, and found I was near my old friend Miss Ruth Truesdale. That was a help, and I found groups of revival brethren here and there. By joining these brethren in fellowship, I began to grow in the Lord. It was a time of joy. I was young and unmarried, and my delight was to go by bicycle—later by motorcycle—to visit brethren on the weekends. These fellowship groups were very close knit and kept in touch with all the others. Anywhere I went I only had to introduce myself to be received with joy. Since I was an Agricultural Assistant, I had to visit a lot of farmers, so I also made Christian contacts on the way. Martha and I met as young Christians and now we are just into our 22nd year of marriage. Ruth Truesdale is still our friend, and the Lord has kept us one in the faith.

### They Call Him "Noah"
Reuben Nyaki, Embu
(As told by Zakayo Kariri)

Reuben Nyaki was getting old when he was taken captive by the Mau Mau in his vegetable garden. He had been cultivating his sweet potatoes when they came and seized him. They took away the digging tool he was using and tied a rope around his neck, taunting him, "So you say you are a 'Jesus man'—well, let your God rescue you now— ha ha! We have you for sure and are taking you away!" He said nothing; he had always been a quiet man. It was broad daylight and there were a lot of fighters surrounding him. They took him up into the deep forest of Mt. Kenya to a clearing where they were administering their oath. They tied him to the trunk of a tree and left him there, saying, "We will kill you soon! Pray to your God now!" He prayed and waited calmly for hours while they were giving people the oath.

The Lord had mercy on him and showed His power. Someone shouted, "The enemy are coming! Government soldiers!" Immediately, the whole crowd of Mau Mau vanished into the deep forest. When the soldiers reached the clearing, one of them cut the rope that tied Reuben and he was free to go home. He went to the Chief's place to report and they kept him there. He didn't live on his farm again until the danger was over. He always felt that the reason God had delivered him from the guerillas was because of their taunt that God couldn't help him now!

Reuben was no stranger to danger. In the late 1930's as a demonstration of his faith in God, Reuben deliberately started to cultivate a good plot of land which was considered by tribal priests and elders to be sacred and untouchable. It was used for their offerings to spirits and tribal gods. When he began to dig a garden there, tribal war-horns were blown to alarm everyone and call the men together to put Reuben to death. When he saw they were determined to kill him, he hurried to Kigari Town to a well-known man, Mr. J. Kamuri, who was also a church leader. Kamuri asked him if the Chief had been notified, and he said, "No." Mr. Kamuri wrote a letter for him and told him to deliver it to the Chief. When the Chief heard that people were gathering to kill this man, he called for his horses and rode with his elders and the Rev. John Connely to Mbogori Market, about 6 miles away. There they found a great many angry people milling about looking for Reuben. The Chief and his men dispersed the crowd with their whips and staffs until they all left. So Reuben was saved from lynching.

Later, after the escape from the Mau Mau, his friends began to call him "Noah" instead of Reuben because he had stood firmly, and almost alone, on God's side through two times of great danger.

### TORTURE WITH DELAYED PAIN
#### Samuel & Sara Muhoro, Kiruri, Murang'a

Samuel: As a schoolboy, in 1928, I entered the class for baptism and learned to recognize sin. But I was often badly defeated by it. By 1936 I began to hate myself and my wicked heart which was full of lust, jealousy, self-effort, anger, self-justification and hypocrisy. Even so, I began preaching to other young fellows, telling them what an evil thing sin is, and I became well-known as a church worker. The elders recommended me for training in the Divinity School, and I entered in 1946.

On the 17th of April in Holy Week that year we were reading John 17, and in that passage I read that "eternal life is to know God and Jesus Christ whom He sent." I asked myself, "Do I really know God?" I was compelled to answer no. I was sad to think I was in a school to learn to teach others about One I did not know myself. This thought made me cry to the Lord about my sins, telling Him all about them, and He cleansed me! Now I realize it is quite possible for a man to be doing God's work for a long time and yet not know the One he is serving.

I wrote to my wife at home and asked her to forgive me for all the wrongs I had done to her. I used to beat her and revile her and mock her in a disgraceful way. I also wrote to others I had wronged, and asked their forgiveness too. Some of them I saw face to face. All this time God was preparing me for the trying time ahead.

When the reign of terror began, I was gripped by great fear of the Mau Mau. But I prayed that the Lord would give me victory over this sin of fear, and He did. Soon I became very bold, and I went to each church in my district to share with those who were saved and to tell others how the Lord had taken away my fear. At this time the Mau Mau were forcing people to take the oath by using great violence, and many Christians were badly hurt. Dead goats, cats, and moles were being hung up where they could be seen around our area as a warning. In the Njumbi church a he-goat was slaughtered, all its limbs broken, and then it was straddled across the prayer desk with a letter warning of the deadly curses to come on the person who removed it. Many church members gave way and took the oath under this pressure, but others stood firm saying death was preferable.

On February 8, 1953, after the horrible and triumphant deaths of Gadson and Rebeka Gachigi, I was preaching in the Kiruri church. I urged people to make haste to meet God because evil days were at hand. The following Thursday the Lord spoke to us and showed us we were sheltering beneath His wings and He would not leave us. I was given courage to witness to the Mau Mau, telling them that if they did not leave their evil ways they would not be saved. Also I spent time strengthening Christians in their resistance to the oath. I spoke to the government people who had said publicly that all Kikuyu had taken the oath, and told them that was not true. I gave them a list of names to prove it. All this exposed me to the anger of the Mau Mau.

During the night of February 13th, 1953, at about 2 a.m., I was deep in sleep when my wife was awakened by the sound of someone outside calling, "Samuel! Samuel!" She tried to waken me without success. When they realized I wasn't answering, they broke down the door. Their last blow woke me up with a start, but after my first startled fear, the Lord restored His peace to me. I had prayed that night as usual that He would be our guard.

Sara: Now I know why the Lord came to me and showed me my sins, and saved me and helped me tell others about it, because He knew there was a battle coming in which I could not stand by myself. He knew I had no inner strength of my own. And sure enough, He was with me that night.

At the time when the Mau Mau came to our house and began pounding on the door, I found there was no fear! The Lord gave me strength and boldness even when they attacked us, because we had firmly made a decision—and told them so—that we would never, never take their oath.

Samuel: When the intruders got into our house, my wife opened the bedroom door. Immediately two of them came at us with long knives. They were young fellows whom we did not know. We asked them what they wanted. They replied, "Give us your money quickly or you will die on the spot." Then they asked for the keys to our boxes and cupboards. After tying our hands behind our backs, they began opening our cupboards and searching through everything.

During this time I was cut with a knife three times, and blood was blinding my eyes so I couldn't see exactly what they were doing. I was sitting on the side of the bed. One of the young Mau Mau fighters kept cutting me for a long time without respite, while the other was passing out our belongings through the window to those outside. There were many others outside, both men and women.

When the one who was attacking me turned to my wife, he asked, "Why are you smiling?" He viciously cut her on the head and she answered, "Because I feel no anger toward you." Then he cut a deeper slash, and broke one of her fingers on the left hand. Her finger has never healed properly.

All this time we talked with them in a friendly way, but they only replied angrily to us, "Why have you refused to cooperate in the good work we Kikuyu are doing these days?" We urged them to repent and come to Jesus. We prayed for them, "Father, forgive them and show them Your way." But they responded by further beating us all over our bodies and deeply cutting the tendon of my left heel.

Then they tried to force us to take the oath. But I told them, "No! We have drunk the blood of Jesus and that is sufficient for us." The name of Jesus always made them fiercer, and they pierced my back at the waist so that I thought they had cut my kidneys, and I cried out, "Lord!" in a loud voice.

"Why are you calling on the Lord?" they asked. I could say nothing in reply as I was almost unconscious, having lost much blood. Then the two young Mau Mau men took some of our blood and smeared it over our lips. When I tasted my own blood, I began vomiting until I was utterly exhausted. Finally, their anger spent, they released my hands, laid me on the bed and began to leave.

Just then our youngest child began to cry, and they asked Sara if she wanted her killed. She answered, "No!" "Well then, shut her up," they ordered.

Sara: I asked them for a blanket for the child. It was very cold. They threw her one and something for each of us to use to cover ourselves. They said, "We are going now, so don't forget to pray for us!" And we did pray that the Lord would help these young men so that they would repent and be forgiven and come into His salvation. The more I think of all that happened that night, the more I am convinced that our dear Lord was right there with us and in us. An amazing thing was that as long as the men were cutting our bodies we felt no pain, and we could talk to them calmly. The pain came later.

In the morning, we heard that our dear Andrew Kanguru had gone to heaven. Brethren from Weithaga Mission got news of us on their way to a convention and came to get us. It was Heshbon Mwangi, Neville Langford-Smith, and Nathaniel Wainaina. How we rejoiced in our pain to see them! On the way to the hospital, they took us by Muthiria to greet the brethren at the conference. Everyone stood and sang praises to God, some with tears for God's deliverance of us and also for taking Andrew to heaven.

Now, years later, He has also taken my dear husband Samuel to be with Him, and the more I realize all He has done, the more I am confirmed in my faith in Him.

(From Sara's personal telling and from Samuel's written testimony recorded in *From Mau Mau to Christ*, K. N. Phillips, Stirling Tract Enterprise, London, 1958.)

## "YOU CAN'T KILL ME!"
### Phares Muhia Wahinya, Kendongu, Kiambu

I was a nominal Christian who did not really know Jesus. I thought I knew Him though, because I had been baptized and confirmed by the bishop. But I was a heavy drinker and an adul-

terer, and I was living in many other sins not fitting for a Christian.
In 1946 I came face to face with Jesus. It was when I heard a
woman speaking about God. She said that in His eyes the person
who is living in sin is a child of Satan. I realized that I was one of
those living in sin. I admitted to God that I was a drunkard and had a
filthy lifestyle. Then I was overwhelmed with grief when I saw
myself as God saw me. I sat down and began to pray earnestly to the
Lord Jesus, asking Him to save me from my sins and wash me in His
blood. He did that. Then I went to those who were preaching and
told them that Jesus had saved me. Everyone confirmed it lovingly.

With joy and some uneasiness I ran home to my wife, Rachel, and
asked her to forgive me for beating her and leaving her for other
women. She forgave me even though she did not yet understand
what I meant by "being saved." The next day she also received Jesus,
and we two became witnesses together to the Lord Jesus Christ. Our
parents and families were angry and told us not to talk to them about
it again. But we kept standing firm in the grace of the Lord, praying
for our loved ones that they also might be saved. Later some of them
did come to know Jesus.

Soon we were persecuted by some of our friends who were angry
at our testimony. They came and took away most of our household
goods—all of our dishes, blankets and everything they could carry—
to punish us and make us stop talking about Jesus our Saviour. But
we accepted the loss of these things and went right on praising Jesus.
When our friends saw that we weren't disturbed and didn't come
begging for the things—because our brothers and sisters in Christ
had helped us with what we needed most—they returned our belongings. In the morning we found all our stolen things there in our
yard, so we had more than before! One of the things taken was a
corn-cutter knife that I had borrowed from a neighbor lady. When it
was lost, she was upset and demanded it, so I had paid her three
shillings for it. But when they returned our things, the knife was
there so I gave that back to her also. When my elder brother, who had
declared I would never inherit any of our father's land, saw all of
this, he was convicted in his heart and soon he also was saved. Now
two of our family were Christians.

Then in 1954 there were problems of another kind. The Mau Mau
oath-taking reached us and the fighters insisted that every member
of the Kikuyu tribe must take it. I told them, "We will not take that
oath. You are saying 'Jesus is a white man.' I don't know about that,

but I know He is my Saviour!" Therefore I was condemned to death. The fighters did not kill me right then because they thought if they killed me in a Kikuyu reserve, government troops would burn down many houses, including theirs. So they made plans to kill me when I went to Nairobi City.

One day some of us were preaching at the Machakos Bus Station in Nairobi when I saw a car without a license plate being driven toward me at high speed. They came and asked me if I was Phares Muhia. Even though I knew what they had come to do, I said, "Yes, I am." So they tied me up in a burlap bag, dumped me into the car and took me to the place where the Mau Mau held court in Nairobi.

When I was asked my name I answered, "I am Phares Muhia and I have been saved by Jesus." They ordered me to pick up soil from the ground and put it in my mouth so that when I was dead, people would call it a suicide. I replied that I couldn't do that because I belonged to Jesus. Then they ordered me to take the oath, and I said I couldn't mix the blood of a goat with the blood of my Saviour who has satisfied me.

The court officials were sitting there in a row with seven guns aimed at me. Their leader said, "Now you will die!"

But the Lord helped me at that moment to reply to the judge, "You won't be able to kill me, because you are not the one to decide the day of my death. That has been decided in heaven just as your death also is in the hands of God."

He was startled and confused, but he said again, "You will be killed!"

And again I told him, "You can't choose the day of my death; it is in Heaven's control and there is no black market. Only God knows the day. If this is the day ordained by God, you will be able to shoot me. But if this isn't the day, your guns cannot hurt me."

He was very quiet. Finally he told me to go and they would decide about me later. But when I had taken a few steps, I was brought back. They went through my pockets to see whether I had letters from the government showing I was working for them. Of course I had none, I only had Jesus. Finally the judge said, "Go! And live your life as a saved person."

So I left them and went right back to the place where we had been preaching. The other brethren were amazed, having assumed that I had been killed. I started to preach again, telling how the Lord had delivered me.

After three months, the "judge" who had tried to give me the oath, and who had told me to go back and live as a saved person, deserted from the Mau Mau and began to work for the government. When I saw him he had become a Chief in the Eastleigh District. I called him by the name the Mau Mau were using when he was their judge, and he responded. I reminded him of my trial and said I was doing what he had told me to do—living as a saved person! He told his guard, "Don't bother this man. We tried to kill him, but we couldn't do it. If you see him in the city, leave him alone; he's really saved."

From that time until now the Lord has been helping me to keep going on in the the road to heaven, and I thank Him.

## IT'S A MIRACLE!
### Stephen Ng'ang'a Wairegi, Murang'a

Both of my parents were witch doctors, so our house was filled with their paraphernalia of magic and traditional worship. When I was five or six years old the first missionaries (of the Africa Inland Mission) visited Gathera, where we lived. My parents would have nothing to do with them, but all of us boys were fascinated with the reading and writing they showed us. One of my older brothers ran away to go to school at Kijabe to find out what it was all about. He even got a new name, Francis!

My father died when I was about seven, and my mother depended on us boys to herd the goats and cattle. But one at a time they left for school and I was the last one at home helping her, though she knew I was longing to learn to read. Finally, when I was eleven or so, she softened enough to agree that I go to the nearby school in the morning and herd the animals in the afternoon. When the government brought an examination to sort out which students could go on to the Intermediate Boarding School at Kagumo, I was chosen as one of the four to go from our area. Mother was distressed because she couldn't pay the fees, but I knew she had changed when she said, "Well, I'll talk to the other boys about it." From them she got the fees and I was able to go. Of course by then I knew I was a Christian—the teacher had told us so, and I could see I didn't do some of the bad things other boys did, so that proved it.

Those days in Kagumo the person who most influenced me was Pastor Elijah Gachanja in the nearby Anglican church. We looked up to him and loved him and I was one of his young people. But I didn't really understand what he was teaching us about salvation until 1945 when we went to a convention at Githumu in August. Reading Jesus' words in Mark 7, I saw that the real filth in my life was inside—the evil, dirty thoughts and words, my stealing—even from my mother— and much more. I cried to the Lord to save and wash me and He did. I was so happy I wept tears of joy. Oh, how wonderful it is now to have Jesus with me all the time and to walk with Him and with my brothers and sisters in the fellowship. I learned much from them, especially from Heshbon Mwangi and John Kanguru.

One grief was that my AIM missionaries weren't happy about my new testimony, even though they were earnestly preaching this very same salvation by the blood of Jesus. But in 1950 they were happy when I married Naomi Wanja, who had been brought up by AIM missionaries, and they took part in the wedding together with all our other friends who were Anglicans, Presbyterians and Baptists. That was a memorable occasion! Then our first-born son was given us at the end of 1951, and we went on to have five daughters and three sons.

Before our first son was born we began hearing about the new Kikuyu oath, but we weren't interested in any oath of this kind. What our tribesmen wanted to do was to get rid of the white people, who had stolen our land, and their Christianity. Naomi and I prayed together in our home, saying, "Lord, we have already taken our oath to go on to know You and to be saved, so we can't take anyone else's oath."

We knew perfectly well that the fighters had sworn to kill any who refused their oath. We also knew that for us who belonged to Jesus it would be a sin to take it, so we each asked the other, "Are you ready to go to heaven?" We both were. But my mother who was still living then was very sad, knowing that we would certainly be killed. I told her laughing, "Mama, God is much greater than people know, and He is able to protect us."

The war time, called "the Emergency," began near the end of 1952, and there was a great time of testing. I was teaching school across the valley from my family on the next ridge, and also studying in the seminary. I said to my dear Naomi, "Come, let us leave our home and fields here. Bring the children and move over to the school compound." She was willing, so we took what we could carry and while we were going down the valley we made up a little song something like, "Dear Lord, help us! Dear Lord, lead us!" All of this area was a dangerous war zone.

I went on teaching school, and I taught the school children: "You know that the One we have asked to protect us is the Almighty God, and we know He can do it." School went on during the day, and night after night we heard the noise of guns, as the war heated up. We had no gun, but we weren't afraid, because we kept putting ourselves in God's hands.

One night in 1954, the Mau Mau decided to attack the government soldiers who were stationed in our area. They were burning buildings and shooting any people they saw. Some came toward our house, but they heard a loud Voice saying in Kikuyu, "What's this? Who said you could attack this teacher? Don't burn that house! If you do, we will punish you severely." They saw no one, only heard the Voice, and they backed up.

Inside, we were lying on the floor with the children. Our little miracle was that we were able to pick up the babies and put them on the floor with us and they didn't cry! God gave them a deep sleep that night. Outside and over our house there were guns and cannons going PWAOOO! PWAOOO! PWAOOO! We were right in the middle, between the Mau Mau and the police. But God is amazing; not one of us was scratched, nor did we lose anything.

It was well known in our area that Nancy and I had not taken the oath, and that God had protected us. One day I went on my bicycle to see how my mother was getting on and to take her a bag of sweet potatoes. She seemed all right and said, "Go safely. Greet Naomi and the children. God will protect you."

I was traveling fast on my bicycle and passed some Mau Mau, one of whom was a giant of a man who had been strangling with his hands those who refused the oath. He turned, and when he saw me going by he shouted, "Where does that enemy think he is going?"

He grabbed a bicycle and a gun and started after me. Someone along the way motioned me to stop, but I shouted, "I'm late!" and sped on. I was coming to a steep hill, but the Lord gave me strength and I didn't even slow down on it!

I whizzed through the little market town of Kalela. When the giant got there, he stopped, aimed his gun at me and then put it away. He told people there watching, "That must truly be a man of God. You better not try to attack him. When I tried to shoot him with this gun, my hand wouldn't function!"

So I reached home safely and that was another miracle the Lord Jesus did. I also count it a miracle that I could go up that steep hill so fast and wasn't exhausted.

Another day, I was walking on the road with my wife, who was now a teacher, and with six other teachers we were going to Kangare. The road went along the base of a steep hill. It was late afternoon and there were Mau Mau lying in wait on the top of the hill. One who had a gun saw me and said, pointing at me, "That one there is wanted. I'm going to pick him off." About then the Spirit prompted Naomi to look up and she saw the face of a man who had been a very strict teacher of hers at Githumu. She saw the gun pointed at me and waved her hand. The gunshot went high over our heads so we hardly noticed it, and we arrived safely at Kangare.

During the evening meal my wife asked me, "Did you notice anything strange at Kimaingi?" I said no. "Well," she said, "they tried to take your life there. There was a man named Kimani on top of the hill with a gun pointed at you, but the shot went high. I knew him quite well and know he has joined the Mau Mau."

All through the war years God was with us and we saw Him do amazing things. How we praise Jesus and know He is good! All our lives He has blessed us. The children are grown. At one time a missionary named Kendall helped me to study for two years in Columbia Bible College in South Carolina. Now I am an ordained minister in the ACC&S (African Christian Churches and Schools). I am most grateful for the fellowship of the brethren—it is precious to us because it includes people of every race, tribe, rank and denomination with no discrimination. It keeps us steady and listening to our Lord as we go on together toward heaven.

## LASTING SCARS
### Ephantus Ngugi, Kandara, Murang'a

I was born in 1914 into a non-Christian home. When my father died in 1929, my brother Rufus and I went to live with our father's brother at Githumu, according to Kikuyu custom. This is where we managed to start school and, with our uncle, became "people of the Africa Inland Mission." I loved my American teachers, Miss Blakesley and Ruth Truesdale. I learned to read God's Word in our language, and got a good primary education.

I first heard about "revival" in 1933 when a man came from South Africa and told us about the revival in America under Charles Finney. He gave me a pamphlet about it, and we wondered what it meant to be "born again."

The visitor said, "If revival comes here, you will all be testifying to people and preaching and they will be saved!" We promised that we would begin to pray to God for revival to come to our area too, and we did. We didn't have to wait long, as our Revival had already begun in Uganda. In 1936, William Nagenda and a few others came from Uganda to our area of Kabete. They spoke of having been "saved" by Jesus. We were excited, but that year only two understood and received this word. They were Obadiah Kariuki (later our Bishop) and Elijah Gachanja (now a Canon). When the Ugandan evangelists came the next year, John Mwangi Kanguru, Tiras Kariuki, Spira Njoki and some others became powerful witnesses to Christ's salvation.

On April 3rd, 1938, I cried to God saying, "Lord, these people who are speaking Your word are saying that they have been 'born again' so please, I want this new birth too!" Marvelously, Jesus by His Spirit entered into me and showed me I was a sinner. He forgave me and said, "Go free, but do not live in sin again." Then I realized the preciousness of the blood of Jesus and of His salvation. I was filled with joy by the forgiveness of all my sins, and by the close fellowship with others.

At first in the Murang'a area we were just three—Elijah Gachanja, John Kanguru and I, but soon Heshbon Mwangi joined us. As the group kept growing, others were openly confessing their sins and asking for forgiveness. Some of the church elders felt that this was a new religion and spoke against it. After a while they ruled that we, "the heretics," should not come to the Lord's Table for communion. We comforted each other in our fellowship meetings that Jesus was daily teaching us the power of His life and of the blood shed for us on the cross. He Himself had come to live His life in us, and this was true communion.

Church leaders refused to let us use the church building for our meetings, so we gladly went outside and sat in the shade under a big tree. Maybe this helped, because out there many young people came to Jesus to be forgiven and born again. A few elders joined us and even some ordained pastors! We saw there was no limit to what God could do.

For eight years after I came to know Jesus, I remained unmarried and He kept me pure. In 1944 I married Mary, a sister in the fellowship. God blessed us and gave us a farm and ten children, five girls and five boys. They are all still living.

When the Mau Mau oath-givers reached our area in 1950, I told them, "I have already taken the body and blood of Jesus who died on the cross for me, so I can't possibly take another blood with a different oath," they said, "You just wait—we'll get you—you'll see." In 1952 they came to my house past midnight and broke down the door. I had a knife, but I put it away because Jesus had affirmed that we should not kill. They dragged me outside and demanded that I take the oath. I told them, "I will not drink the blood of your goat, because I have already taken the blood of Jesus."

They slashed me in many places, especially my face and mouth. They knocked out all my front teeth so I would stop preaching Jesus. Many of the cuts were deep and I carry the scars today. They broke up a megaphone I used when preaching outdoors, and jubilantly said, "This will never speak again!"

One of them shouted, "That's enough! Leave him now." They left me but took my wife and cruelly forced her to take their oath.

It took me quite a long time to recover enough to eat solid food. We were taken into protective custody at a police station where the officer in charge was Idi Amin, a mercenary from Uganda. When brethren came to request our release, we gladly joined the others who were living close together at Weithaga, where Rev. Obadiah Kariuki and teacher Heshbon Mwangi led us in fellowship. We planted a vegetable garden in that area, took care of our children and comforted those who lost loved ones. We all prayed, "Lord, help us to glorify you as our brothers Shadrach, Meshach, Abednego and Daniel did in Babylon, and we will speak of You to everyone."

One day without realizing it a few of us walked into the middle of a battle between the British army and the Mau Mau. They shot at us with shotguns and pistols, but the Lord put up an invisible shield and we were not hit. Nevertheless, that day we were trembling in fear and alarm. The man who had been the driver for the British Governor of Kenya was there, and he asked us, "Why are you shaking? Aren't you trusting in God?"

We cried, "Lord, forgive us and make us strong to trust You wholly." We relaxed and then the man said, "Now you can tell others what He has done for you." God Himself spoke to us through this stranger, giving us new courage.

We were able to return to our farms in 1957, and the Holy Spirit has kept us testifying for Jesus until now. He is a mighty Saviour!

## LEFT FOR DEAD
### Simeon Rikura, Meru

I was brought up entirely in the traditional way. I did not go to school, and as a young man I went to work in the town of Isiolo. There I heard someone preaching about Jesus. I liked it and I began to wish I could read about Him in the Word of God. I prayed, "God, if You will teach me to read so that I can read Your Word, I will be delighted and will become Your preacher to tell others about You." Of course I didn't know to close my eyes to pray, I just talked to Him looking up—but God is good. A roommate of mine began to teach me, and slowly in 1950 and 1951 I learned to read Kiswahili, the trade language. I went to church, and was taught and baptized. I married my wife and also learned tailoring in 1952; and that year I had a personal encounter with Jesus Christ.

By God's grace, one Friday afternoon I stopped in the marketplace to listen to a man preaching. He was Joshua Ichang'i, from Nyeri a teacher in the local school. He saw me there listening and carrying some books. When he finished, he asked me, "Where are you coming from?"

I replied, "From church."

He asked, "So you know about Jesus?"

"Oh yes, I do," I said.

"Has Jesus saved you?" he questioned again.

"No, not yet."

"Why not?" he pressed.

"Well, I'd like to be saved, but I don't know how to go about it," I said.

At that, he walked home with me and invited me to his house for supper. There he told me about Jesus and how He really wanted to save me. Finally he said, "Let's pray, and ask Jesus to forgive your sins."

I fell on my knees and prayed, "Lord Jesus, please wash me! I give myself to You—and from now on I will belong entirely to You." When we said "Amen," he hugged me and sang the Hallelujah song. Then we sang it together.

From that time on, Joshua taught me the way to walk in Jesus' love. He nurtured me spiritually, welcoming me into his home every evening after work for a year. Instead of going home, I went to Joshua's house for fellowship, and we often ate together too.

In 1953, the Emergency had begun and was spreading, and Joshua was moved back to Nyeri. In 1954 I got permission from the Asian shopkeeper I worked for to return home to Meru. I went alone, leaving the family there. The fighting was going on all around; people were being killed, and many had been sent to the detention camp at Manyani. But the Lord was with me as I was talking about Jesus along the roads, in marketplaces and in church.

I arrived at my home in Thura, and on the third day I went to bed early at about 8 p.m. In the middle of the night, I heard pounding on the front door, so I got up and opened it. Some men said, "You are Rikura, we know you!"

I answered, "Yes, but I don't know you."

They said, "We are those who are called 'Mau Mau.' We hear you are one of the 'saved ones' and we have come to give you our oath."

"Wait a minute," I said, "Jesus has saved me. He has given me His blood to drink and that is all I ever need. It is impossible to mix the blood of your oath with His blood."

They began to beat me with their knob-sticks and cut me around the head with their great knives. They dragged me outside, put a rope around my neck and dragged me bleeding, on my back, along the ground half a kilometer to the road. All the while they were beating me until I was unconscious. When they thought I was dead, they threw my body into some bushes, taking my shoes and watch and shirt. About 3 a.m. I opened my eyes. Toward morning I felt cold and was able to sit up. It was then I noticed that I had no shoes or shirt. Slowly I got up and stumbled home, where I had some more clothes in my travel-box. When I talked it over with my brethren there, we agreed that I should go back to Isiolo to my work and my family there.

After I had been at work about a month, some government soldiers who were looking for Mau Mau sympathizers found a few of us together in a home having a fellowship meeting. They didn't believe us and were suspicious that we were not what we said. So they put us in their vehicle and took us to the Home Guard camp at Kinoru where they locked us up with the Mau Mau, who told us that some of them had been tortured and killed there.

The Mau Mau couldn't figure out who we were. "Who gave you the oath?" they demanded. They pointed out one of them who had been a fighter in the forest and asked, "Is he the one?"

We said, "No, we never took the oath, and we don't know that man."

Along with the Mau Mau prisoners, we suffered from hunger and beatings. The government soldiers tortured us to make us confess we were Mau Mau. But I kept on gently sharing my testimony of Jesus. Although there were just four of us from Kirua, we continued to have fellowship every evening and to join together for prayers in the morning. On Sunday there was usually a preacher who came from outside the prison. After four months, we were moved back to the camp near Isiolo and there we were released.

I was grateful to go back to my family and my tailoring job. I have never been able to stop thanking the Lord Jesus for taking me through those difficult days. He says that His thoughts are not our thoughts or His ways our ways (Isa. 55:8) and His plans for us are perfect. One of the good things that happened during this time was that the Lord saved my wife, whom He had given me, and He also gave us four children.

Then the Lord took my dear wife. Two years later God gave me another wife, a sister in the Lord, and we had five more children. All of my children are now grown up. God is good. My wife and I have fellowship every day and pray to be "like a tree planted by the rivers of water, bringing forth fruit" (Psalm 1:3).

## An Immovable Witness
### Hudson Wainaina, Murang'a

I was born in 1905 in a traditional Kikuyu home. As first-born, I was expected to herd the family goats and to learn all the worship and protection offerings and rituals of our tribe.

I was 29 years old and married with one child when I first attended a church—at Githumu (Africa Inland Mission). We liked it and went ahead to be baptized and have a Christian wedding in 1937. We learned to read, attending school with the children! Later we built a church at Ndugamano and moved there. We also opened a school, though we were just ordinary lay people. I was made a church elder and I preached in this church. Later our church joined those who separated from the AIM and began the ACC&S (African Christian Churches & Schools). This was because at that time the AIM did not sponsor any schools above primary. They felt God had called them to evangelism, but we wanted to give our children more education.

In 1945 I was saved, accepting Jesus Christ as my Saviour. Though I had preached Him a long time, I had never seen my inward sins, only the outward ones. It was in reading the Bible that the Holy Spirit convicted me of my selfishness and unforgiveness and taught me to take these, and others He showed me, quickly to the blood of Jesus to be washed. I really knew Jesus then, and was walking with Him, staying near the cross.

When the Emergency started I was a preacher, and it seemed to me that everyone was taking the Mau Mau oath. Jesus told me not to take it, and soon my wife and I were the only ones around who had refused it. We kept on going to church, the two of us alone, as everyone else had gone off into Mau Mau activities. That was 1952.

Finally the Mau Mau came to our house, pounded on it until they broke in the doors and windows, and dragged us out of bed. They beat me and beat me until I was unconscious. They beat my wife too, but someone with authority said, "Leave her now!" They blind-folded me and carried me off, my wife and children trailing behind. Maybe the Mau Mau thought I was dying, because they took me to the river and plunged me in to revive me, then carried me on to a place where they were administering the oath. They read me the oath, but finally they gave up and took me home.

In the morning I went to Murang'a and the brethren took me to the hospital, and from there they took us to stay at Weithaga Mission where the brethren were camping. I asked the Lord to cleanse me in His blood from the defilement forced on me that day. Apparently the Mau Mau realized that I was never going to follow them as others did who left the church and their faith. (I went on with Jesus and later some of those who had beaten me turned to Jesus and were saved!)

When we returned home to live, government people had taken over our church and house and made them part of a camp for the Home Guard in that village. They put up a small mud house for us and told me to sleep there, so I did, with my wife and children and mother.

One day a man appeared in the village with some guns to be repaired. He was beaten up by a soldier and died. The next morning everyone in the village was told to gather in one place, everyone including the children. So I went there, so did the teachers and the Home Guards—we all stood there. Government officers said many words, then told everyone who had a gun hidden in his house to go and get it. Finally the one in charge said, "If anyone has anything to say, let him say it."

I spoke up and said, "My name is Hudson Wainaina and the Lord

Jesus has saved me." Everyone listened, including the government officers, when I gave my testimony.

After that the British District Officer took my arm and said, "Come over here." Then privately he told me to go back and ask the people if anyone else wants to be saved. So I went back and said, "Who else wants to be saved?" I preached, but no one spoke up. So they were all told to go home.

Our Chief told the District Officer, "This man's job is to preach to everyone; but if he gets hurt, don't be surprised." This was because he knew that the people didn't like Jesus and they could kill me for preaching Him. Nevertheless, now it was my job to preach to the whole village morning and evening with a loudspeaker, and the Home Guards had to be there too. There were some people who saw that what I was telling them was true and they were saved. At least, from that time everyone knew that for me this was no game, and nobody tried to change me again.

Until this day I am still preaching the Word of God in the church and to all people. Each day Jesus is my strength, and I am 85 years old. I know of nothing on earth that has any value compared to Jesus.

SHOT SIX TIMES
Robinson Maina Kamau, Murang'a

My parents were the first Christian converts in our area, Njumbi, so they brought me up in the church. But then because my father died when I was eight years old, I became the ward of his brothers. His younger brother who was a Christian took me, but in 1945, when I was finishing sixth grade, he died also, so I never got any further education. The next year, however, I was asked to help teach in a bush school, and I did this for three years.

In May of 1949 I was in a Bible Class that was being taught by Pastor Elijah Gachanja in our church. I saw that though the church elders spoke against him, he knew Jesus personally and was walking with Him. He asked me questions that made me realize that I too needed to be saved, and that year Jesus washed my sins away and my life was changed.

Early in 1952 I went to Nairobi to look for work and found Pastor Elijah there, who let me stay in their home. By July I was selling groceries in a food store operated by a man of our tribe. I didn't know that he and his helpers had all taken the Mau Mau oath.

One afternoon a young fellow, a friend of mine who hadn't taken the oath, came by and wanted me to come outside a bit so we could talk. The manager gave me a short break to go with him. I didn't know that the day before my friend had been forced to take the oath. There were five of them, and they grabbed me and tried to force me into their car. At first they couldn't do it, but some onlookers helped them and I was pushed in. The car sped off to the Athi River, ten miles outside the city. There they took me into a forest clearing and said, "You are going to take our oath!"

I said, "Never! Absolutely not!"

Ignoring this, they produced something to drink, and began reading: "You shall not keep company with Christians. You shall not read their Bible. . . ." I got more and more angry as they went on. They began beating me on the head and then pushed their pole into my eye. I was bleeding so much they took me back to Nairobi. When I managed to stumble back to Pastor Elijah's home in Pumwani he was with a man named Mkinyo, and they saw I was in real trouble with my head bleeding and some fluid running out of my eye, so they quickly got the police, who took me right to the hospital. After my wounds were dressed, I was able to go home, but couldn't go to work for two months. When I could work again, I returned and went on to the end of that year.

In July of 1953, I began to hear whispers: "We want Maina. . .we want to see to him." Someone from my home area came and told me that it had been asked in a Mau Mau meeting, "Who will get rid of him?" And he told me who it was who had volunteered to kill me.

First of all, I forgave all these people including the one who had signed up to do the job of killing me. My informant said he had to be very careful because if they knew he had warned me, he would be strangled.

I began to be fearful and tremble, and wondered if I should report to the police the name of the man who wanted to kill me. But I knew if I did, they could arrest him and hang him, but God would require an accounting of me. I heard this man had a wife and two children, and I was not yet married—so I made up my mind and told the Lord I was willing to die for him instead.

Then the day came when my friend told me, "The man who is after you has a gun now and can kill you at any time—at work, or leaving work, or at home in bed." My friend and I used to meet after work and I would make tea for us, using some of it to put hot compresses on my eye; then we would pray together, shake hands and say, "Lord willing, I'll see you again."

That happened to be Bible Week, and I went straight to the meetings after work. My pursuer was waiting for me every day after work on my usual route, and I never showed up! But then one day on my way through Kibera District I heard someone behind me calling my name. I turned to see who it was and saw a tall, good-looking man and didn't realize he had a handgun. He shot me, and the bullet went clean through my arm; then he shot again and again, six times. When I tried to run away, I fell on the road.

I was picked up by the police. One of them was a British Inspector who took me straight to King George Hospital, where I lay under treatment for a month. My arm was in a cast because the bone was broken, but the greatest difficulty was with the shot that punctured my lung. The arm didn't heal straight, and I had to continue breathing exercises for seven months; also a gastric ulcer developed, but the Lord kept me alive!

Later I was able to get married and have seven children, who are now grown. No wonder I love Jesus and, with my wife, we are full of gratitude to Him.

## A STRONG TOWER
### Rufus Karaka Manjeru, Murang'a

In 1928 when I was just a little boy, my uncle, with whom we stayed after our parents died, took us to church at the Africa Inland Mission station of Githumu. I remember those early missionaries: they loved God very much and taught us well. We were blessed. In 1932 I was baptized under the water. I loved God and began right away to tell others about Him. At that time, Kikuyu people in rural areas were still wearing goat skins.

After primary school I was accepted in a government intermediate school at Kagumo in Nyeri, and studied there for three years. Mr. Kenneth Downing, my pastor, used to come to visit me. On his recommendation, I was asked to teach the Bible class for the students in the morning. I used to go out to pray in a hiding place I had in the woods. One time I heard a noisy hyena coming right toward me, so I prayed hard and trusted God, and he passed by me without trouble. Because I excelled in my examinations, I was chosen to study in Alliance High School for two years. Kenneth Downing even visited me there. The missionaries trusted me completely, because I followed all the church rules.

As I grew older, however, and lived farther from the mission,

Satan began to take me over, even though I was still telling the other students they ought to follow God. In 1942 when I became a teacher for the mission, I was seducing girl students to such an extent that I was expelled from the church for a year. The next year I taught in an independent school and married Marion, a church girl, after she became pregnant. She was good at teaching children and was a trained midwife.

My older brother, Ephantus, whom I loved very much, had been saved since 1938. He has been very close to me all my life. He even loved me when I was disgraced in my sins, and kept right on telling me what Jesus could do for me, as did my missionary friend Ruth Truesdale, who never gave up on me. In 1947 I was one of the founders of the new church group, African Christian Churches and Schools, and was its first General Secretary. By 1950 I also was a half-hearted follower of the Revival Movement.

The Mau Mau oath became an issue in our area in 1950. I decided not to take it because it seemed to be satanic in part. By 1952 my brother Ephantus was coming to my house every evening. We read in *Daily Light* together, prayed and shared. It was painful that our own Kikuyu tribe looked on us as enemies.

The night of January 8, 1953, we read in *Daily Light* that the name of the Lord is a strong tower; the righteous run into it and are safe (Proverbs 18:10). In the morning, we talked about this strong tower—Jesus—as we pedaled on our bicycles to the village barber to get haircuts. We were still talking about Jesus on the way home. Along the road we met some Mau Mau fighters. A man jumped out of the woods with a pistol and shot at us! We both shouted "JESUS!" He shot at us again—and my brother and his bicycle fell down. Both of us began shouting in Kikuyu: "TOWER! TOWER! TOWER!"

Jesus did help us, for amazingly neither of us was hit that day. No one came out of their houses to see if we needed help, because we were considered to be enemies. Then we came to the house of a woman in our fellowship, who saw us and began to wail, calling us to stop. Her child had run home saying there were more fighters lying in wait on ahead to kill us. We turned around and went back to the place where we had first cried TOWER! God is amazing, because there was a car with British soldiers in it. We stopped the car and they took us with them, having recognized us as non-Mau Mau people. We asked someone we knew to take care of the bicycles.

The soldiers took us to the military camp near Githumu and

brought in our wives and children for safety. We could pray together there, but we didn't want our children exposed to the cruelty and evil behavior of some of the soldiers. Idi Amin, who later became dictator of Uganda, was there as a mercenary in charge of this camp. We were much relieved when Heshbon Mwangi and Neville Langford-Smith came and got us released to come to stay at Weithaga with the brethren. While there I came into a revival experience and could truly testify that Jesus had forgiven all my sins and filled me with His joy.

With my family, I was soon moved to Kahuhia, where I taught in 1953 and 1954. In 1955 I was sent to teach at Gacharage. I was a teacher for 32 years, loving and serving the Lord until now when I am 73 years old.

### KILL THE HEADMAN!
#### Jimna & Josephine Kimori, Murang'a

Jimna: I remember hearing about the First World War when I was a boy, but what was really hurting me was that both my parents died in those years and I was left an orphan. I went to live with my grandmother whom I called "Shosho" (Granny). She appreciated my help, but was embarrassed because she had no means to provide my food. So we had lots of trouble scrounging in the countryside for something to eat. When she died, I went to a distant relative who had land and cattle, which I herded for milk.

When I heard other children talk about going to school, I left the cattle unattended for a few hours and went to school. When my relative found out, he was furious and never wanted to see me again. At school I found another boy who had run away from home and we teamed up. At first we followed other children home until we found a kind mother who would feed us with her children, but we were ashamed to keep doing that and they got tired of us, so we ran away to Kiambu. We had no school clothes, only a cloth to tie on the shoulder, so we decided to work on a coffee farm until we could buy clothes and a blanket. This took four months, then we went to Thogoto to attend school and looked for a place to live. An African family gave us daytime work and we went to school in the evening. That was 1929 and we were "big boys" then.

The controversy over female circumcision (see List of Terms) nearly emptied the schools and churches, but we stayed in our school until 1941 when we completed it and were full grown.

We went to Naivasha and started a business selling used clothing out in the open in the marketplace. There I met a girl named Wambui and came to love her, and she loved me. I wasn't a church member, but from childhood I had always listened for God's guidance. God told me to go to her parents and tell them my situation exactly as it was. So I did. I explained that I wanted to marry Wambui, but I was penniless, had no parents or brothers to help me, and not even the inherited land in Murang'a which my parents had farmed. "If you want to refuse me," I said, "I'll accept that."

Her mother asked, "What are you planning to give me?"

I showed her my empty pockets, and said, "I'll get it from here."

They thought about this for a while, talked to their daughter, and then the mother answered, "Who can refuse an honest young man like this?"

Delighted, I promised, "Mama, I'll work hard, and my first ten shillings I will bring to you!"

We did work hard and finally I had saved 200 shillings, which I hurried to take to Mama. She said, "Well! You said you were poor, but I see you are going to get rich. Take this back and invest it in your business and earn more. Then bring it."

We were finally married, Wambui and I, and she has been a good wife. God knew she would have to be strong to endure all the trouble I caused. After four years, we moved back to my hereditary district, even though I owned no land and didn't know which part had belonged to my parents.

Wambui (Josephine): Josephine is my baptismal name. We were church people. I had been baptized and loved God. When we moved to Murang'a, I would go with our baby and visit all our neighbor ladies to chat, help them with their work, and speak of the Lord. I knew what the "saved people" said, and on December 24, 1946, I broke down, confessed my sins and knew I had been washed clean by the Lord Jesus. I hurried to tell brother John Kanguru and Hagar. They rejoiced, and so did all the fellowship folk, who received me gladly.

I always loved Jimna, but now I loved him more than ever. He sometimes drank too much and would come home and fall asleep with his shoes on. I had the strength to take off his shoes and carry him to his bed. He didn't like my testimony and sometimes beat me when he was drunk. And, of course, the money was gone, so we couldn't buy clothes or things for the baby.

Jimna: When we moved to my home area where people knew me, someone let us sleep in a tiny hut. My wife is very friendly, and she would visit the neighbors and help with their work, and they would give her food for the baby and even some for us from their gardens. When I could earn a little money, I went to buy the supplies we needed. My relatives, who were occupying my parents' land, were amazed that I didn't take them to court to get my inheritance. We just lived there quietly. Finally they gave us a half-acre plot and we were happy to be able to plant a vegetable garden of our own. Later they gave us another small plot, and I found out that this had been my father's. And gradually I was able to buy some more.

I got a job working for the Chief, and in 1946 he asked me to become the Headman to help administer our district. I accepted, and then we were able to build a house of our own. From 1950 on, I was under pressure from the Mau Mau because I was one of the few civil servants who was too conscientious in my job to take the anti-government oath. The fighters wanted badly to get me to take it. One day a great number of Mau Mau activists came from Nairobi to our area, and began seizing people and forcibly giving them their oath. Several people came running to me to inform me what was going on. Some fighters saw this and decided they would have to kill me. I was in our house with a government veterinary officer, my wife and children. They surrounded us and started pounding on the door. We made big noises by pounding bottles on pans, or whatever we could find. Then we heard them say they would burn the house down. I couldn't let them burn up my family, so I said, "I'm going outside!" The gang seized me and marched me away.

Josephine: After Jimna went out, I saw they had already set the house on fire. I cried out, "Dear God, come! Please put out this fire so the children won't be burnt up in the house!" I ran out and picked up some branches that were lying outside and beat at the fire. To my surprise, it went out; that's a miracle for a grass-roofed house! Then I looked all around, calling for my husband, but no answer. The children were crying for him. Some government soldiers came asking where he was. They searched the area as far as Kahuro without success, and left two soldiers with us overnight. I said to them, "Come, let's look in another direction."

They replied, "We don't go out at night." So I waited quietly with Jesus until morning.

Jimna: When I stepped out, there were at least thirty people there.

They seized me and walked me away, cutting me with their great knives (the deep scars are still on my face and body). They intended to kill me, so all were cutting me as hard as they could. But God did not permit them to kill me. My last word to them was "Let's go!"

They answered, "Where shall we go with you?" but I fell down unconscious and they left me for dead.

God spoke to me and said, "Get up! They will return." He strengthened me to stand on my feet. Then He said, "Don't go home. Go in that direction. They will return."

I ran in the strength of the Lord until I came to a house. In it I found a woman who had just delivered a baby that day. I was covered with blood and I asked if she had a burlap bag I could lie down on. She laid one out for me in back. She said, "Lie down and be quiet, I hear people coming." The people asked her about me but she said, "He isn't here."

In the morning, some children went to call my wife. She came, saw me, and went for the doctor at the nearest clinic. He came with his helpers and they carried me to their ward. The Mau Mau found out I hadn't died, and posted a guard outside the clinic to kill me when I came out. When I was well enough, government officers took me, under guard, to their training school, where I attended classes for a while, but as always there was a Mau Mau outside waiting to kill me. They tried again and again, but each time God protected me. One day I was being taken with a truckload of students to a meeting. The Mau Mau had bribed the driver to kill us. The truck turned over and many were hurt—my injuries were the most serious of all. My arm was so badly crushed they thought I would never use it again, but God has healed it enough so I can use it some!

Before I was saved, I drank with the other Headmen and officers, and enjoyed their dances. But one day in 1967 it was my time to come to Jesus. The evening before, a few of the saved ones had been at our house praying and planning for the next day's large meeting. Josephine was one of those chosen to travel in the car. But she was too sick to go. They asked, "Who will take her place?"

John Kanguru said right away, "Jimna will." I said nothing, so it was decided.

In the car on the long trip they were singing from the heart the songs of God, and I began to ask myself, "What about me?" The Spirit of God clearly answered me, "Now you will be saved." I asked the others to stop singing and told them, "I am being saved by God!" I repented and was forgiven all before we reached the meeting. The next day in the meeting I stood up and told everyone how Jesus had saved me.

My wife had been saved for 21 years and had lovingly cared for me in my drunkeness and sin. But from then on we have lived together in great peace. I know that God's grace is unbelievably great, for He led me from my youth, saved my life and delivered me many times out of great danger even before I learned to walk with Him!

# 4

# THEY GAVE THEIR LIVES

*"Others, refusing to accept freedom, died under torture in order to be raised to a better life. Some were mocked and whipped, . . . they were killed by the sword. . . . The world was not good enough for them!*
Hebrews 11:35–38 (TEV)

*". . . the scripture will come true: 'Death is destroyed; victory is complete!' . . . Death gets its power to hurt from sin. . . . But thanks be to God who gives us the victory through our Lord Jesus Christ!*
1 Corinthians 15:54–57 (TEV)

*"Then the Lamb broke open the fifth seal. I saw underneath the altar the souls of those who had been killed because they had proclaimed God's word and had been faithful in their witnessing. . . . Each of them was given a white robe, and they were told to rest a little while longer, until the complete number of their fellow servants and brothers were killed, as they had been.*
Revelation 6:9–11 (TEV)

## INTRODUCTION

Harassment and torture of Christians by the Mau Mau began a year or two before 1953. (See Heshbon Mwangi's story in Chapter 3.) But the actual killing of "uncooperative" Christian adults in the Kikuyu, Meru and Embu tribes apparently did not begin until early in January of that year, after the declaration of war. These "political murders" occurred both in the west of Central Province on the Aberdare Mountains (Gadson and Rebeka Gachigi) and on the east side of Mt. Kenya (Evangeline Mataria). Their stories are in this chapter.

At first the Mau Mau leaders firmly believed that the killing of a few "traitors" would intimidate all other resistant Christians into joining in with the freedom fighters. This proved true for over 80% of both churchgoers and government servants—and it is no surprise, because these tribes have traditionally had an almost psychotic fear of death and dead bodies, which they didn't even dare to touch. (See the List of Terms, and Silas Muchina's story in Chapter 5.)

What shocked the guerilla generals, therefore, was to find that a strong minority of their own tribespeople had truly lost their fear of death. They not only ignored the tribal taboos and held funerals, but they used these occasions to celebrate life! (See the first paragraphs of the Introduction to Chapter 2.)

These accounts are factual. Some are from eyewitnesses; others are from the martyrs' relatives or those who participated in the burial of slain Christians. Some facts about the martyrs came to light from accounts given by the killers after they came out of the Mau Mau army.

You will recognize that these who died were ordinary people, living simply in rural areas for the most part, but beloved of God and dear to their fellowship family. You will see that the killing of these unarmed, loving people had a profound influence on their communities, both on Christians who had defected and on the Mau Maus who killed them.

The number of committed Christians was not depleted by these deaths, but rather it grew. The joy, peace, forgiveness and freedom that came with losing the fear of death proved very attractive to young and old. Christian sharing groups began to include a good number of ex-Mau Maus. By the end of the war, revival fellowships were larger, stronger and more confident than they were at the beginning. Churches were both rejuvenated and growing. As in many other periods of church history, it was true in Kenya that "the blood of the martyrs is the seed of the church" (Tertullian, 2nd Century).

### THE FIRST MARTYRS
Gadson & Rebeka Gachigi, Njumbi, Murang'a

A young Christian couple, Gadson and Rebeka, lived in Njumbi, near the forest of the Aberdare Mountains, at the time when Mau Mau guerillas were based there. Rebeka taught at the little Mioro school and Gadson was a carpenter and the church leader. It was a home full of loving-kindness and thankfulness to God for their first child, Timothy, who was over a year old; and they were expecting a second. (The birth of Timothy was a great embarrassment to the powerful tribal priests, who had firmly declared that a girl like Rebeka, who had refused the tribal circumcision rites, would never bear children!)

Jesus had taught this couple to love their enemies, so Gadson and Rebeka were kind to the freedom fighters when they saw them—but they had refused to take their oath to kill. On the other hand, Rebeka had given a drink of tea to some very weary British soldiers passing by, which made the Mau Mau furious. This couple was marked as traitors to be killed.

These two, living in the joy of the Lord and in His peace, were not greatly concerned about the danger they were in. On Friday afternoon of a special weekend early in January 1953, they walked several steep miles with their neighbor-brother Nathaniel Wainaina to participate in a large weekend meeting of Jesus' people at Mucharage. They enjoyed being with those they loved and who loved them. They had been challenged and blessed by the messages they heard. Rebeka went home Saturday afternoon to pick up Timothy from his grandparents and to teach Sunday School. On Sunday afternoon, Gadson walked home with Nathaniel. At the path where they parted, Gadson, as usual, said cheerfully, "Goodbye, brother, I'll see you tomorrow if the Lord hasn't come."

That night the Lord did come for Gadson and Rebeka. Mau Mau fighters broke into their house while they were asleep in bed. They tied ropes tight around their necks and strangled them in bed, then tied the other end of each rope to a leg of the bed. They didn't bother the baby, who was asleep in the other room.

The Mau Mau went on to kill the nearby Subchief and his soldier guard. Then they started to cross the valley to kill Nathaniel in his home. At the first rays of dawn, they began to argue as to whether they could finish the job and get back into the forest before daylight. (All this they confessed later, when they surrendered.)

In the morning, Gadson's parents, who lived nearby, heard the baby screaming and went to see if they could help. They were shocked to find their son and his wife strangled to death and lying on the floor, one on each side of the bed. They took Timothy home and cared for him.

The news flew all over the hills that morning that Gadson and

Rebeka had gone to heaven, and all the brothers and sisters were invited to the "wedding." "What wedding?" the villagers asked.

The next day the celebration began as trucks and cars full of singing people, both Africans and missionaries, crept up the steep, winding road, passing group after group of others on foot, all singing and praising Jesus. One missionary who was there said, "We praised the Lord the whole way."

The two rough coffins were at the front of the church just where Gadson and Rebeka had pledged their love to one another for life and had received God's blessing on their marriage. It was a triumphant meeting, full of victory. Although all his front teeth had been knocked out recently by the Mau Mau, Heshbon Mwangi preached. He said, "This young couple were married here in this old church of Njumbi. Now they are at the Marriage Supper of the Lamb!" The people shouted in agreement!

After the service was over and the coffins were buried, some leading brethren met together regarding their crisis. They decided that the time had come to move some families out of such dangerous areas. Nathaniel Wainaina did not go home after the funeral but went along with those from the Weithaga Mission to help them plan how to accommodate all who were in danger. They did it by using classrooms and dormitories, with many families building their own shelters. This way they were able to live together for mutual help, fellowship, and comfort until the countryside was safe again.

(Reported by Rev. Samuel Muhoro, Nathaniel Wainaina, Canon Elijah Gachanja, Daudi Karigi and Edith Wiseman in *Martyrs*, Highway Press, London, 1958.)

## LOVING HIS KILLERS
### Andrew & Alice Kanguru, Murang'a

Andrew grew up in the Rift Valley and began farming in the Subukia area, where he met and married his wife, Alice. They both loved Jesus, and Andrew spent all his spare time telling people what God had done for them at the cross. Through his testimony, many came to understand that churchgoing alone was not enough. Eternal life could only be found through the salvation of Jesus.

When the family moved back to their ancestral land in Kiruri, on the Aberdare Range, Andrew became a lay reader and preacher of the Good News in all the villages of that area, assisting Pastor Samuel Muhoro. Andrew was well-known and loved for strengthening the

*Mt. Kenya — a rugged "sacred" peak.*

*Church of the Martyrs in Murang'a Town.*
*(page 26)*

*Church gate — symbolizing the spiritual power given the martyrs.*

Bishop Obadiah Kariuki (right) visiting with President Jomo Kenyatta at the State House, Nairobi, in 1971.

Revival leader Heshbon Mwangi in 1956. (page 86)

Obadiah Kariuki, first African bishop of Kenya. (pages 23, 27)

Phillip Kibotho, evangelist.
( page 40)

Paul Kibe, evangelist.
( page 36 )

Daniel Muthomi Theuri. ( page 48 )

*Rev. Nathaniel Kamunye (left) and Daniel Gathiomi. ( pages 36, 55 )*

*Three "Freedom Fighters" set free in Christ.*
*Left to right: Charles Riria, Justus Thiruaine and Zekaria Mutunga.*
*( page 46 )*

*Jason Njara Njogu. ( page 64 )*

*Peterson and Phoebe Wambugu.  ( page 67 )*

Blind soldier Justus Mwangi. ( page 53 )

Stephen Kehia. ( page 70)

Lawrence Kimotho in his animal-skin suit. ( page 57 )

*Simon Ng'ang'a and his church. ( pages 38, 83 )*

*The Rev. Canon Heshbon and Elisheba Mwangi. ( page 276 )*

*Abinjah Wacheke. ( page 93 )*

*Phares Muhia Wahinya.*
*( page 103 )*

*Ephantus Ngugi and wife. ( page 109 )*

*Robinson Maina Kamau. ( page 116 )*

*Jimna and Josephine Kimori. ( page 120 )*

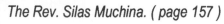
*The Rev. Silas Muchina. ( page 157 )*

*The Rev. Canon Elijah Gachanja.*
*( page 150 )*

*Solomon Maina. ( page 165 )*

*Joel and
Susana
Buku.
(page 168)*

*Walter Maitai
and wife.
(page 175)*

*Joshua and
Miriam Ichang'i.
(page 177)*

*Abishag Hannah Wanjiku. ( page 181*

*David M. Munywa. ( page 182 )*

*Peter Munge Wohoro. ( page 188 )*

*Walter and Pauline Njiru.*
*( page 222 )*

*Walter Mwangi Rurie.*
*( page 194 )*

*Left to right: Joel Mwigaruri, Francis Ndigwa and Canon Bedan Ireri*
*( page 232)     ( page 258 )          ( page 207 )*

*Chaplain Geoffrey and Rachel Ngare.*
*( page 228 )*

*Arthur Kihumba, teacher and herbalist.*
*( page 238 )*

*David Mutembei.*
*( page 243 )*

Obadiah Gakunju Nthukire. ( page 254 )

Eunice Kagio.
( page 263 )

Hagar John Kangoro.
( page 256 )

Felix Imaita.
( page 265 )

Moses Mahugu. ( page 275 )

brothers and sisters in the fellowship groups. He helped them to stand fast in the grace of Christ as the rumblings of the underground rebellion came nearer. He was glad when some saved teachers were posted to their school—believers who took a stand for Jesus, publicly saying that they could not follow the majority of their fellow Kikuyu in drinking the blood of the Mau Mau oath. This was a great encouragement to Andrew.

One night in February 1953, there was a massive attack by a whole company of guerillas on the homes near the church and school of the people who had refused the Mau Mau oath. A number were slashed and tortured and had their goods stolen, and Andrew was killed. Before his death, he told his attackers of the love of Christ for them, and forgave them for what they were doing. Alice, his wife, was badly injured and nearly unconscious when Andrew died.

The next morning, February 14th, help came from the police and from Weithaga Mission. Heshbon Mwangi and missionary Neville Langford-Smith found and cared for the body of Andrew, carefully tended the wounds of the others, and took the most seriously wounded ones to the hospital.

Heshbon says, "That morning Neville and I both forgot about fear and loving our own lives, and determined to be on call day or night whenever we were needed. The boldness and peace of the suffering ones gripped us. Dear Alice, our semi-conscious sister, was saying in an almost inaudible voice, 'My spirit is still on the way to heaven to meet the Lord Jesus!'"

The Farewell Service for Andrew at the Kiruri Church was in an atmosphere of high celebration. Hundreds arrived singing and praising God, and all marched to the grave singing "Onward, Christian Soldiers!"

(Reported by Alice Kanguru, Heshbon Mwangi, William Macharia and others.)

### TRIUMPHANT DEATH IN A PIT
#### Mary Wangechi, Murang'a

Mary was a young wife and mother of three small children, living with her husband in the Njumbi region. She was attracted by the joyful faces and kindliness of her neighbors, Pastor Elijah Gachanja and his family, and she liked to visit them when she could. She became good friends with Rebeka, who was then an unmarried girl living with the pastor's family to help them with their work so she could go to school. The pastor and his wife often talked about Jesus, who had changed their lives, forgiven their sins, and showed them how to walk with Him. Mary and Rebeka sometimes wondered about this, wishing they had the peace and assurance that the pastor and his wife had.

Pastor Elijah's family planned a short trip for a few days of rest and renewal. They had the use of some empty teachers' houses on another hill and invited Rebeka and Mary to come with them. Mary was able to arrange it, so they both went along. It was during those days that both girls were able to accept that Jesus had died for them too. Each knew He had washed her sins away and become her Saviour. They came back home full of joy and praise, telling everyone Jesus had changed their lives.

Mary's husband was furious when she told him. He beat her, and complained bitterly to her parents that she was no longer the kind of wife he needed. Mary's mother was very upset and she sent word demanding that Pastor Elijah must come to see them. When he came, Mary's mother met him with a big stick and said she was going to beat him soundly for ruining their daughter. With a warm smile, Pastor Elijah replied, "Yes, if helping her to know Jesus as her Saviour has ruined her, then you are right, I did it, and you may beat me." Mary's mother was too surprised to do it.

Mary went quietly about her work, often singing softly, and quietly telling her children about Jesus and teaching them to sing. No matter how often she was beaten by her family, she would not change. Finally she was told that she could not eat food in either her husband's or her parents' house, even when she had grown and prepared the food! So after her work she would visit the pastor's home, where she was always given a good meal. She was able to help Pastor Elijah's family too. One day word got back to her family that Mary was on the grass roof of the pastor's guesthouse, helping a workman to rethatch it with bundles of dry grass. By tribal law, that kind of work was taboo for women, so her father furiously marched up there and shouted at her to come down. She came down and followed him down the path. When they were out of sight, he beat her with his walking stick to teach her not to disgrace the family. When he had finished and started home, Mary asked, "Is that all?" He nodded, so she went back to help finish the thatching.

Pastor Elijah was transferred from his church at Njumbi, first to

Nakuru, then to Nairobi City, before the Emergency was declared. But when he left, there were plenty of loving brothers and sisters in Njumbi who helped and comforted Mary. Her friend, Rebeka, had married a Christian brother named Gadson and moved away, and she had heard the good news of Rebeka's first baby.

When the Mau Mau oathing began, Mary was still telling people what Jesus can do. Her family continued to be distressed at this and they discussed how taking the Mau Mau oath would settle her down. Soon her husband ordered her to go to her father, who would tell her what to do. She went to him and asked, but he said, "No, go to your husband." She went back to him and again he said, "No, go to your father."

Then she asked herself, "Now what shall I do?" She had recently heard of the deaths of Gadson and Rebeka and their triumphant funeral, and knew this could happen to her, but she decided to do nothing. This gave her family the impression that she had been persuaded to agree with them. When she realized this, she stood up before them all and said, "One thing I am not ever going to do is to take this oath. Jesus is my Saviour, and I could never turn my back on Him." At this they were more angry than ever.

Since all of her family were Mau Mau adherents, it is no surprise that word got back to the forest fighters. Guerilla fighters came for her one night, strangled her to death, and stuffed her body down a pit latrine in the neighborhood.

For a week the brothers and sisters of the fellowship were looking for her and asking everyone, "Where is Mary?" Then someone discovered that there was a body in a toilet pit. One brother, Silas, who reported it to Pastor Elijah in Nairobi, said, "Of course Mary's body smelled awful when we pulled it up, but we hardly noticed that at all because we loved her so much!" Her body was tenderly cleaned and cared for, and with great praise she was buried in the churchyard with Gadson and Rebeka.

After some time, Mary's mother went on a journey to visit another married daughter of hers. In crossing a swollen river, she was swept off her feet and drowned. Afterwards, Mary's father started going to church and became a believer. So he was saved. Eventually all three of her children also were saved. They are proud of their mother, Mary Wangechi, who died for Jesus Christ.

## A WITNESS UNTIL DEATH
### Evangeline Mataria, Martyr of Meru

Before Evangeline's husband died in 1949, he had built a shop in the local marketplace, in partnership with Charles Mathiu. So when she became a widow with three children to care for, she continued as a partner in the business. She also earned some income by cultivating their fields. The family lived on the northeast slope of Mt. Kenya, not far from the dense forest. She was much loved by the fellowship group with whom she regularly met. To care for her, they built her a house, helped her with cultivation, and met other needs—as these groups have always done for widows.

Sadly, her brother-in-law plotted a way to take the shop's business away from her. This man had taken the Mau Mau oath in 1952 and was a friend of those who were fighting in the forest. With the local leaders of the rebellion, he arranged a time and place to give their oath to a group of women of Evangeline's community. He knew she would refuse it and could then be put to death by Mau Mau law. Charles Mathiu was involved with the plan and told Evangeline to come to a certain house that evening for the distribution of profits from the shop. This way she was tricked into going to the house where the oath was to be given. A neighbor of hers was there, Ezekiel Ntombogori, whose wife Tabitha was a sister in the fellowship.

Musa Ntoagiri, who was in charge of the oathing, announced that Evangeline must take it first. She jumped up and said in a strong voice, "Never! The blood of Jesus has changed my life, and His blood can never be mixed with a goat's blood!" At this, they angrily shouted that she would die, and pushed her out the door. Then they went on giving the oath to others.

Outside the house, the waiting guerillas tried every way they could to persuade or force her to take the oath. But she refused, and they knew they would have to kill her. They urged her neighbor, Ezekiel, to persuade her. He warned her that if she refused, she would surely die and leave her children orphaned.

With a smile, she said, "I am quite ready to go to heaven, and God will take care of my children very well. But I can never take an oath to kill people and disown my Jesus!"

An old man sitting there, Ntoitunga Ntoithiri, begged the Mau Mau not to kill her and offered them seventy shillings (a large sum then) if they would let her go, but they refused.

Finally, a gang of the guerillas tied her hands and marched her into the forest. On the way she peacefully told them about Jesus' love and how He died for them so that they could be forgiven and live with Him forever in heaven. This made them even more angry, but two were touched and moved over to one side. They hid among the trees but followed along. Finally they reached the place where there was a grave dug. "Here is where you will be buried," they shouted, "if you don't take the oath!"

She warned them that God saw everything they were doing, and that all they did in secret would be known openly. They tied her up in a cloth and threw her down. She prayed, "Father, forgive them, they don't know what they are doing!" When they started strangling her, she prayed, "Lord, receive me into heaven!" She died there and they buried her in the grave they had prepared.

The two who had hidden and listened saw it all but took no part in the killing. They were disturbed by Evangeline's words and victorious death; they deserted from the Mau Mau and reported the matter to the British authorities. Ezekiel Ntombogori, the neighbor, also defected and trusted Jesus as his Saviour and shared what had happened with the fellowship brethren. He says even today, "Her boldness and unshakable stand for Jesus cannot be compared with anyone else. It was her testimony that moved me to stand strong and give up everything in order to get Jesus. She totally lost her fear of death—I have never seen anything like it."

Together with the women who were in the house when she was seized, Ezekiel and Tabitha reported to the police the names of those who killed her. Her body was dug up and the story confirmed. A number of the men involved were caught, tried, and convicted of Evangeline's murder and sentenced to death.

(From reports by Ezekiel Ntombogori and Tabitha, David Mutembei, and Fred Valender's book, *A Mustard Seed Mission*, U.K., 1988.)

## A FORGIVING TEACHER
### Edmund Gikonyo, Murang'a
#### (By Apolo Kamau Kamau, his "son")

I called Edmund my "father," because we were closely related. He was born at Mihuti, and his parents, Karinja and Wahuya, were not Christians. Edmund was a clever young man and was sent by missionaries to be educated in Mombasa at Buxton School. He was on a scholarship so his fees were paid, and he was trained as a teacher. He came to know the Lord as his personal Saviour about 1949. He had married, and his wife is still living. When he was teaching here in Rwathia School in 1953, I was his co-teacher.

We had a problem in the school because most of the parents of our students had taken the Mau Mau oath and now refused to let their children attend a Christian school. These parents wanted their school to be independent, but Neville Langford-Smith, the Education Secretary for the church, said, "No, if you want an independent school, build it somewhere else."

Even though there were no children, Edmund and I walked every day to the school, about 3 kilometers from home. There were four of us teachers and we stayed there all day, knowing that this area was full of Mau Mau all around us. After school hours, we all went home. Edmund and I shared a great deal together—having good fellowship talking about Christ and how He was helping us daily. His public testimony was, "Jesus has saved me. I have not taken the Mau Mau oath and never will." Mine was the same. Often I stayed in his home in the evening, sometimes until midnight. Then I went to sleep in my little round hut nearby, where I lived alone.

Rumors began circulating that Edmund and I were secretly going to Nairobi to report on the activities of the Mau Mau in this area. This was not true, but the lies were being spread because we were resisting the oath. Perhaps the Mau Mau planned to use this accusation as a pretext for killing us.

Before long we each received a letter from the government stating that we were in a "special area of high risk." We should leave our homes at once and stay in a government post for safety. Edmund suggested that we should go to Weithaga, where there would be no guns but much good fellowship.

We had heard there was to be a meeting of the young people of the fellowship at Kahuhia. Edmund said that I should go to attend the meeting on Thursday, then on Saturday he would go to Weithaga and I would meet him there. However, Edmund did not leave in time. On Wednesday I made the journey to Kahuhia and on Thursday we heard on the radio that teacher Edmund of Rwathia School had been killed on Wednesday night!

That night, my sisters and brothers, who lived very near us here in Mihuti, heard and saw what happened around Edmund's house. They said that a group of the Mau Mau were pounding on his door.

From inside the house Edmund heard his own brother calling his name at his door, "Edmund! Edmund!"

My sisters and brothers slipped outside quietly and climbed trees so they could see and hear everything. They saw Edmund open the door and come outside. When he saw their gun, he said to the Mau Mau, "I have forgiven you for what you are going to do now." Angrily they put the gun to his mouth, but before they shot and killed him, he cried out, "Lord, receive my spirit!"

Hiding in the trees, they heard the gun and saw Edmund fall. Then they saw the gang go straight to my hut. When they saw the padlock on the outside, they shook it until they were sure that no one was inside; then they returned quickly to the forest.

I didn't go home after the Kahuhia meeting. Instead I went and stayed with the brethren at Weithaga, as we had planned, for the duration of the war. Together we were able to keep on praising God and we still are.

With the help of the brethren, I married a sister in the fellowship who is still serving the Lord with me until now. After I retired from teaching I became a pastor, and Jesus is still merciful to forgive me every time I run to Him in repentance. I love Him more and more each day.

## A MOTHER CHOSE DEATH
### Mariam Ndago, Meru

Mariam's husband, Samuel, was a Mau Mau, and he reported in their council that she was saved and had refused to take their oath. Ten fighters volunteered to kill her. On April 11, 1954, Mariam was sitting with her little daughter and two other women, doing some work together. Suddenly they were surrounded by these Mau Mau fighters demanding that they come into the forest to take the "freedom" oath with the blood of a goat. Mariam said, "I have taken the blood of Jesus, and no matter what you do I won't take your oath."

At this, the men forced all three of the women into the forest, leaving the little girl behind. The men tried to frighten Mariam by telling her they would break her back with a club, but she was firm saying, "It doesn't matter what you do. I have taken the blood of Jesus and He will take me home to heaven." She fearlessly continued to give them her testimony while she watched them dig a grave for her. This took place in the woods near the thickest forest. When the hole was deep enough, they threw her into it and covered her with dirt up to her neck. Still she sang praises to God and said in a loud voice, "Listen, every one of you. God is watching you and you will answer to Him for what you do. But I have no debt to you for I have told you about Jesus. He is with me, and I plead with you: receive Him and be saved!" Then she prayed the prayer of Jesus on the cross, "Father, forgive them, for they do not know what they are doing."

They continued to throw dirt on her while she was still alive. Then they cruelly killed her and closed the grave. We do not know whether the other women took the oath or not, but we do know they were not killed. Also, someone reported what happened that day. Later, Mariam's husband was killed in the fighting.

A great memorial service was held for Mariam in Chogoria Presbyterian Church. Her testimony strengthened all the brethren mightily. The little girl who was left behind is now an officer in the Department of Agriculture, having earned a degree in the University. Like her mother, she too has trusted Jesus—praise God!

### WAITING FOR JESUS
Geoffrey Mwiruri, Murang'a
(By his wife, Ziporah Wanjiru)

Geoffrey and I were married in January 1942. Twelve years and seven children later, Geoffrey left me for his heavenly home during the Mau Mau war.

I was saved in 1949 during a meeting I attended at Kahuhia, where the banner in front of us read: JESUS IS THE HEAD. I kept thinking about those words and realized that Jesus was not "head" of my life. Instead, I was following my own desires. When I admitted this, the Holy Spirit showed me all the things in my life that were grieving Him and He took me to Calvary for cleansing. He saved me at that time and I am still following Him today. The next year Geoffrey went to a large meeting at Kyonyo, and Jesus saved him there.

As the Emergency was starting, we agreed that we would not lean on each other, but should each walk with the Lord, listening to His voice. Then we would each have a personal testimony and assurance of going to heaven, no matter what happened. We had to be separated frequently because we were cultivating some plots at Githunguri, some distance from our home in town where Geoffrey worked. I stayed on the farm with our children and the livestock. When it came time for Geoffrey to leave us in January 1954, we prayed together and again agreed that we would each walk with Jesus until we were reunited. I never saw him again.

He had been invited to sleep in a teacher's house because the three teachers and two children wanted a godly man with them to lead evening prayers and teach them the way of God. Most of the people of the town had been moved to special camps or villages. Geoffrey had refused the Mau Mau oath and was very outspoken about it, influencing others. This angered the Mau Mau and they were watching for him.

During the night of January 30, Mau Mau fighters pounded on the door of the house. They broke in and began cutting all four of the men in the room, wiping their knives on the clothes of the children, even when the young ones crawled under the bed. The teachers in the bedroom heard the commotion and climbed into the attic. The guerillas asked each one in the sitting room, "What are you doing here?"

Geoffrey answered, "I am waiting for the Lord Jesus to return." They kept on cutting him angrily. At last Geoffrey prayed in a loud voice, "Lord, don't hold this sin against these men!" And before he died, he cried out, "Father, receive my spirit!"

I heard about it the next day from the children who had been in the room when he was murdered. Neighbors had taken their bloody clothes to wash and given them something else to wear.

Our Christian brothers and sisters rejoiced and sang as they buried Geoffrey, celebrating his entrance into heaven. They have stood by me wonderfully through the years. When I had no money, they paid school fees for our children, one of whom has become a church minister. I continued farming and raised our food, selling some in the market. As a family we went on praising God as we are doing today, waiting for Jesus' coming.

GLORY FOR A CHURCH PLANTER
Paul Muswita Kamende, Kirinyaga
(Told by his eldest daughter)

When he was a boy, Paul Muswita's family moved to Mombasa and there he attended school and church and became a believer. When he returned to Kirinyaga, his family's home area, he began a church at Kiariza in Kathare area. First, by himself he built a shelter of woven banana leaves on a frame and began to invite a few people at a time to come and pray with him. He taught the ones who came, and before long many more people were coming. Together they built a better building of poles and mud plaster with a thick grass roof. From this beginning, they became one of the established churches in the Anglican parish of Mutira. Those who were obvious leaders among the believers became church elders. They were Joshua Kariguri, Jeftha Mwai, and others. They too were inviting people and bringing them to church to learn about Jesus. With the help of these elders, Paul began a bush school to teach people to read and write, and a Sunday School for children.

One day when Paul went to the church center at Mutira he met a Christian girl, and they agreed, together with the local church people, that God wanted them for each other. They soon had a church wedding, and together went back to Paul's new, growing church. We children were born, and grew up in a Christian family where we learned about Jesus—as we also did in school. On Sundays after church our home became the gathering place for many, with mother cooking for everyone who came. There was much joyful singing, and all of this attracted new people.

As time went on it was apparent that Paul had become an important man in the community, and he was chosen to be one of the trusted Counselors in that area. The Chief depended on him a great deal because he himself was illiterate. Paul never drank, nor was he ever found cheating or oppressing anyone. He was openly a "Jesus person." He was kept in the position of Counselor for more than twenty years. To help him in the church, Jeftha Mwai became a lay reader, assisting in every way he could.

The politics of rebellion reached that area in 1950. Then came the Emergency, and in 1953 the Mau Mau arrived. Paul said plainly that he belonged to Jesus and could never take the oath which they demanded. We children were still living at home until February 1953, when I, the eldest daughter, was married and moved to my own home nearby. By then Paul and his family had a large, well-built house of stones set in cement, in European style, with all the furnishings they needed. He was loved and much appreciated in the community, and this no doubt protected him for a while from the guerillas.

But one night in February 1954 he was called to the door of his house by men whom he knew and recognized. When he opened the door they seized him, threw him down on the floor right there in his doorway, and shot him in the head with a pistol so that he died instantly. His wife was not at home, but one of the sons who was awakened by the noise went running to call her. The police also came, and took his body to the town mortuary. I, as the married daughter, their first-born, was expected to take charge of the funeral. Those were days when the government restricted all travel, so Bishop Obadiah Kariuki was unable to come. Rev. Musa Mumai did manage to come and he conducted the service. There was fear everywhere because most people had taken the Mau Mau oath. The service and burial were at our home. Jeftha Mwai was there and very helpful.

It was not very long after that the Mau Mau fighters took Jeftha Mwai and killed him also—because he refused to take their oath, was constantly praising the Lord Jesus, and was telling everyone about Him.

## A FEARLESS MAN OF PEACE
### Jeftha Mwai, Kirinyaga
(Reported by his wife, Sofia Wangechi, and others)

Jeftha Mwai had married by tribal custom before the time he personally met the Lord Jesus and was born again. After that, his and Sofia's marriage had a new oneness—because she had also been saved shortly before, in a Bible class taught by Pastor John. So they decided to have a second wedding in church. It was a peaceful home with the joy of the Lord. God gave them five children, three boys and two girls.

Besides being a farmer—growing corn, beans and bananas for the family—Jeftha was a church evangelist. He gave his testimony whenever he was teaching new believers for baptism and everywhere he went. He helped Paul Muswita build the Kathare Church near Kerugoya Town, almost directly across the road from Jeftha's house. He was a good man who never quarreled and was trusted in the neighborhood.

When the Mau Mau threat of death came, he said, "That's nothing to worry about—Jesus is in all of this and He is going to be glorified." Neither Jeftha nor his wife took the oath, and as fighting grew worse the danger to them increased. Jeftha continued to say, "We will live in peace as we are, even with danger, until the time comes for Jesus to take us home. We won't run away!" They lived through many days of warfare, and Jeftha helped to bury a number of those who were killed for their faith, including his dear Christian brother Paul Muswita.

Then one day he left home to go to work on some land given them in Mwea, several miles south of Kerugoya. His wife reports, "I stayed at home with the children. Three days later someone coming from Mwea brought me word that my husband had 'disappeared.' Actually, the Mau Mau had found him, taken him away and killed him, but the newsbearer only said that he was gone. When I realized what had happened, I could only praise the Lord through my grief. Jeftha had lived courageously, and we rejoiced that now he was in heaven with the Lord."

They never found his body to bury it, but years later when the fighters were finally released from detention, and were "confessing to the government," some mentioned the name of the village in Mwea from which they had taken Jeftha Mwai and talked about his death. Still, no one admitted to having been involved in it.

"There have been times since the Lord took him," confided his wife, "that I wished God could have taken me and left Jeftha, because he was able to help so many. But I am grateful for the time we had together and I keep praising the Lord."

Another brother, Henry Nguti, was killed the same year, 1955, in his own home when he refused to take the Mau Mau oath. All the believers knew that they needed to be prepared to go to heaven at any time, night or day.

## "NEVER LEAVE JESUS!"
### Reuben Gitau, Kandara, Murang'a
#### (By his wife, Rachel Wairimu)

We were both quite young when we were married in December 1940. After our marriage, Reuben went on to become a school teacher and an evangelist, both of which he did better after his encounter with the Lord Jesus in 1947. In 1950, the Lord also saved me. So when the Mau Mau recruiters came to our area, we were able to trust the Lord together and prepare to go soon to be with Him. We absolutely refused to take the Mau Mau oath.

In 1953, our house in Kagumwini was burned down by the Mau Mau. So the pastor of our church, Rev. Heshbon Gawia (later a bishop), with whom Reuben worked in Githungiri, took our family into his home! We were a crowded but loving family.

One day in April 1954, Reuben left home as usual to teach in the Kariguini School, which was situated about 5 kilometers (3 miles) away. In the afternoon, as I often did on Fridays, I walked to the school to return home with him. About 3 p.m. regular classes were finished, and he gathered the children to teach them the Word of God.

On our way home about 4 p.m., we saw a Mau Mau guerilla on the road running toward us. He ran straight to Reuben, grabbed him and knocked him down. Reuben said to him, "Do what you must—I am ready to go to heaven." Then three other fighters appeared and, recognizing the danger, Reuben turned to me and said, "Go home to the children. Train them well, and never leave Jesus!"

First I ran back to the school and told the other teachers, who came with me to the place where my husband was seized. The Mau Mau had shot him with a pistol, cut him with their long knives, and then they had run away, leaving him there. Soon some Home Guards came with the Subchief, who saw his body and left him there, taking me back with him to make a statement. I had not recognized the Mau Mau who attacked him, so I could not give him their names.

The brethren of the church came and buried Reuben right there where he had been killed. It was hard at that time to get permission to take a body somewhere else to be buried. I was not present, because from the Chief's place I was taken to Murang'a and then to Thika and to Nairobi, to give reports, before I could come home. The children were all right with the pastor's family. But we did not stay there long, because missionary Cyril Hooper came and took me and our seven little children to Weithaga, where the brethren could help me to take care of them.

Late in 1955 the fellowship brethren built us a small house in Githungiri near the church, where we stayed until 1960 when we were able to move to the place where I still live in Kagumwini. The children have grown up and one is a Subchief.

Reuben's last words to me, "NEVER LEAVE JESUS," have stayed with me all these years. I have walked close to Jesus and will never leave Him.

### THE BURNING BUILDING
#### Three Brothers in Christ, Meru
(Told by Felix Imaita, David Mutembei and Fred Valender)

On one occasion during Mau Mau fighting, we had a preaching team in the Kithirune Market on one of the northeastern slopes of Mt. Kenya. Some visiting brethren stayed overnight and slept in a shop belonging to one of the church leaders, in which was stored lumber and other building materials.

A party of Mau Mau came during the night and raided the market, taking all they wanted from the shops. When they broke into the church leader's shop and saw the people sleeping there, they poured a four-gallon tin of kerosene on the timber and set it on fire. Ibrahimu Murungi and others on the ground floor escaped through the back door, but three brethren who had climbed into the attic died and their bodies were burned up completely. They were Stefano, Stephen and Samuel. Ibrahimu cycled down to the nearest mission station to report, and another brother came to tell us at Katheri.

After the first shock, our rejoicing in the Lord became a very big celebration, and increased as brethren gathered from all around. Rebeka Philip and I were among those who gathered up the ashes of the slain men. We sang praises to God as we made coffins of the scorched timber. The unsaved people in that area were utterly amazed that none of us was afraid that the Mau Mau would come back to attack us the next night. "Where does this fearlessness come from?" they asked.

Methodist missionary Fred Valender reports: "I went up to conduct the funeral service wondering what I could say to the grieving wives, families and friends. But as I got out of the Land Rover at the church, I could hear joyous singing. Soon I saw a procession coming from the marketplace. The men were carrying shoulder-high three coffins made from the debris of the burned shop, and all in the group were singing songs of victory over death. They had dug three graves near the church and they stopped singing only long enough for me to read the funeral service. They sang again throughout the time they filled in the graves. Then they took the poles on which they had carried the coffins and made three crosses. They positioned these on the graves, facing the forest where the Mau Mau were hidden. There was no need for a sermon, the crosses said it all—for the people all prayed, 'Father, forgive them, they know not what they do!'"

Some Mau Mau were watching from the edge of the forest and were amazed that we forgave them. From then on, in our area, the word passed among the guerillas to avoid killing the "saved ones" for fear of punishment by their God! This whole experience brought renewal in our Meru fellowships and many more believers lost their fear of death and joined us.

### A YOUNG TEACHER AND AN OLD GOATHERD
Pithon Machari, Murang'a
(Robinson Ndirangu tells what he remembers of Pithon)

Pithon Machari's parents were Kikuyu who never learned to read and did not go to church, but their son, Pithon, went to primary school in Nairobi where the family lived when he was a boy. When he finished primary school, he got work there. Then the church elders of Kangema called him to come and learn to be a teacher at Kigari Training Center. So Pithon became a school teacher; in fact, he was my teacher in 1945. When he finished his training, he came here to Kangema to be our teacher, and lived very near us. In 1948, he was saved by the Lord and became a loving witness for Him. I was also saved that year, and we were in the same fellowship. So we went through many things together in the Mau Mau Emergency.

In 1953 Pithon was teaching at Gatuya Ngweiri (near Heshbon) and refused to take the Mau Mau oath. Then, because he was sharing Jesus with the schoolchildren and they were being changed, their parents were angry. They despised, scorned, and fought against him. They threatened to kill the carpenter who was building Pithon's house, so he left the job and went home. But the Lord gave Pithon another man to build for him, and before long his thatched-roof house was finished. The people of the area continued to hate him as a traitor, and began looking for an opportunity to seize him and force him to take the oath.

Pithon moved to Weithaga to stay through the dangerous time, but his wife, who had not yet been saved, didn't go with him, keeping the children with her. One day he went back to his home on his bicycle to take some food to his family. On his return to Weithaga, Pithon was ambushed by some Mau Mau fighters near Kangema Town. They dragged him into the bushes and asked him about the oath: "Did you take it?"

"I never will," said Pithon, "I have taken the blood of Jesus and am satisfied. I can't take another oath." They stabbed him deeply with their knives, hid his body in the bushes, and left him to bleed to death.

It happened that just at that time there was an old man herding his goats in those woods. The same guerillas found him and asked him if he had taken the oath.

He said, "No, the blood of Jesus is all I need. And if this is the time for me to go to heaven, I will go willingly." They also stabbed him to death there.

Following a radio report that a teacher and a goatherd were missing in this area, policemen began looking for them. They found the bodies and took them to Murang'a Hospital. Then they brought them back to be buried near their homes. A whole busload of people, singing joyously, came from Weithaga for the burial. People in this area were stunned that Kikuyu would be singing and rejoicing over death during this time of great danger to all. Even the British soldiers were totally amazed at them as they buried the bodies of their beloved brothers who had gone to Jesus before them. Bishop Obadiah led the service which was full of praise.

## TEACHERS ON BIKES
### (By George Mbijiwe, Meru)

August 1954 was a time of danger and hard fighting in Meru. Each month, we who were headmasters of mission schools were expected to come to Methodist headquarters in Meru Town to receive the wages for all the teachers in our school. Each one's wage was in a marked envelope and we were supposed to take these back and distribute them. One morning at the end of August, the time came for me and the other heads of schools in Kirania District to pick up the wages. We traveled by bicycle, close together as a group, through the forest. It was a frightening trip, but we arrived safely.

After we had received the wages for our schools, I explained to the others that I could not start out with them then because I had matters to settle with the person who was building my house. I said they should go on, and I would try to catch up with them as soon as I could. I saw them start out in close formation, just as we had come.

As they neared the Ncheru Forest, the two in front, Francis Ontiria and Joseph Ntokiumba, became alerted to danger. They saw a group of men beside the road ahead of them dressed as policemen. They recognized that they were Mau Mau in police uniforms preparing to rob and kill them.

One of them shouted to the other, "Better be shot in the back than face them!" Both yelled and speeded up, going as fast as they could. Those two got by safely. The rest, close behind, then saw the danger, jumped off their bicycles and ran into the thick growth of the forest. Most of these teachers were caught, killed, robbed, and piled up as firewood is stacked!

When the two in front reached a Home Guard camp, they reported breathlessly: "Help! The teachers following us have been attacked by Mau Mau who tried to stop us. They must have been injured or killed!"

The Guards laughed and said, "Ai! How come they were killed and you escaped? There are no Mau Mau in there that we have seen. You are lying."

A little later Rev. Johana Mbogori and another man came hurrying along out of the forest on this dangerous road. Joseph and Francis asked if they had seen any Mau Mau. They said they hadn't.

Teacher Joseph repeated, "Our friends have been beaten!"

The Guards again said, "You are lying. We will beat you."

"But," he insisted, "if they weren't stopped by someone, where are they? We were traveling close together!" When word of this ambush reached the Chief, he went to search for the teachers in his car. By then, one of the teachers who had been left for dead had regained consciousness, managed to roll off the pile, and crawled to the road. The Chief found him and took him to the hospital in Meru Town.

● ● ●

When I finished my business in town that day, I started out fast to catch up with my friends. But when I came to the Public Works Department Depot, I was stopped and turned back by a man named Paul who said, "Along that road things are bad." I had to return to town.

By six p.m. the report had come to Meru Town that people had been killed along that road, and one was in the hospital. I went to the hospital and talked with the teacher the Chief had rescued, but later that evening he died.

The next day when people went out to look for the others, they found our friend Gitonga lying in the bushes very badly cut up but still alive. The six others were dead and their bodies were brought back for burial. That was a very sad day.

Later we learned of another reason for the ambush by the fighters who attacked us that day. They not only wanted to rob the wages and use our bicycle frames to make guns, they especially wanted to capture a teacher named Festus Migwaa, who knew how to burn bricks, something few people know. His wife had taken the oath and told the Mau Mau about Festus, that he was a saved man who had not taken the oath and would probably be traveling with us to Meru Town. But by the grace of God, Festus was not in our group that day. He would certainly have suffered a great deal if he had been captured.

BRIEF ACCOUNTS
Nine Martyrs of Embu
(Reported by Canon Bedan Ireri, James Njogu, Erasto Kamwana)

Shem was a church elder who was born-again and zealous in serving the Lord and caring for people. His wife also loved the Lord, and although they were childless they were satisfied in Jesus. They adopted an orphan girl, Edith Mugure, who became a sister in the Lord and married a Christian engineer and architect, Epafara Ireri Muturi.

Shem was one of those in Kigaari who helped the many Christians who took refuge at the mission, camping there during the days of the Mau Mau war. One day Shem left the relative safety of Kigaari and went to teach the catechumens of the Anglican Church of Mbukori. On the way he was ambushed by Mau Mau and killed. His body was never recovered.

### Abinjah Igoki

Francis Njoka of Kiriari was being hunted by the guerillas. When they came to his home in 1953, he managed to climb up into the attic of his house. His grown daughter, Abinjah, who was his first-born and soon to be married, was in the house when the Mau Mau came. "Where is your father?" they demanded of Abinjah. She refused to tell them. She also had refused their oath, so they knocked her down and killed her with their knives.

### Timothy Mujuga
#### (By Zakayo Karigi)

Timothy was my first cousin. He was killed by the Mau Mau in June of 1953 for two reasons. He was the first church member at Kiriari to testify that he had received Jesus as his personal Saviour—which seemed at that time a strange religion. Also, he was among those few Kikuyu who had refused to allow their daughters to be mutilated in the tribal rite of circumcision (see List of Terms: Female Circumcision). He was seized in the Mbubori Market near Mt. Kenya. They tied him up and dragged him away into the forest and strangled him. We don't know where they took his body, for it has never been found.

### Parmenas Ndwiga

Parmenas was living with Canon Bedan Ireri in Kigari in 1953. He was a strong Christian and did not take the oath. He was intercepted one day on the road near his home. The Mau Mau took him away and his body was not found.

### Josephine Kiura

(See the testimony of her husband, Erasto Mushiri, Chapter 5.)

## Ephantus Kiura

Ephantus was a very quiet man, a teacher and a Christian who would not take the Mau Mau oath. So the Mau Mau found him one day in his home, took him outside, and slashed him with knives until he died. His brother's wife was also killed because she would not help them find her husband.

## Benjamin Kairichi

Benjamin was a faithful Christian and a lay reader in his Anglican church. He was the father of our Christian sister Nerea Wathumu. He didn't want to take the oath and was killed by the Mau Mau. When his body was found, it was obvious that his death was the result of repeated slashings. He was buried by the brethren.

## Jemima Njoka

Jemima was a girl who loved the Lord Jesus and had refused the Mau Mau oath. One day the fighters came to their home and told her father that he must join them and discard Christianity or die. He refused, and while they were searching for his wife he escaped and climbed onto the roof. When they couldn't find either her father or mother, they asked Jemima where they had gone. She refused to tell them, so tragically, they killed her instead.

## Elijah Njeru

Elijah was not killed by the Mau Mau but by British soldiers. He was a first cousin of Canon Daudi, and was not the man the government was searching for. Thinking he was Elisha Njeru, whom they considered a traitor, soldiers beat Elijah and killed him. Elisha is still living and tells the story. When it was told to Canon Bewes, CMS Secretary for Africa, he charged the British government with killing innocent persons. The body was exhumed and the charge confirmed, so Canon Daudi was compensated for the care of Elijah's family.

OTHER MARTYRS WE WANT TO REMEMBER
We List Their Names:

<u>Murang'a District</u>
Ben Karume
Peris Mwangi

Pithon Mwangi
Rachel Nyambura Kirugumi
Grace Wachoro Nduhia, Mbiu
Penina Zakayo, Micobio
Absalom Maina
Pithon Ngeri

Nyeri District
Johana Wanjau Gakaara
Gideon

Embu District
Nahashon Muchera
8 of the 12 buried on the Joseph Gakonja Kariuri Mountain

Meru District
A Roman Catholic nun

Kirinyaga District
Wilson Muriuki
Erasto Katindi
John Mungai
Peter Maganjo
Henry Ng'uti
Naaman Kiambati
Mwarage Gacheru
Joseph Gatore
John Kahuki
Daughter of Chief Siera
Granddaughters of Chief Siera

# 5

# NO FEAR OF DEATH IN DANGER

*"Jesus himself . . . shared their human nature . . . so that through his death he might destroy the Devil, who has the power over death, and in this way set free those who were slaves all their lives because of their fear of death."*
Hebrews 2:14–15 (TEV)

*"Don't be afraid! I am . . . the Living One who died, who is now alive forevermore, who has the keys of hell and death—don't be afraid!"*
Revelation 1:18 (TLB)

*"Don't be afraid, . . . you are mine. When you go through deep waters and great trouble, I will be with you, . . . you will not drown! When you walk through the fire . . . the flames will not consume you."*
Isaiah 43:1–2 (TLB)

*"Even when walking through the dark valley of death I will not be afraid, for you are close beside me, guarding, guiding all the way."*
Psalm 23:4 (TLB)

## INTRODUCTION

Bishop Obadiah Kariuki (see Chapter 1) wrote during the days of danger:

"After our Lord's ghastly death, the disciples trembled behind locked doors for fear of the Jews. But Jesus came to them and said 'Peace be unto you,' and their fears melted away. We were like that when we realized we had no soldiers to protect us; we trembled exceedingly, yes, very much. But Jesus has come to us too with His peace, and our hearts also are glad. We know that even if bad things happen to our bodies, we are all well and in peace with Him."

Obadiah went on to say that it was when they surrendered themselves wholly to God that they really knew peace, adding: ". . . we who learned in danger tell you this with the love that God has put into our hearts."

In early 1953, in Karatina Town, Nyeri, both Solomon Maina and Silas Muchina knew they were high on the list of enemies that the Mau Mau War Council had ordered killed. When they heard of those in Murang'a who had already gone to heaven by violent deaths, they agreed that none of them had long to live. In fact, neither of them expected to see the end of that year, nor made any plans for 1954. "Each day that we were still alive, we were surprised, and praised the Lord in the evening with our brothers and sisters," said Solomon. They decided that each of them would search his or her heart, surrender everything to God, and be cleansed in preparation for death. After they had done this, great blessings followed. Now they had no fear at all and went anywhere at any time that the Lord sent them. They were free!

They were part of a large company of men and women who apparently lived in total peace during the war years. However, they fully expected martyrdom at any moment of day or night. Theirs was that special peace coming out of total surrender, and it included genuine love and concern for those who wanted to kill them. In all ages, even as now, there are people in our world who have been or are living under a similar threat of death for the Lord Jesus' sake. It is largely for those who are presently in such danger that these Kenyans who learned this costly peace are telling their stories.

† † †

### A PATRIARCH OF REVIVAL
Canon Elijah Gachanja, Njumbi, Murang'a

I was born right here at Njumbi, high on the slopes of the Aberdare Mountains, about 1900. Though my parents knew nothing of Christianity, they brought me up well and I loved them. As children we were proud of our stretched ear lobes with their showy ornaments.

It was in primary school that I began to love Jesus and to preach. I even walked down into our valley and up onto the next ridge to tell people what I had learned of Him. Whenever I found a circle of elders drinking beer from a large pot through long straws, I would politely ask if I could come and stand in the center. This always made them laugh and they would say, "What! Is a child now asking to drink with us?"

And I would say, "No, I just want to tell you about heaven." Then I would preach Jesus to them. When my father was annoyed and asked what I thought I was doing, I said, "I just want to plant some seeds for God."

When I finished our village school I wanted to know more, so I went to Nairobi and found a Mission there. It was located on the land where the Kenya Parliament Building now stands. The missionary then was Mr. George Burns. I wasn't old enough to be baptized, so I continued in the preparation class, and I preached on the streets to the rickshaw men who were waiting for a fare. Before long I began to teach reading and writing to others, and was wishing I could learn to be a real teacher. Then Mr. Burns said, "I am going to England on leave, and on the way I will take you down to the coast to the training school in Mombasa. That was in 1922. When Mr. Burns returned, he brought me back to Nairobi to teach. Later he took me to Mombasa again to be trained for ministry, and I was ordained in 1928.

My work at first was in Nairobi. We had our first visitors from Ruanda and Uganda in 1935 and 1936. They were telling openly what Jesus had done in their lives, and in their countries, and we were amazed. I remember Josiah Kinuka and a brother named Ernest. They came not only to Nairobi but went to Maseno, Kabete, Taita, Mombasa, and elsewhere. While in our area, two of them were assigned to stay in my home. I knew they were praying for me, because they went into their room to pray by themselves. I wondered why.

In those days, Mr. Burns used to have an early morning Bible study which I liked very much. Then he took us on a retreat for prayer. That is where the Lord began to speak to me. The Lord Jesus himself began to show me all my sins. I was groaning in agony and felt I would surely die. Then Jesus showed me a vision of His cross, and said to me tenderly, "*You* don't need to die for your sins; *I* died for them all on the cross!" I believed in Him in a new way and soon I was filled with joy.

I went home to my wife and told her how I knew that Jesus had forgiven and cleansed me. I told her all the sins He had shown me, which I had never wanted her to know lest she be angry at me. Gradually I was able to tell others about it too. At first nobody understood.

I hadn't been getting along with the elders of the church. They saw me as a harsh man trying to be their boss. In the next elders' meeting I realized that I had been quarreling with them, and I asked their forgiveness. There were others also that I had to apologize to. This was unheard of, and made many people uncomfortable. This happened in 1937 when I came into a revival experience of the Holy Spirit.

People began complaining that my preaching had changed a lot, because I "talked about sin too much" and kept urging them to be saved. This was uncomfortable and they didn't like it. Nevertheless I also noticed that many more people were coming to church than before, hoping to hear about salvation. I prayed, "Lord, please help me! And help some people to understand what You want to do for them."

One day we were on our way to church and it was my turn to preach. As we walked I had the feeling that this was the day they would start to be saved. After the service, I retired to the small anteroom as usual, and a man came in with tears flowing freely and began to tell us what bad things he had done, and I knew God had touched him. Then two more came in the same way, and I was certain God had begun His work. It went on like this—and the church elders said I would ruin the church. But I knew the Lord was doing this work. Then we began to meet regularly for fellowship with those whom the Lord had touched, openly sharing our needs and listening together to the Lord's voice in His Word. Frequent fellowship was the custom in Uganda, and it became the pattern in all of Kenya too where God was bringing salvation.

In my church, there were more and more complaints about me. The elders said I would spoil the church and asked that I be sent home to where I came from. So the bishop sent me back to my home church at Njumbi in Murang'a. I began to preach to the people. These also saw that my message was different from what it had been and were angry about it. They decided not to give me the usual monthly allowance of a pastor. When I asked about it, they said there was no salary for the preacher. The treasurer simply put it away. So my wife and I went on without it and grew our vegetables.

When I invited people to a fellowship meeting, elders said, "We won't go to his 'fellowship' either." But one man who had lived in Nairobi and known me there asked the elders, "Has Pastor Elijah been tied up so he can't have a fellowship meeting?" and they said no. So he said, "Well then, I will go with him!" He came, and gradually a few others did too.

There were young people who came to our home. There were two or three young girls whose hearts were open. They came to ask questions and listen. Two of these, Rebeka and Mary, came with us for a few days when we went to have fellowship with some people on another ridge of our mountain. Both girls met the Lord there and were saved. We had thought they were shy girls, but they began to boldly tell everyone they met about Jesus and what He had done for them. Rebeka later was married to a young carpenter who knew the Lord, Gadson Gachigi Mwangi. Mary was already married to an unbeliever and her testimony caused her much suffering at home.

When Bishop Stanway from Australia came to visit our area, he asked the church elders why they were not giving their pastor his allowance, and they had no answer. "Is it because you want to get rid of him?" he inquired, and they agreed. "All right, you tell him to leave and I will tell him where to go." He sent me to Nakuru Town for a year. There I found the people hungry for the message of salvation. The message reached them with God's power, and they always gave me a salary!

Then I was assigned to Nairobi, to a church and school in Pumwani. I had an inner urge to keep finding people who needed Jesus. I went one day to visit the Nairobi Club in which were Muslims, Kikuyu, foreigners and all sorts, and they gave me permission to speak to the people. They listened a long time and said, "We never heard any of this from our leaders!" They were open.

I also went to the jail to tell them about Jesus' salvation and they listened attentively. Thieves began to confess what they had stolen, and I knew God had begun His work.

There weren't as many people in the city then, and I began to talk to people on the streets, and one by one they responded. Even now you can preach on street corners—that is what I did.

Then the missionaries chose me to go to Limuru to be in charge of the Divinity School there while the principal was on leave in England, and I was given Obadiah Kariuki to assist me. He also had been spiritually renewed in 1937.

After that good year in Limuru, I was moved back to Nairobi, this time to St. Stephen's Church. During those years, 1940 to 1950, we kept in close fellowship with the brethren in Uganda and Ruanda, Obadiah Kariuki (later our bishop) and I went to visit them and had fellowship with them in the Namirembe Convention of 1940 and the Kako Convention of 1950. The Anglican Church in Kenya was still questioning and resisting, but we also were able to have revival conventions: at Kahuhia in 1947; in Embu in 1948, at Kigaari Runyenjes. Dr. Irvine was there and Neville Langford-Smith came from Kiambu. Again at Kabete in 1949, and we held a great convention at Thogoto in Kiambu in 1950.

I continued serving at Nairobi's St. Stephen's Church all during the Mau Mau Emergency. I was in the hospital with tonsillitis when word came early in 1953 that two of our dear young people, Rebeka and Gadson Gachigi, had been murdered at Mioro! I was filled with envy that they had reached heaven before me—how I wished I could have gone instead! Then others followed rapidly—our dear Mary Wangechi, then Andrew Kanguru, and on and on. Robinson, a young brother staying with us in Nairobi, was shot several times but survived. He was married to Rebeka's sister, Ziporah, who was strong and helpful.

From 1960 on, revival spread rapidly and Jesus' salvation was becoming known far and wide. The doubts of church leaders were disappearing. Those of us carrying the message were able to travel far and wide. We had Heshbon Mwangi, Silas Muchina, Tiras Kariuki, and for a while Sospeter Magua (later Bishop) free to go when we were needed at conventions. We went to Tanzania and Uganda as well.

My last word I want to give you is from Jesus' parable: When you have done all that He has given you to do, say, "I am an unprofitable servant" (Luke 17:10). We are His unprofitable servants who love Him.

## HE TOUCHED ME!
### George Kimani, Murang'a and Eldoret

I was born at Kangema in Murang'a District, the last-born of my parents who still wore goat skins and sheep skins and knew nothing of Christianity. My mother loved me dearly because I was black like she was, and all the rest were brown like my father. My brother tried hard to help me learn to read, begging my parents to let me go to help him for a few months. In six months on his farm I learned to read and write Kikuyu. Then I determined to also learn English, but it was very difficult to get that little bit of education. When I applied for a job on the railways, I couldn't frame an English sentence. So I copied other people's applications and printed my name on it. Then I worked at it—I got a dictionary and an English grammar and other books, and kept studying them after I had started working for the railways. I also learned mathematics without a teacher. If someone gave me an example, I would work on it until I figured it out.

By 1940 I was married and living in Kajiado, working on the trains that carried out for export the bicarbonate of soda mined in Lake Magadi. Elijah Gachanja from my home area came to stay with us a few days. He was telling us of the salvation he had found in Jesus. After he left, while I was drinking tea in my house with my wife, the Lord laid a great weight of conviction on me for my evils. I found I was mixing my tea with my tears. Then I realized that a woman would see a man's tears—which was unthinkable in our culture. So I ran out into the bushes to hide myself. Then I fell flat on the ground. I asked the Lord to save me—as Elijah, the man of God, had said He would. But then I didn't know what to do next! Why hadn't I asked Elijah? Now he was gone. I was wondering and weeping and seeing Jesus, and kept on saying, "Save me, Lord!"

But the devil sneered, "Do you think God can save anyone here on earth?"

I said, "Yes! If He cannot save people here on earth, why did His Son come here to die on earth?" So the devil ran away.

Then I began to cry out, "Save me at any cost—even if it means I lose my job on the railway and I become the poorest man who ever lived; even if I am beaten and put in prison for my thieving. I will speak for You there. Even if my wife leaves me because she cannot stand living with a saved man, let her go—only save my soul! Even if to be saved by You is to die on the spot, *save me!*"

Then He touched me and I actually felt the weight of my sins lifted from me. The tears stopped. Was someone there doing it? I looked around. There was nobody. Then I said aloud, "What is going on?"

The Spirit of the Lord said, "You have been saved." He had to say it a second time—then I felt as if a full bucket of cool water had poured over me; then a second bucket. I was transported into a new heaven, new joy, newly alive.

I took my Bible, dusted off my clothes, and went to tell the good news to my wife. She looked at me as if I were a madman. I went down the street telling the neighbors, and they all thought I was crazy. I tried telling the evangelist at our small church—and even he didn't understand it.

I went to the railway officials and told them all I had stolen and done wrong in my work, and they forgave me, only asking me to return 100 shillings for the money stolen. I paid it and still have the receipt in my file. When people asked what I was doing, I said, "I have been convicted by the scripture which says 'God is light, and in Him is no darkness at all' (1 John 1:5). So anything I have done in darkness must come to the light and be straightened out with the ones I have wronged. If something was stolen, I must take it back, whether it's a knife, a pen, a book or money."

I was convicted about having stolen poll tax for twelve years. I had not paid it to the government, so the Lord told me, "Go to the District Commissioner and report yourself."

So I went, trembling. It was not easy. As I left the house, I told my wife, "Goodbye, I'm going to be put in jail."

I went to the office and told the truth. The first officer went and talked it over with his boss. One of them came and asked me, "Why didn't you pay it?"

"Because of sin." He bowed his head.

Finally they told me, "The government forgives you six years and you have to pay six years, but you may pay it little by little." It was only 12 shillings a year then, and I was able to pay the whole 72 shillings that day.

Everything the Spirit touched had to be put right for Jesus' sake, and every act was met with great blessing. I would start out trembling and come back transported with joy. I went on until my mind was clear and nothing remained that He was pointing out.

I had to tell everyone I met about Jesus, and after two years the stationmaster asked to have me moved from there because I was troubling people by constantly telling them about Jesus. I have been like that all through my years since then.

My wife and I were eight years without a child; then we had seven children, two of whom have died.

When the Emergency came, we were living in Eldoret Town, and were known by all the people. The great wonder was that nobody thought I might possibly be a Mau Mau, and no Mau Mau dared come to ask me to take the oath. The government did not treat me as a Kikuyu, and therefore a possible Mau Mau, because the railway officers all vouched for me.

My eldest brother was a Chief at Murang'a, a big man at that time. His name was Joshua Kogi Kiberu and he had much trouble with the Mau Mau people who were trying to kill him. He barely escaped. I told him, "Do not fear, I am praying for you; you are not going to die this way." He was not a saved man then but he was saved later, and his wife was also.

I knew Tiras Kariuki well. He was my friend and colleague for a time in the railways. I know he was beaten but not straightaway killed. Much later he died of the internal injuries caused by those beatings.

I love God and am waiting for His coming.

## A Surprised Polygamist
### Silas & Rebeka Muchina, Karatina, Nyeri

Silas: My family were not Christians, and I was an only son with five sisters, so it was very important to my father that I marry and have sons. I felt I must, according to the tribal custom, marry three wives in order to be sure to produce heirs. My first wife was not yet bearing children. So I married a second, who already had a son by another marriage, and I brought them both home. Then I also paid the dowry to the father of another young girl—to be my third wife.

I had heard that the church in our neighborhood—where there was singing which I liked—would allow a man who already had several wives to join the church without requiring him to break up his marriages. So when I had firmly married all three, I felt it was safe to go to this church and join the choir.

I was an avid snuff user. But on the way to choir practice, I always hid my little bag of tobacco in some dense bushes at a certain place along the road. One day on the way to choir practice with a friend, I hid my pouch as usual. Afterward, when it was dark, I returned to the bushes, pretending I needed to relieve myself. And lo! right there in that place I met the Lord! Jesus appeared to me in shining glory, and He showed me all my sins! When He had forgiven them, and the glory was gone, I was dazed and went back to my friend who was waiting for me. We went on down the road. Finally I asked if I could borrow his Bible to read, because I had none.

When I got home I woke up Rebeka, my first wife, and told her that Jesus had appeared to me and saved me. I told her, "All my tobacco is yours now, including the supply of it here in my box."

Then I called Mjenge, the second wife who had a boy child, and told her, "Jesus has saved me just now—this hour. So tomorrow morning you must take your son and your things and return to your father, because now I can't have you as my wife." Then I got up very early in the morning and went to the home of the third girl I was marrying, named Ndunge. I found her outside the house pounding grain with a wooden pestle and mortar. I greeted her and then said, "Yesterday Jesus met me and saved me, so I won't be able to take you as my wife after all."

I went out to the road and found her father and told him about it, and he said, "Oh no! You can't do that! What is joined together can't be separated. The dowry is paid and she belongs to your family now." I explained that I had no brothers and my father was too old to marry her, and I gave him my testimony. Eventually he had to accept the situation.

On the way home a friend of mine said I was crazy and told me of another Christian in the church who had three wives. And my father was furious because the second wife hadn't come that morning to herd his cows. When I told him what I had done, he tried hard to persuade me to get rid of the first wife and keep the second. When I refused, he beat Rebeka, the "childless one," and drove us both away from his village.

So we went a little distance away and cut saplings to build ourselves a little grass hut. We had nothing to put into the house or to cook with. But nearby there was a house that had been deserted with everything in it, because the mother of the home had died in it. The Kikuyu say that when that happens, her house is cursed and must be left just as it is. Anyone who touches anything in it will be cursed and die. Kikuyu are very, very afraid of death, and very superstitious. But now, since seeing Jesus, I wasn't afraid of any curse, and Rebeka went with me into the cursed house to get the things we needed. We even took some grass off the roof for our little house. This caused a lot of trouble with my father, who reckoned me as cursed and dead, as did all the people in the community, who then avoided us. No one would come near our place even to ask for a cup of water. When we asked a neighbor to sell us a bottle of milk, he filled it half full. This was his way of telling us we couldn't buy any more milk from him.

On Sunday I gave my testimony in church, and then went out with my Bible and spoke about Jesus to a woman and her daughter on the road. They believed and started to follow Him! My first sermon! I started going to school and teaching my wife to read too. Some white people gave me work guarding their property while they were away, so I did this and studied hard. There was one pastor in the church, Josiah, who taught Bible classes, and these helped me very much. Before I finished the primary school exam I decided I wanted to go somewhere for Bible training, and I was accepted at

Machakos Bible School (Africa Inland Mission) in the Kamba tribe. My wife and I went there in 1937. From then on the Lord blessed us with children, and the first two, born in Machakos, were boys!

In 1940 I found fellowship with three students who had come from vacation in Kikuyuland . . . saying they had been saved. That first night together we went about all night preaching—we didn't sleep. I also gave my testimony with them in a very large meeting of church people that Wednesday, and many were saved. But this upset the church leaders and they said of me, "If this fellow is like that, we won't let him preach in our churches any more." They didn't actually expel me from school, however, so I was able to go on.

In 1942 we returned to the family home in Kikuyuland and my parents were delighted with my little boys. My father blessed me in Kikuyu fashion, saying, "My cattle are all yours and also the goats." And he added, "I want you to buy me a coat so your mother and I can go to church with you." I knew, however, he was saying this just because of our boys, not because he believed in Jesus.

One of our missionaries, Rev. Phillips, came and asked me if I would be willing to go to Chogoria for nine months, where three of the church evangelists were leaving to go to Bible School. I agreed, and went to Chogoria where I found Dr. Clive Irvine. When he heard my testimony, we became great friends and began to travel about together preaching. Soon we wrote to Uganda to invite Brother William Nagenda, an evangelist of the East African Revival, to come. In 1945 he came and preached salvation. Many, many people were saved in the Chogoria area. When the team returned to Uganda, I was left with the care of all these new brethren who were just beginning to get together in fellowships.

Rebeka: Jesus saved me too in 1945. He showed me my many sins, had mercy on me, and brought me into His family that year. He saved me from my boasting, self-pity and stealing. From that time on I really loved my husband and thought of his welfare—something I hadn't been doing. I also began to love the work of God, and I learned to quickly repent of what grieved Him.

Silas: How grateful I was to have new fellowship with my wife! There in Chogoria I no longer had time to teach the classes in the church, but I traveled around in Dr. Irvine's car with a loudspeaker, preaching to everyone and encouraging the brethren.

Before the Mau Mau Emergency began, Brother Geoffrey Ngare came to this area, which was a great help. We were all saying openly that we could not carry guns. Jesus would not allow us to kill the freedom fighters because they were people for whom He had died and who needed Him to save them—as the British soldiers also did. We felt we were facing death on the center cross with Jesus, hung between two other crosses: on one cross was a thief (the British who had taken our land), and on the other cross a murderer (the Mau Mau)! Our job was to offer salvation to both, as Jesus did. We really were in the middle: the Mau Mau were trying to kill us, and the government put a lot of us in detention camps because we refused to fight with them!

After the war started, we moved back to Nyeri, our home area, where we then heard that I was on the short list of those the Mau Mau most wanted to kill. I was required by the Home Guard to move into Karatina Town. I personally didn't feel the need to move into a safe place, because if God gave the Mau Mau permission to kill me that was all right, it would be His will. If not, I was perfectly safe anywhere. Evidently they didn't get permission from the Lord, because I traveled all around during the Mau Mau time, preaching and encouraging my Christian brothers and sisters.

Rebeka: During the Mau Mau danger, we had to leave our home and move into Karatina Town. I was strong in spirit by then and knew I could never deny my Lord. When I was moved onto the Tumutumu Presbyterian Mission Station, with three other ladies, Dr. Brown gave us a little house among those who had leprosy or tuberculosis. We rejoiced to be there and were loving the Lord. At night we could hear the guns firing all around us, but we were never afraid of being killed. In the daytime we could go out and tell others what the Lord had done for us. God is so good!

Since the Mau Mau time, we have gone on praising the Lord. I have been able to give hospitality to many many of our brothers and sisters in the Lord, so besides bringing up our five sons and two daughters I also have many spiritual children like Roda Kariuki, Naomi Gatere, Phoebe Njoki, and Joshua Ichang'i. The Lord be praised!

Silas: Now in my old age, I am still praising Jesus, spreading His Good News and waiting for His coming. Recently I presented my dear wife, Rebeka, with a silver loving cup which is engraved: "For the best wife in the world."

## Fellowship Wins
### David Karigi, Kagaari, Embu

I grew up in a tribal home, but in 1937 I went to school at the mission because I eagerly wanted to learn to read and write. Of course I was also taught the Word of God and went on to be baptized and confirmed. In those days, anyone who learned to read well was expected to teach others, so I became a teacher and a church elder while I was still a young man. So I took on Christian culture, at least on the surface.

In 1949, a Gospel team from Murang'a and Kiambu came to preach here, and each one told how he or she came to have a personal encounter with God, a cleansed heart, and a new kind of life and walk with Jesus Christ—they called it being "saved." The Holy Spirit used these testimonies to show me my sins. I found a place to be alone and began to pray, "My God, I am seeing now that I am full of sins; please forgive me and wash me clean!" I began giving them to Him—my fornication, dirty thoughts and songs, the witchcraft spells I dabbled in, and so on. By the time I went back into the church, I knew He had dealt with these and set me free. I was filled with joy and couldn't help telling everyone that Jesus had accepted me. Then the Lord went right on showing me more—the fights I had been in, the lies, the stealing of food from white employers, the charms I had worn, and on and on. All were forgiven and washed away in the blood.

More and more people came to know Jesus personally until there began to be a revival in the church, so that in 1948 we could hold an all-Kenya and East Africa Revival Convention at Kigaari! Some brethren came from Uganda and we learned from them their Hallelujah chorus "Tukutendereza Yesu!"—the first stanza of which translates as: "Let us praise Jesus, Jesus the Lamb of God, for His cleansing blood has reached me! All glory to the Saviour!" We sang it and its various verses not only in Luganda, but versions of it in English, Swahili and Kikuyu.

The dangers of Mau Mau began for us in 1952. Many of our tribe, with grudges against the white rulers, took the oath (to fight and kill for freedom and to drive Christianity out). These people turned on us, saying, "You Christians are 'whitey-lovers'! Jesus is just a white man! And we hate you for taking on white people's beliefs and customs!" We were told that we would surely be killed if we didn't join them and take their oath.

I began to pray earnestly for my brothers in Christ because some were afraid to die and took the oath. I saw that Jesus had not been afraid to die for me to heal my sinful heart, and I knew that if I should be put to death for Him, He would give me boldness and courage, and take me to heaven.

At first, I kept my big corn-cutter and another sharp knife near the front door. I left the door unlocked, because I heard that if it is locked they will break it down. I reasoned: When they come they will be too many for me, but before they kill me I will fight valiantly. But as I prayed and knelt before the Lord and searched His Word, I saw I was on a wrong path. Jesus taught us to love our enemies and do good even to those that injure us. I felt I should love even the ones who might come to kill me. Jesus reminded me that when He was crucified He didn't strike back at anyone, but He prayed, "Father, forgive them!" I also prayed that He would forgive me for wanting to fight the attackers, and I put the big knives so far away that when they broke in I would just be praying for them.

We were given orders by the government to spy on the guerillas and report anything we knew about their movements or where they were mobilizing. They also forbade anyone to feed or give food supplies to the rebels, and anyone who did would be jailed and punished. But we found these orders did not agree with what Jesus was teaching us and we told the officers we could not obey them.

It helped a great deal that we frequently met for fellowship. Together we prayed for the fighters on both sides and for each other, and shared deeply with one another what the Lord was doing for us, delivering us from fear. At the end of every fellowship time we said to each other, "If I don't see you again here, I will see you in heaven!" We could not know what day or hour one of us would be seized and put to death, or sent to a detention camp. We did know we were prime targets for Mau Mau attack, and that government officers were suspicious of us too.

We kept hearing reports of dear brothers and sisters whom we knew, along the Aberdare Mountains and north of us in Meru, who were attacked and killed or badly injured. I prayed earnestly to the Lord that when they seized me I would be without fear and able to testify to Jesus who has saved me. Neighbors came and asked me, "Are you really refusing to take the oath? You will surely be killed!"

We lived very near the edge of the forests of Mt. Kenya. At one time Mau Mau scouts came to our church during a service, as spies, to see if any people who had taken the oath were there. That day some of them came to my house and found no one at home. They didn't go in but said to bystanders, "We won't stop until we have given the oath to everyone in our tribe—even those who are refusing will take it or be killed. Just wait! You'll see we mean what we say." That day God really helped me, because I was openly going about on God's business and they couldn't possibly have missed seeing me. In fact, I must have greeted them on the road and told them, as I did others, that they really need to be saved! Perhaps they laughed, but I am sure if it had been at night they would have killed me for that. However, when they burned down our church and school, I did move to live with the brethren in Runyenjes Town.

One of our elder brothers, Ezekiel Njiru, was dragged by the Mau Mau into the forest by a rope around his neck and would have been killed, but he escaped when the alarm was given that soldiers were coming. Someone carried him out of the forest and to the river, where he revived and was able to walk into Runyenjes, where we received him!

When we were holding meetings in the marketplace, sometimes former church members who had taken the oath from fear came and told us they were sorry now and wanted to repent and come back to the Lord. Some joined us in Runyenjes, and we rejoiced.

One night all the grass-roofed houses in which we were sleeping on the Runyenjes schoolgrounds were burned to the ground. By then the government officials considered us trustworthy, so they built a whole section of safer stone houses for us. Then when they were going for an attack on the guerillas they called us to come and fight with them. I said we were willing to come, but could not kill the enemy because we were under God's law—"Thou shalt not kill." There was grumbling among their people, who said we were unworthy of the houses we had been given to live in.

Another time two white officers came and picked me to show them where in the forest they could find the Mau Mau. I was reluctant, but they were pushing me along. One of them cursed me soundly in English and I said, "Thank you." Then he shot into the ground right under my feet, and I jumped and ran straight into the forest very scared. I waited and prayed there, but they didn't follow me, so I returned home. These happenings let us know that those who had given us housing were our enemies too.

I decided not to stay there any more, but to go home first and then go out in search of our brothers in Christ who were scattered and in hiding around the countryside. I found one place on Mwea Plains where a group of brethren had an encampment where they slept and cooked and prayed. They were delighted to see me and get news of others and encouragement. I could travel the roads of our District on my bicycle with a pass I had been given because the authorities knew and trusted me. I found another group on Mwea Plains and wondered if they had turned to become Mau Mau, so I greeted them with "Tukutendereza Yesu!" and immediately saw they were on Jesus' side. We shared testimonies of His leading and were mutually strengthened.

Before long the time came when the British blockade around the mountains was so successful that the forest fighters were starving. Then the government proclaimed amnesty by radio and by leaflets dropped from planes flying over all the forest areas, saying that anyone who walked out of the forest unarmed and holding up green branches in both hands would not be killed but treated fairly. Hunger brought many out, and among them were those who wanted to repent and come to the Lord or come back to Him. We gladly received them!

Brother Epaphras Kariuki and I felt we now ought to go to preach in the government-protected villages where so many people were living. So we went to the British District Officer for permission. He not only gave us permission, he gave us a Land Rover and a driver who was told to take us to whichever village we wanted to visit and introduce us to the one in charge. This was amazing, for the ones in control of these villages immediately announced on their loudspeaker that all must come to hear what these men from the District Officer had to tell them. We were shocked that the people came in fear and with heavy frowns. It seems that they expected punishment, or more forced labor. They were thin and we pitied them, but gladly told them we had come with the Good News of the living God who loves them and offers anyone who is willing to come to Him new life in Jesus. Some really listened to the word of the cross, and it was not difficult to begin Bible classes with them—which soon became fellowship meetings.

All of us who came through those days of constantly expecting death were surprised in the end to be alive! We learned then to trust God every moment, and we still trust Him like that today.

## PEACE OVER FEAR AND HATE
### Solomon & Martha Maina, Gaini, Nyeri

Solomon: I was born in 1929 and was taught all the traditional Kikuyu customs by my parents. I had only one year in school, and then obediently worked for my father tending the goats. I married my wife, Martha, in the traditional way.

Martha: My mother died when I was born and my father and older sister took care of me in the Kikuyu way. They had little time because we were living on a white settler's farm near Timau and they were both working for him. The day I discovered I had no mother, I cried, and my father said, "Don't cry, Gakenya, I will be both father and mother to you. If you want it, I will even buy you a dress like the schoolgirls wear!" (We had always worn just a piece of cloth tied around the waist.) That dress changed me. Suddenly I began to notice the schoolgirls and their homes and loving parents. I prayed to our god on Mt. Kenya, "When I'm a big girl, please give me a kind husband like some of the fathers of the schoolgirls I see."

One day some preachers from a distant Presbyterian church came to our village. It was the same day that the tribal elders had killed a goat for Satan to keep him from troubling us. Father brought home some of Satan's meat for our meal. The preachers wouldn't touch it. So we girls didn't either, because we liked the visitors. These teachers advised us to run away from home and come to their village where we could go to school. When a whole group of us did, the Christians took us into their homes. After we had learned to read and write, we went home. Father was very angry and whipped my sister.

But when he started to whip me, I said, "Father, if you whip us like this, we will all run away again." He stopped and said he wouldn't do that again, nor would he bring home any more of Satan's meat.

My sister and I kept on going to church and we were both baptized in 1945 on the morning of the celebration of Victory Day for World War II. I now had the name Martha, but we went from our baptism straight to the victory party with all the boys and young men and we danced all night. From then on we totally forgot our Christianity. (Solomon) Maina was one of those boys, and we got married in 1948 in Kikuyu fashion with a dowry paid to my father.

Solomon: After I took a wife, I left home with her and went to Meru where I learned tailoring. There I worked for an Asian shopkeeper and used the sewing machine on the front porch of his shop to sew clothes for people.

In that same year, 1948, I heard some young people telling everyone what Jesus had done for them. They said He had given them victory over their sins, and assurance of everlasting life. I had never heard anyone talk like this before, and I really wanted what they had. In December of that year, I accepted the Lord Jesus and was saved. That was a happy day and I couldn't sleep that night for joy, knowing that my name was written in the Book of Life! I began telling people about Jesus, and going out preaching. In 1950 I went with Martha to the East Africa Revival Convention in Thogoto and heard Dr. Joe Church, Festo Kivengere and William Nagenda, and saw that the fire of repentance and salvation was spreading all over East Africa. I then moved back to Nyeri, which was my home area.

When the Emergency began in 1952, spokesmen for fellowships gathered at Kahuhia from all over Kikuyuland to seek together what the Lord was telling us to do in this war. We were challenged by the story of the twelve spies in Numbers 13. Only two stood firm, trusting the Lord fearlessly, while all the rest were afraid of the giants and wanted to turn back. We saw the Mau Mau fighters as the giants and knew that almost all Kikuyu people, including Christians, were taking the oath they demanded. But we determined to be the two who obeyed the Lord, and were ready to die for Him.

Martha: We were living nicely in Meru Town; then my husband ruined our peace by getting "saved." When that happened, I wished I hadn't married him. For seven years I did everything I could to show him how angry I was about it. Then in 1952 we moved back to Nyeri District near the town of Karatina, onto his parents' farm. About the time of the declaration of Emergency, when the war was getting intense, I bore our first child. My husband's parents and I took the Mau Mau oath of course, but Solomon didn't. Freedom fighters from the forest passing by our farm knew they were welcome and would come in for a meal. We sometimes carried cooked food out to them in the forest. But life became difficult. The Mau Mau began to distrust me, thinking I might give their secrets to my husband; and the government police didn't trust him because they thought he might send information to the Mau Mau through me!

Solomon: My wife hated this salvation I spoke of. She took the Mau Mau oath and made life hard for me. One night a friend of mine, who then was in Mau Mau leadership, secretly brought me word that the War Council had named me as one of the top four on their list to be killed because we associated with white people. My friend also said he would be killed if they heard he had warned me. He advised me to leave home and find a safer place to live. So I left and went into Karatina Town. There I found a small house near the shop where my sewing machine was. Others joined me, who were also on the hit list. One was Silas Muchina, and our fellowship grew. We had much joy in the Lord, even though we heard shooting day and night and knew people were being killed.

We heard of the brothers and sisters in Murang'a District who had been killed, and this drew our fellowship group closer together. We were sure that none of us had long to live, and that we would be attacked by the Mau Mau any day. So we agreed that each of us should search his or her heart and be cleansed and ready to die. I had a quiet day with the Lord and gave Him everything, surrendering my house, my family, my body, my life and everything I had, saying, "Now I am ready to come and live with You." After we had done this, great blessings followed. Now we had no fear at all and went anywhere at any time that He sent us. We were free!

None of us expected to see the end of 1953, and we made no plans at all for 1954. Each day that we were still alive, we were surprised, and every evening we met with our brothers and sisters to sing and praise the Lord. The Home Guards in our town heard us singing and rejoicing at night and grumbled, "You fools! Why are you singing when everyone else in town is crying? Where do you get your strength; do you have some secret sources for getting food?" We replied, "No, we have strength because we are satisfied with Jesus. Jesus is our food and our life and we keep seeing Him in new ways." That was really true for me from the day I gave everything to Jesus. I was saved in a new way and loved Him more because I knew I would soon be with Him in heaven. I felt He was saying to me, "I want you now to give yourself wholly to Me to serve Me in any way that I choose." I agreed, and said I was ready to give up my tailoring any time He said so. If He wanted to send me to a difficult place, I would go. When I did get locked up with a bunch of hard-core Mau Maus, I was not as brave as I meant to be, but Jesus taught me through it. (See Chapter 6.)

Martha: In two or three years, our second child was born, and after he began to grow I was restless and began to remember the convention at Thogoto I had attended with Solomon in 1950, where the words were written large, "'Come now, let us reason together,' says the Lord. 'Though your sins are like scarlet, they shall be as white as snow,'" Isaiah 1:18 (NIV). I remembered they said that even if your sins are very many, He can cleanse you and take them away. It was through that verse that I was saved in 1956.

Solomon: So we went through the worst Mau Mau years, and a wonderful thing happened in 1956. Martha came to Karatina to see me and she had shining eyes. She wanted to stay for the fellowship meeting, and there she stood up and said she wanted Jesus to forgive her many sins. She was saved and became my sister in the Lord. All the sisters and brothers affirmed her forgiveness and warmly received her into fellowship, some leaping for joy. Martha and I were so happy we wept together. Peace has come to our home as we love each other and both testify to what Jesus can do. Now we have nine children, six girls and three boys, and the youngest son has been saved by Jesus. In our old age we are still asking Jesus to lead us and protect us from evil until He comes.

## A WEDDING IN WARTIME
### Joel & Susana Buku, Murang'a and Nairobi

Joel: Although she was not a Christian, my mother brought me up well. My father died when I was very young. In 1937 when I was about eleven I was able to start school, and I went straight through primary and intermediate school. In 1945 I entered Alliance High School.

Susana: A pioneer missionary named MacGregor came to Kangema, our family home district. My mother's older brother went to his school, taking along his two younger sisters, so my mother learned to read. She became a Christian and married another new Christian. My father was one of the first to allow his daughters to go to school. That is why I could go to school young and continue as far as teacher training at the high school level. I began teaching school in 1946 and have always enjoyed teaching the Bible.

Joel: I had been baptized in 1944, and a year later I was confirmed and became one of the student Sunday School teachers from Alliance High School. When I left Alliance in 1948 I got a job as clerk to the Supervisor of Schools at Weithaga Mission, who was Neville Langford-Smith from Australia. I also taught Sunday School there.

I learned a new kind of life with the older young people at Weithaga and went to their dancing club, and soon they elected me their secretary. Fortunately, I had not yet started to drink or smoke, but I soon would have done everything the others did.

One Saturday night we danced all night, and the next morning I had to go to teach my Sunday School class. The lesson was about the three Wise Men who were trying to find the young Jesus who was born to be King of the Jews. It was King Herod the Lord used to touch my heart. As I told my class, he only pretended to be eager to go and worship the Child, while his plan was murder. That was the word the Lord used to show me myself. I was a hypocrite. There had been another king in my heart ever since I started attending the dancing club: the devil was taking charge of me, just as he had King Herod. For three days I struggled with this, and the devil tried hard to prevent me from going to the Lord. But on the last night of 1951, I made my decision and accepted the Lord. By the time I knew I was forgiven it was nearly midnight, and there was a meeting of the fellowship brothers and sisters who were waiting for the New Year. Imagine their surprise when suddenly this young clerk, Joel, burst in shouting, "Now I have accepted the Lord Jesus!" They were all thrilled. They hugged me and sang, receiving me warmly.

Susana: While I was teaching schools out in rural areas I went to church faithfully and served in the church. So the elders thought I was a very fine girl. But they didn't know that I was also spending time with other young teachers whose lifestyle was very different. They were getting involved in the underground political rebellion and gladly taking the Mau Mau oath. I also saw that many so-called Christians were taking this oath, and the only ones who seemed able to resist this pressure were those with a testimony of being truly saved and who would rather die than take it. The pressure on me to take the oath was becoming great, but I thought I was strong. Just in time, at the beginning of 1951, I was moved to Kahuhia to teach in the Teacher Training School for Girls. There I lived in the dormitory with the students, which for me was a much safer place.

That year we had a Christian Life Conference for the girls led by Miss Ruth Truesdale and two saved girls she brought with her. Miss Ruth brought a message from Song of Solomon 1:6, which says: "They made me caretaker of the grapevines, but my own plot was neglected." Suddenly I saw what I had been doing. As a teacher I had been telling others the way to the cross but never taking it myself. I was like a woman who helps her neighbors dig their gardens but never digs her own. God showed me all my inner hidden sins and my fear of not being able to hold on to Him. When I completely gave myself to Him, He assured me that He would hold *me*, not I *Him*. He has done that for me all these years. The girls were astonished that a teacher would stand up and admit she had sins and praise God for saving her. Soon many of the students were saved also, and are still walking with Jesus today.

Joel: In the new year, 1952, when I had newly found the Saviour, the devil pestered me about leaving my peer group and going around with older people. But the Lord helped me to say goodbye to the devil and tell him, "No! I now belong to the Lord. I'd rather have reality!"

I went back to my dancing club and told them I couldn't be their secretary, saying, "I am no longer coming, because I have now given my life to the Lord Jesus." From then on I had real friends. Some were fathers to me—like Heshbon Mwangi and Obadiah Kariuki and others. So the Lord really did change my life.

That year after the Emergency was declared, many of the brethren suffered and died. I was still at Weithaga with Neville Langford-Smith and his wife, Vera. At first I was very afraid of death! Then one day I read some words in Isaiah 8:11–13: "With his great power the Lord warned me not to follow the road which the people were following. He said, 'Do not join in the schemes of the people and do not be afraid of the things that they fear'" (TEV). I was strengthened by those words and from then on I was not afraid to die. I could sing hymns with the others when we heard of Andrew Kanguru's death and the deaths of other believers. I could even go out at night with Cyril Hooper to pick up injured people and take them to the hospital. In my job as part of the supervisory team for schools, I had to travel with others throughout the area, sometimes through the forests, to pay the teachers' salaries not only in Murang'a but also in Nyeri and Embu. On our visitations I had come to know Susana, now on the teacher training team at Kahuhia. I praise the Lord for giving her willingness to be my wife.

Susana and I got married in April of 1953 when the fighting was fiercest. The Mau Mau had said there must be no church weddings, but we went ahead anyway and were married by Bishop Obadiah Kariuki. Susana's brother gave her away and Neville and Vera Langford-Smith were there.

Susana: We were married at a very dangerous time; even my parents couldn't come to my wedding because travel was so dangerous and passes were impossible to get. But we were surrounded by a great community of brethren living close together because of the war. Many families who could no longer stay on their farms had moved into Weithaga, where we fellowshiped together and comforted each other.

During those dangerous years one after another of our community was killed by the Mau Mau. But we went on praising Jesus as we lovingly buried our dead with singing and testimony. For instance, in 1954 Ernest Maina was killed. He was a teacher who had come to live at Weithaga with his wife and family, and had been going every school day on his bicycle through some forest to his primary school at Iyego Ihiga. One evening he didn't return, so Heshbon Mwangi and Neville Langford-Smith went out to look for him. Sadly, in the forest they found his body, which they brought back to the station that night. So we buried him the next day in peace, singing Hallelujah! Ernest's son is still there in the Iyego Ihiga area and is well known in the coffee industry. Another teacher killed during that time was Pithon Mwangi. This was a painful time in many ways, but it was wonderful the way the brothers and sisters strengthened each other. These teachers were not afraid of dying, and day by day they went to school and returned fearlessly.

In our encampment, the women and children slept peacefully at night. But the brothers took turns standing guard around us—not with weapons but with prayer—ready to alert us. On the whole we were not afraid, for we were ready and expected to go to heaven at any time. Of course fear came sometimes, but we quickly took it to the Lord and He lifted it away. Our daily Bible studies together were our source of spiritual strength and physical well-being. Heshbon and Obadiah were used by the Lord in leading us.

Joel: For seven years after we were married we had no children, yet we loved the Lord. Then when the time came, we had five children and adopted another. In 1957 we were moved to Nairobi where I began to serve our Anglican church as Secretary to a body handling church finances, called Church Commissioners for Kenya. Many times in our family life, in the fellowship, or at work, we have faced problems which could have turned into battles. But we learned to run to the Lord, who said in Matthew 11:28, "Come unto Me, all you who labor and are heavy laden, and I will give you rest."

A COUPLE ON THE GO
Tiras & Madlin Kariuki, Kiambu
(By The Most Rev. John Gatu & David Mutembee)

Kariuki Kahindi was born at Kanyariri, Kabete, about 1907. In his
mid teens he decided to get an education and become a man of
consequence. First he joined the local Presbyterian church, was baptized "Tiras" in 1923, and was confirmed the same year. Moving fast,
he started formal schooling in 1924 and the next year he passed the
upper primary examination with such high marks that he was able to
enter Alliance High School in 1926! He graduated with a teaching
certificate in 1929, taught for a year and then took a job on the East
African Railways. He married Madlin Nyambura in the Kabete Anglican Church in December 1932.

In 1939, he attended the meetings of the revival team from Uganda,
and the encounter he had with the Lord Jesus completely changed
the direction of his life. He wholeheartedly turned from his sins and
received the forgiveness and cleansing offered. He was one of the
very first in central Kenya who, with Obadiah Kariuki, began to walk
with Jesus, becoming an enthusiastic witness to others and a help to
those who received salvation. In 1944 he gave up his employment
with the railways in order to have more time for preaching God's
Word as a free-lance evangelist.

Although from time to time he operated businesses on the side, such
as a bus service, shops at Kanyariri and others, these were definitely
on the side. The needs of the brethren, the church, and the calls to
preach were his priority. He is counted as one of the first strong
leaders of the Revival Movement both in Kenya and elsewhere.

He and Madlin were not blessed with any children of their own,
but their spiritual children are scattered throughout East Africa and
beyond. Their residence at Kanyariri became a home and for many
young people a place for spiritual and practical training. These young
people helped in the offering of hospitality to God's people of any
tribe or nationality who came.

Tiras was a man of great courage and Christian conviction, always
telling the truth in love. He refused repeated offers of ordination, but
served the Presbyterian Church faithfully in several important areas,
especially in leadership training. He respected other denominations
and was at home in any gathering where the name of the Lord Jesus
was honored. Usually Tiras and Madlin went out preaching together, on foot in the early days. They preached in every province of

Kenya and in nearby countries including Tanganyika (now Tanzania) and Nyasaland (now Malawi).

In 1952, they sent out a request to the Kenya fellowships for a young man to take charge of their household while they were absent. Young David Mutembee was sent from Meru, and he lived there all through the time of the Mau Mau fighting, not returning home until 1957. To his surprise, one of his first duties was to learn how to take care of an infant only a few weeks old! This happened because a sister in the local fellowship, who already had six young children, died in childbirth. It was generally agreed that Frederick, the father, could not care for an infant then, so Madlin gladly offered to take care of the baby and took him home. They named him Moses, and whenever she needed to be gone for a while, she entrusted him to David.

David reports what he saw and learned in their home. Very quickly he discovered that this was a home open to all people of God and all seekers. There were always a few young people there who had been disowned by their parents for becoming involved in "the Ruanda Heresy." These stayed, being discipled and helping with the work until they were married and established. There was also a constant flow of guests. People from many places all felt at home and well cared for by the generous host and hostess and their young people. Therefore, supplies and financial help kept coming in from brethren who could help, and somehow there was always enough.

When the Mau Mau fighting began, Tiras and family were named on the fighters' list of people to be killed, both for not taking their oath and for openly preaching Jesus. On the other hand, British army officers watched this house with suspicion. Some in the War Department wanted to prove that this rebellion was fueled by communists. They watched with suspicion the unknown white people who so frequently visited. They saw there the Kikuyu who refused to carry weapons to fight the Mau Mau. Also there were frequent visits by unknown Africans and Asians. Could this house be a center for communist infiltrators? So they sent in an expert inspection team who thoroughly examined every book, paper, shelf, and drawer in the house and attic, looking for incriminating literature, letters, or any other evidence. During this process, the household stood together in the living room singing the Hallelujah song and praying. Of course the inspectors found nothing, but sternly ordered Tiras not to travel anywhere. He gave them his testimony and explained that that was impossible because he and Madlin were obeying the orders of the Most High God. They kept on traveling as they were needed.

They also continued their weekly evening Gospel meetings when neighborhood people crowded in for the joyous singing, testimonies, and exhortations. Since everyone was welcome, the Mau Mau fighters twice came to this meeting with guns in their pockets, and mingled with the crowd. They were planning, as they later told Tiras, that when he stood up on the table to preach they would shoot him and end his objectionable talk about Jesus. But the Spirit of God was strong in that place, and both times when the one with the pistol in his pocket pulled it out, one of his fellow Mau Mau grabbed his arm and they began fighting. The scuffle might have ended the meeting, but Tiras stepped down from the table and began singing the Hallelujah song, which almost everyone sang with him while they gently helped the fighting men find their way out. Then the meeting continued.

Every evening during the years of active fighting, this family knew, as did many other households, that this could be the night of a Mau Mau attack when they could all be killed. So every evening after supper when they came together for prayers, they seriously committed themselves into the hand of God either to protect them or receive them into heaven with joy. They said good night to each other with, "See you in the morning, here or in heaven, the Lord be praised!" Then they went to bed in peace and slept soundly.

The local Mau Mau made a plan to get into the house so they wouldn't have to break in. Their General Kayuitina was chosen as the one most likely to be able to masquerade as a guest in the house and to sleep in a guest room. Then he could quietly kill Tiras in his sleep and slip out. The general did sleep in the house and his men could never figure out why he hadn't killed Tiras. Later he told Tiras that that week he had had an encounter with Jesus and his sins had been forgiven, but for the time being he had kept quiet about it!

Tiras and Madlin were not surprised to find out later that there had been frustrated attempts to kill them each year from 1952 to 1956. They had quietly gone on with their work and travels as God guided them, with no apparent fear or anxiety.

After it was over they went right on with their preaching and open hospitality to those who came, no matter at what hour of day or night they arrived. God used them in the leadership of the Revival Fellowship Movement, sometimes to help prevent the kind of divisions so common to such movements, then again to reconcile those who had "withdrawn" for one reason or another.

After some illness, Tiras was called home to heaven on September 2, 1972. In the farewell message, Brother John Gatu said, "We can hear Brother Tiras saying with Job, 'I know that my Redeemer lives, and on the last day He will stand upon the earth; and after my skin has been destroyed, yet in my flesh I will see God!' Therefore, our hearts should not faint."

## A Scientist Learns the Way
### Walter Maitai, Entomologist of Nyeri

My father was the first converted Christian here in Ihororo, and I was born in 1920. He died while I was still a child, but my mother brought me up as a Christian. After finishing Alliance High School, I went to study entomology at the Scott Agricultural Laboratories. I was the first Kenyan to specialize in the science of insects relating to agriculture. So I have had a chance to travel and do field work in Tanzania, Uganda, and in different parts of Kenya. (A new insect he discovered is called by his name.)

I was a "good Christian," in the Presbyterian Church, and had a church wedding. But I was living in sin. I was a drunkard and a chain-smoker, an adulterer and a thief.

In 1949 my place of work was in Ruiru, and that year revival meetings were being held at the Kambui church. This was the first such meeting I had heard of, and I felt an urge to go. When I went I learned three important things. One speaker said, "What good is Christianity if it can't take you to heaven? If you are in sin, religion can't save you." And all the sins he named were mine.

The next speaker said, "I was a slave of every sort of sin, but when Jesus saved me He gave me power to give them all up and I have never done them again." I thought he must be lying, but the words penetrated me. The one leading the meeting said at the end, "All of you who have been saved tonight, come up here to the front and we will praise God together."

When they came, he said to them, "If Jesus should come just now for His people, He would say of you, 'These I have washed in My blood and they are Mine,' but unfortunately some others have turned away." I was standing in the back and saw that those who went forward were all poor and uneducated—no upper-class people there. But they were praising God joyously with all their hearts, and I was terrified.

I returned home and knelt down in my bedroom and said, "Lord Jesus, I have heard that my Christianity can't take me to heaven, and that You are able to make people stop sinning, and that if You come tonight I can't go with You because I haven't been washed in Your blood. I am asking You now to wash me and save me like You did those people in the church who were praising You. Lord, even me, please save me!" I remember that was November 27, 1949. The Lord Jesus came in and saved me! He took away my thirst for liquor and the craving for tobacco. My adulteries ended, stealing stopped.

The things I had stolen from the government in my work, the Lord told me to return them. So I took these things, six American sheets and two towels, back to my director, saying, "I am returning what I have stolen because Jesus has saved me." He was very much surprised, but he forgave me. Then the Lord helped me to share with my drinking companions, and those with whom I had sinned, and all whom I worked with, that Jesus had saved me. Some said, "Oh, Maitai can't stop drinking—just wait a month and see." But I never went back. The Lord helped me to go on sharing my testimony until some of them were saved. My wife shrugged and said in her heart, "Ha! Yes, he'd better get saved, he has so many sins!"—and didn't believe it was possible. She waited seven years, and the brethren all loved her and forgave her, prayed for her and testified to her until one day the Lord saved her!

When the Emergency started, we were stationed at Jacaranda for our work. People began taking the oath everywhere. We heard that all Kikuyu had to take it—or else! But my Christian brothers and I said to each other, "The blood of Jesus has satisfied us; we simply can't take their oath." When I told this to other workers at Jacaranda, they hated me violently and some told me they would kill me. One day a man who was known to be cruel and had taken more than one of the oaths was looking at me very fiercely while we were working. I remember saying to all of them at work, "I am ready to die at any time." By this they knew that I would never take the oath. Even the white people we were working with knew that Maitai would never take the oath. Those in charge knew that those who were praying with me were really Christians.

When the Home Guard was started, we declined to join it, saying, "We can't fight. Our job is to pray for the Home Guard and to pray for our land, but we can't carry guns or other weapons. Our weapons are prayer and the Word of God, that's all." At that time I was attending a small prayer fellowship of revived brethren near Kambui on Friday evenings, returning home after dark on my motorcycle through Mau Mau territory without fear. One night I was ambushed and hit on the back with a heavy pole, probably a tree trunk, but I didn't fall and kept going! When I told the brethren next day, they said, "That settles it! From now on, Walter, you won't go out at night. We will pray here and then all go to bed." So we did that. We were surrounded by Mau Mau, but we kept on praying steadily and Jesus kept us safe from all dangerous people.

Finally the Mau Mau fight was over, and we went on telling people about Jesus. Many people were saved at this time, and my wife, my sister now, also was saved. He kept us faithful and testifying and He is still doing that today. There are so many things He has done for us as we have been living with Him.

Four basic things I need for life with Him:

1) I need to be genuinely walking with Jesus, allowing Him to cleanse me all the time. When He sees a "small" sin in my thought life or a careless word, He helps me to repent immediately and come back into fellowship with Him.

2) He has taught me the importance of continual Bible study.

3) Prayer is important. I guard special times for prayer and keep up a conversation with God all day.

4) Another thing is singing hymns and gospel songs. I'm no singer, but I hum them and play records that refresh me. Finally, I know that I am a foreigner in this world, just passing through, waiting to go to my home in heaven.

## A Girl and a Man Unafraid
### Joshua & Miriam Ichang'i, Nyeri

Miriam: When the first missionaries of the Church of Scotland Mission came to Nyeri and started a church at Kyamwangi near where we lived, my parents became convinced Christians. Even though he was illiterate, my father sent all his children to school, both boys and girls. He also followed the missionary doctor's advice and did not allow his girls to be circumcised according to tribal custom. Those church members who disagreed with this started an independent church which followed more of the tribal customs.

Every Sunday morning we went to Sunday School and church as a family. And in the afternoon we went out together visiting homes and villages, singing hymns and telling people about the Word of

God. In those years, when I was six to eight years old, the church seemed full of fire.

When I was ten years old my father became sick. As he saw his illness increasing, he had a talk with my mother. He said, "I feel that I will soon be going to heaven. Now I charge you to see that all of my children, both boys and girls, get all the education of which they are capable."

So we all went to school, first in the village and then to the boarding school at the mission in Tumutumu. Three of my sisters became village school teachers. But God helped me and I did very well in the Kenya African Primary Education Examination. So I was chosen to be one of ten girls from all of Kenya to be in the first class of the new High School for Girls. In spite of negative advice from some church women, my mother chose to follow her husband's request and she let me go.

There was no school building for us there at Thogoto, just a long Quonset hut. It was divided into a dormitory, a dining room, a classroom and a washroom. Miss Jean Ewing was our very capable teacher. Our school was not far from the Alliance High School for Boys, and on Sundays, both morning and evening, we attended services in their chapel. A zealous Christian, Mr. Carey Francis, was the headmaster and brought in outside speakers when he could. In our second year, 1949, William Nagenda and his revival team from Uganda had meetings and gave their testimonies for several days. I knew I was a very good Christian, often urging fellow students to live good lives, and reproving the boys who were beginning to smoke secretly. But the preaching of William and the others was strange to me and touched me with a sadness which I couldn't understand. I knew that my father used to sing about being washed in Jesus' blood and about His second coming, and he knew for sure he was going to heaven. Why, then, did I get so uncomfortable at what this team said?

Then some high school boys went to Chogoria for school vacation, and returned saying they were saved! Two of these were my special friends, and they said, "Miriam, we have been saved!"

I answered loftily, "I don't swallow this revival thing—our church refuses it."

"Look, Miriam," they said, "a lot of times we have stood right here talking and you told us to be 'good Christians'—to stop lying and smoking and breaking other school rules—and we couldn't do it. Now we tell you that Jesus has made us able to overcome these bad habits and you get mad!" I was speechless and went home puzzling over this.

That night when the girls were asleep, I knelt down by my bed and prayed, "Lord, if this teaching I'm hearing is my father's faith, please show me. But if it is a heresy, let me know. If it is from You, I will follow You all my life and never turn back."

I began to sing softly, "Into my heart, . . . come in to stay." I asked Him to clean up my heart and take it over. The Spirit of God did come in! The girls were all sleeping, so I jumped up, got under the blanket, and praised Him in whispers. By morning I was singing out loud, "My cup is full and running over!" I remember that day was July 27, 1949. The girls were amazed and a little scared, but the joy of Jesus' presence was with me, and it has stayed for the rest of my life.

After teacher training, I was posted to the mission school from which I had come. I began to teach both boys and girls in the intermediate school at Tumutumu. I wasn't allowed to say a word in school or church about my new experience of salvation. So I asked permission to start a branch of the Student Christian Union, because I knew that there I could speak to students. Many were saved, both boys and girls, and soon revival spread on the mission compound. Brother Silas Muchina had heard there was a saved teacher in our school and came looking for me. From then on we were together in the fellowship meetings.

Personally, I was facing a big problem. Yet I knew the Lord wanted to bless me. There was a young man I had come to know and love in high school who had now gone on to Makerere College in Uganda. We had an understanding, and our parents had agreed, that at some time we would be married. My problem was that before he left he told me, "Miriam, spiritually I have really backslidden." I had been reading about King Saul in 1 Samuel 15 and how he disobeyed the Lord by sparing the fat sheep. The Spirit spoke to me that holding on to this relationship was like that, saying, "Break the bond; be free to serve the Lord." He helped me and I submitted to Him. At that time I decided I would never get married. I would only serve the Lord. God was also dealing with me about small things that I had taken from school property—a needle, a pointer, a book—and I was convicted and returned them.

In 1952 the Emergency was declared by the British governor in October and Jomo Kenyatta was arrested and put in detention. The war began to heat up against the freedom fighters, who were called the Mau Mau. All the Christian students were in danger and so did not go home during vacation. The girls were not allowed to leave the mission compound, and many Christian families came to live at the mission. There was fear everywhere. By December of that year revival swept our compound and spread out into the adjacent village, so I had many opportunities to lift up Jesus.

I went out in the local marketplace and to other towns, sometimes preaching with Brother Silas. We knew that most of the people we were speaking to were part of the Mau Mau army or their followers, but we were completely unafraid.

In our travels, Silas introduced me to another teacher named Joshua Ichang'i and told me of his firm stand for the Lord.

Joshua: A great thing I have learned is that I needn't ever worry about feeling lonely when I am walking with Jesus. I was moved to Ihururu to teach, and dear Silas Muchina managed to follow me there, and brought with him a brother who lived near me, Walter Maitai, a scientist in biology. What a strength Walter was to me! Not only that, it was through Silas that I met Miriam Mathenge, whom God had chosen to be my life partner.

Miriam: In 1953, with the blessing of the fellowship, I was formally engaged to Joshua Ichang'i, who by then was Assistant Education Officer for the district.

Joshua: When I was moved to Isiolo, and later to the Teachers' College in Embu, Silas kept track of me and made sure I was still praising the Lord and finding fellowship. In my new position, I was given a Land Rover for visiting schools and delivering teachers' wages and supplies. There was a rule that everyone working for the government must carry a gun. I said, "No, I can't carry a gun, because I could not kill anyone. And to carry a gun without using it would be a lie. I know that God will keep me safe every day until the day appointed for me to come to Him."

They told me, "No, you will have to choose. On Monday take your gun or you must leave work!"

Miriam: On Sunday after church we were praising the Lord with the others in our fellowship, and Joshua said to me, "Sister, you agreed to marry me knowing that I am the Assistant Education Officer, but tomorrow when I report for work I will be fired. So think it over."

I laughed and said, "We weren't led by the Lord to marry because of your position, or salary, or anything else. It was Jesus who spoke to us, and He broke my strong determination to never get married.

Your job isn't important at all."

Joshua: My testimony and refusal must have been talked about in the whole department, because on Monday when I went to work I wasn't fired. They had a new plan.

My supervisor said, "You go ahead with your work. We know you refused to carry a gun because of your strong convictions. You will be accompanied by two soldiers, one your driver. They won't guard you—as you said God will protect you—they will guard the school supplies and wages you carry to the teachers." So we went out, even through forests, to visit the schools, and were safe. After the war, one of the ex-Mau Mau fighters of our area told me, "We knew where you were traveling but never interfered with you because we heard that God was with you."

Miriam: In December of 1954, though the battle was still going on, with God's grace we held a week of evangelistic meetings where many people turned to Jesus. The week culminated in our wedding!

In 1956, while the fighting was slowing down, Brother Tiras Kariuki and Dr. Philpott of our church went through all the towns and villages of our area preaching Jesus. Revival spread through the whole district. By 1960, our Presbyterian church leaders held a great convention on the Tumutumu mission grounds.

After our marriage, I stopped teaching and looked after our home and the children. Walking with Jesus and studying His Word daily to find out what He wanted us to do has been the secret of victory in our lives and home. After the children were grown, I worked for some years in the Central Bank. When some of our children began working there too, I retired in 1980. Joshua and I are still serving and praising our Lord together on our little farm.

## "A Mother in Israel"
### Abishag Hannah Wanjiku, Kangema, Murang'a

My parents knew nothing of Christianity as I grew up, so I was taught only Kikuyu customs and worship. In 1918, while I was still an unmarried girl, I decided to get an education if I could. So I hid from my parents and then ran away to go to school in Jumbe. My parents disowned me when they found out where I was. But I continued in school until I became a "Christian" teacher in 1922. I was married in the church in 1924 and my husband and I followed the customs of church members by dressing up on Sunday morning and taking holy communion.

In 1946, I met the Lord Jesus who truly saved me, and my whole lifestyle was changed. Immediately I was in a battle, because my husband disapproved of this. At that time we had two children, who had finished school locally. Our girl was married and our son had gone to South Africa for further schooling.

In 1952 the Emergency began, and the fighting was fierce, especially against those who refused to take the Mau Mau oath. A brother in the Lord, a neighbor of mine named Edmond, was killed in the first year. With a young girl who was staying with me, I watched from a dark place the night that men called Edmond out of his house. He could see that the fighters had come to murder him, and we heard him cry in a loud voice, "Lord, forgive them, because they don't know what they are doing!" And when they were putting a pistol into his mouth, he cried, "It is finished!" and they shot him right there.

Frightened by Edmond's tragic death, the girl, my sister and I left home. We went to Weithaga Mission station where we camped with the "saved ones" for the next four years.

I worked in the camp with the women and girls, teaching and strengthening them. I showed them how to trust in the Lord and to endure suffering and loss in those dangerous days. All of us had loved ones in heaven, and I often said to them, "Let us stand tall and straight and firm in the power of the Lord, so that we will be ready to go when He calls us."

In 1954 the girl who came with me heard the voice of the Lord and was saved. My sister was too. In fact, it was a time when many of the young people came to Jesus.

When the danger had lessened in 1956, we returned to our homes and helped rebuild what had been destroyed. My husband had taken the Mau Mau oath, so he did not come with us to Weithaga. But in 1958 the Lord saved him! My daughter now has grandchildren, and my son, who was a great help to me, went to heaven loving the Lord. I praise the Lord that even to this day Jesus has kept me strong in Him. God is faithful!

(Abishag was over ninety years old when she reported this.)

## WON BY LOVE
### David M. Munywa, Meru

I was born in 1913. By the time I entered training for medical work, in 1930, I had finished school and been baptized. When I graduated from Maua Hospital's training school in 1937, the government placed me on the staff of the Meru Town Hospital.

I was inducted into the British army in 1939. Most of my time in World War II, I was in Egypt helping with a 2,000-bed hospital for all races near the Suez Canal. My first leave of absence to return to Kenya was in 1944. Soon after arriving I was assigned to go with a medical team to Ceylon.

In Mombasa we heard that the medical ship we were to travel on had been sunk by a submarine. When we were put on another boat, we were frightened all the way, and were much relieved to reach Ceylon. We were taken into a great forest and taught how to live up in the trees with all our equipment, using rope ladders and rope bridges. But when this training was finished the war was over, and I was able to return home in 1946 and resume work in the Meru Town Hospital.

The Mau Mau were active in our area in 1952, so many of our staff moved into protected quarters, but I stayed at home with my wife, saying, "Large towns are safer than the countryside."

I was a preacher in my spare time and very proud of myself, so I fought against the "revivalists" who were advocating another kind of salvation. I said, "They will ruin our church!"

On April 4, 1952, I heard there would be a fellowship of these people in the home of one of our hospital staff. By that time I was curious to know what they said. When I walked in, everyone stood up as if I were someone important, and I was given a special chair. I was impressed and felt their love. I listened to their words about Cain and Abel—how Abel's offering was acceptable to God and Cain's was not. This struck me hard as I began to realize that my preaching was useless because of my many sins. Finally I stood up and said, "Will you please forgive me for fighting against you? I see that I am a great sinner." Ah! How they sang Hallelujah and hugged me! It was during that song that I knew for sure I was saved and had been received into fellowship with Christ.

I was full of joy all that night while I was on duty, and the next morning I hurried home to tell my wife and children, but they cried and my wife said, "He is lost!" My friends wouldn't listen to me either, ignoring my testimony. The brethren suggested I leave my old buddies for a time lest they draw me back. But they themselves began visiting my wife and doing many kind things for her. Then one evening she went on asking them questions and talking with them until midnight—when the Lord saved her. What joy we had then in our home! Later I had to repent of jealousy that her testimony was better than mine!

In those days we were not allowed to have fellowship meetings in the church, so we met outdoors and other places. One day we came back from a fellowship in the Kaaga Girls School and heard that our brother Nashon, a hospital cook, had been arrested and put in remand because a Mau Mau prisoner had falsely said that he had given the oath to him and others of us. So when we reported back to work, the doctor ordered us to turn in our uniforms and report to the police. We were put in jail with Nashon for forty-two days, but when our names could not be found in the list of those who were undoubtedly Mau Mau, we were released.

The District Commissioner told us to go back to the hospital, but the doctor wouldn't have us, so we were out of work. Finally we were put into the detention camp at Kinoru for six months. We spent our time telling other prisoners about Jesus, and giving medical help wherever we could. My wife survived by selling the coffee beans from our plot.

After my release, I was called to work in another hospital in Kiambu near Nairobi. Jesus was our amazing Helper all through that time and we are still praising Him!

## A SCHOOLGIRL CHOOSES
### Naomi Wanjiru-William, Murang'a

I thought I was a Christian by birthright because my parents were Christians. They were active in church work and I always went to Sunday School. If anyone started to tell me the Gospel, I would say, "Go tell the heathen. Even my blood is Christian, so I will surely go the heaven."

One day when I was twelve or thirteen years old I heard it declared: "Even if you are born a Christian and have been baptized and work in the church, if you have not personally repented of your sins and received Jesus as your Saviour, you won't enter the Kingdom of Heaven!" I knew the preacher was talking to me. I was shaken, and right then I received Jesus as my Saviour. I had always thought I had no sins, but the Holy Spirit showed them to me: I had been angry and fighting with my brothers and sisters; I had rebelled against my parents, disobeying them behind their backs; and I was a hypocrite. I confessed this to Jesus. I asked for and received His forgiveness. The preacher introduced me to the loving fellowship of those who were saved and always praising God. They received me as one of them even though I was a little girl.

But when I gave my glad testimony to my parents and to the church, my church put me out and told me not to come back to worship there again. My parents despised me and told me they would not give me any clothes or food until I came to my senses!

I was in primary school, and my mother worried about me. Though I couldn't eat with the family, my mother would whisper to me to look in a certain cupboard where I would find some food she had put there for me. Although life was difficult for me, I was grateful for my mother's kindness. Much more help and support for me was in the revival fellowship, and in talking to Jesus in prayer. He always assured me that I belonged to Him and to His Kingdom.

When the time of the Mau Mau war came, I boldly said to the oath-givers, "I will never drink the blood of your goat because the blood of Jesus is all I need."

So I too was on their list of enemies to be killed. One of them told me, "We want your head!"

I replied, "You may take it—I give it to you for Jesus' sake." But every day the Lord protected me, and I was learning to live close to Him. Before long all of us in the fellowship moved to live at Weithaga Mission. There were teachers there to teach us and I was able to work in the home of our brother Joel Buku. When it was safe, I returned to my parents' home.

From then on I couldn't go to school. My parents wouldn't allow it. They told me that if I wanted more education I would need to give up my fanatical views of salvation. My father was well-to-do and said he was prepared even to send me to England for further education, if I chose that. He gave me three days to think it over. During those days, the Lord spoke to me and said, "Sit still and wait. I will provide all you need."

I told my father, "I choose not to go for higher education. I will be better off to live here with Jesus."

My parents said, "All right, you have made your choice."

I had learned dressmaking, and was called to work at Kahuhia School. There I lived with the girl students and taught them sewing. Eventually I became the Matron of the Girls' High School.

While I was there I met and became engaged to a brother in the Lord, William Macharia. My parents agreed to our marriage and it wasn't long before they too came to Jesus and were saved. The Lord gave us six children and two of them have been saved! In our life together we have gone through both good times and hard times and we have always witnessed to God's grace. Three of our children are teachers and three are in medical work. God has blessed us, and our children have blessed us too.

I am so happy that I chose Jesus—what good would it have been to go to school in England without Him? Now I have been blessed by entertaining in my home here a dear couple from Britain, George and Maureen Swannell!

## HE'S A FOOL!
### William Macharia Njoroga, Murang'a

My parents and grandfather were so deeply involved in Kikuyu customs and worship that they despised my uncle who was trying to plant a Christian church in our area. As a young boy I naturally sided with my parents and spoke against him too.

Then I started going to school and discovered a whole new world. Other boys had already received new "Western" names. I felt backward and uncivilized, so why shouldn't I get a new name too? All I had to do was attend the catechism class, learn the Ten Commandments and other stuff. It wasn't hard at all to get baptized, and then I had the new name "William"! My parents were hurt and said I was on my uncle's side. I didn't understand that. All I knew was that now I was William.

By 1950, I was in Kahuhia Teacher Training School when a revival team, including Tiras Kariuki of Kabete, came to hold meetings. I was shocked at their testimonies, because to be honest, even though I was baptized, I was carrying a very heavy load of sins. As the team shared, in my heart I was crying to the Lord to rescue me. Jesus changed everything: He took the whole load of sin away! He became my Saviour and Lord and He introduced me to His big, loving family.

When I finished school in 1952, I became a new teacher at Muthiria School where Heshbon Mwangi was the headmaster. When I arrived at my new job with no blanket and no food, I discovered how kind the Lord is. Heshbon took me in as if I were his son, and he has been a spiritual father to me all my life.

After I had taught one term, I was moved to the school at Kiruri, where Samuel Muhoro was church leader and Andrew Kanguru was his\assistant. These brothers were delighted when I came, as they had been praying for a saved teacher for their new school.

When I shared my testimony with the school children, some of them and their parents hated me because the Mau Mau war had now reached this area, and their forest hideout was close by. Nevertheless, I stood firm with Samuel and Andrew and their wives, openly saying in church that the blood of Jesus Christ was all I needed, and I would never take another blood or another oath.

At the end of the school term, I went back home to visit my mother. A gang of Mau Mau burst into her home to take me away and give me their oath. Looking very fierce, they shouted, "Macharia!"

I stood up and said, "I am Macharia, and I have been saved by the blood of Jesus Christ. He is all I need. But listen, I am not fighting against you. Leave me alone and I will never report you or be a witness against you in any place. On the other hand, I am reporting you to Almighty God in heaven. I am telling Him that you want to kidnap me and that I don't want to go with you!" The fighters became bewildered and confused by this, and they went back to those who had sent them, saying I had refused to come, and since they hadn't been told to kill me, they didn't know what to do.

Their leader said, "Well, leave him for now. He's a fool. That's just religious talk. We'll get him later."

So I was free to go, but I never did pass on any information about the Mau Mau or even talk about them. It was enough for me to talk about Jesus. I didn't return to Kiruri, because I was sent to the new Teacher Training College at Kigari, where the area School Supervisor, Neville Langford-Smith, was our headmaster. It was through him and Heshbon Mwangi that I heard about the terrible Mau Mau attack on the Kiruri church and school. Andrew Kanguru had been killed, and his wife and the Samuel Muhoros and Penina Meshak had all been injured. It was clear then that it was a good thing that the Weithaga Mission station had become a refuge for the many brethren who were in danger. On many school holidays I went to Weithaga to be with them. There we could pray together earnestly, and help each other by sharing fellowship and seeking in God's Word together what He had to say to us in this danger.

During this time, I also went to preach Jesus in the camps of the detainees. How we rejoiced when some of the Mau Mau came to Christ, including some of those who had come to take me from my mother's home to give me the oath! It was wonderful to praise God with them and embrace them as brothers!

After my training in the college at Kigare, I taught school from 1955 on. By 1958 the war was waning and I began to feel it was time for me to get married. I had frequently prayed that the Lord would lead me to know who would be right for me to live with all my life. So I shared my desire with my spiritual father, Heshbon Mwangi, and the other brethren in the fellowship who had helped in my walk with Jesus.

They said, "All right, you must seek the one God wants you to marry. We don't know who it is, but God will show you."

After more prayer, I knew. I went back to them and said, "It is Naomi Wanjiru, the school matron." They were happy with my choice.

Since she was working in the Girl's High School, and Miss Jocelyn Murray, the British headmistress, was a good friend of mine as well as hers, she helped us find times and places to talk together. So when I had an opportunity, I spoke to Naomi, and told her what the Lord was showing me. When she asked for time to pray about it, I objected at first because I was already sure. But then I gave her time, and finally I asked her, "What is God's answer?"

She replied, "I am agreeing, but He has told me that I may become your wife only if both your parents and my parents agree to this."

To our surprise and joy, both her parents and mine agreed. Finally the day arrived, April 8, 1958, when we were married at Weithaga, together with two other couples. There was a great crowd of rejoicing brethren. One wedding couple were of the Luo tribe, and one of the ministers was white, because we all wanted to show that, in Jesus, tribal and national prejudices have all been taken away. Naomi and I have lived in the joy of the Lord and the fellowship of the brethren ever since.

## A GIFT OF BOLDNESS
### Peter Munge Wohoro, Nyeri

I grew up in a Christian home, read the Bible and taught others, but I didn't know what people were talking about when they spoke of salvation. At one point I confessed my sins as I saw them, but I didn't get the strength to live right. Nor could I say with confidence before people that I had been born again. So I prayed, "Lord, why is it that I have confessed to You all my sins that I know of, but I still can't tell people about it. Please come and show me what it is that Satan has put in me to keep me from having a testimony. I want to be sure that when I leave this life I will be with You forever."

Before long, while songs about Him were being sung, Jesus showed me that if I did not confess Him before men He would not be able to name me before His Father in heaven. That evening I stood up in the meeting, without even thinking who might be listening, and said boldly, "From this moment I have received Jesus Christ to come and live in me, and I will trust Him to put my name in the Lamb's Book of Life." From that time on I knew I had been born anew and I began to have the confidence within me that I was a child of God. That was January 20, 1948. From then on things went well. Jesus promised me that He would be with me every day until I leave the earth, and He *has* been with me and I have never gone into hiding since that time. I spoke fearlessly in the open air and in offices in Nyeri and Nairobi, in marketplaces and on street corners. I have been beaten up for telling people about God's salvation, but later some of these same people have come to Jesus and preached with me! When they knocked me down, I always got up again and went on speaking. It has been a wonderful thing to see quite a lot of people come to Jesus.

In December 1949, I met some very clever people in Nanyuki who said they had studied a lot. One of them said he was a Christian and was saved. He told me I was still young and untaught and didn't understand spiritual things. He told me that I had gone astray on the teaching of the cross. He said Jesus went up into the third heaven, and which heaven did I think I would go to? I got confused with these questions, and was losing my faith.

Jesus rescued me when I cried, "Lord, help me!" He showed me this was Satan again trying to confuse me. I left them and began to study the Bible carefully. Jesus showed me that I had both the Holy Spirit in me to teach me and brothers and sisters to show me how to walk with Him, staying close to the cross every day. So from that time my strength has come only from His blood cleansing me of my sins, and I don't worry about the third heaven!

I began to work for the Nairobi Water Department in 1950. Then when those of the secret army came in 1952 trying to force me to take their Mau Mau oath, I said, "No, I can't possibly do that. I would rather die as a person who has taken the blood of Jesus Christ and been saved. This oath you offer me is not a good gift. I know it would destroy not only my body but my spirit-life as well." So I was named as one of those to be killed by the Mau Mau, along with my wife and my mother and my father. But I remembered that when He saved me Jesus told me that He would be with me until my last day on earth, so I was not afraid. And He has given me boldness to speak for the Lord to policemen and to government officers.

During the Emergency, I sometimes walked into the quarters of the British soldiers without permission and told them about Jesus our Saviour and what He could do for them. Three times there were white soldiers who wanted to shoot me with pistols for this. I remember telling them, "You have no authority to shoot me. If you do and I die, my blood will be on you and you will be punished for killing a man of God." They let me go.

I was beaten up badly in Nairobi by the Mau Mau. Also some fellow workers in the Water Department were given money to kill me, but, as they told me later, they feared my prayers and could not do it. Jesus gave me special strength in trouble.

Government officers told me, "All who are not Mau Mau must carry a weapon. We need you to fight with us."

I said, "If I must go into battle with you, I will carry the Word of God as my weapon and you can take your gun." I tried to get in to explain this to the British officer in charge, but they blocked the way. Just then he came out of his office and saw me with my Bible and heard what I had said. He turned to his assistant and the local Chief who was there and said, "Leave him alone and let him go." I have learned that the testimony which is given in the power of the blood of Jesus has such strength that it can withstand anything. I was astonished that, in spite of many threats, all through the war the Lord protected me and my family.

Before I retired I was in charge of the Nairobi Water Department, so I have had many temptations, but the power of the Holy Spirit has been with me and my testimony to Jesus is the same today as it was in the beginning.

Since my retirement the Lord has given me special strength many times to go into the home of a brother who has grown cold or strayed from the Lord. I tell him, "Come, let us go back to church. You have fallen, but Jesus wants to restore you." We go together to church and he returns to the Lord and we praise Him together. Jesus has given me much to do and has blessed me.

## Goat's Blood to Jesus' Blood
### Phoebe Njoki Wambugu, Nyeri

My childhood was an ordinary Kikuyu one. I herded goats, carried water and firewood, and helped in the fields with my mother. We lived on white settlers' farms, ending up working for those who were living in a Forest Reserve area.

What fascinated me most was the sacrifice of blood to appease the anger of the great god of the Kikuyu. If there was an epidemic of disease, a drought, a famine or other threat, people looked for a goat or sheep which was all one color, no spots. Then a man must be found, having only one wife and no bodily deformities, and a boy to help, also with no deformities. Outside the village, under the tallest tree, the animal was strangled and all the blood poured out to Ngai. Then the whole animal was burned up as an offering. No one ate it.

From time to time missionaries came through our area and talked to us. I liked them and I was interested especially in their clothes, which were not like the skins or pieces of cloth we tied around us. They were friendly and kind, not like the white farmers we knew. Some boys ran away from home to go to school after these visits, but most of the girls didn't. Nevertheless I began to plan to run away and learn all the new things. I did this when I was twelve or thirteen years old even though I knew my parents would be furious. The missionaries were helpful and I went to school. After I was baptized in 1940 I became a full member of the Presbyterian church. I studied nursing, midwifery and public health, and I got work in the General Hospital in Nyeri Town. I finally went back to see my parents. They were not happy at first about the changes in me, but later became Christians also.

From 1948 on I heard and resented the preaching or testimonies of the "Ruanda revival" people. I felt quite superior to them. I disliked the way they openly told the shameful sins they had committed. I hadn't done these things so I felt I was a much better Christian than they! In my opinion, they were just trying to ruin the church.

When the Mau Mau war began, I was scared and stayed inside the hospital most of the time. We all knew that the Mau Mau were eager to get hold of nurses, taking them into the forest to tend their sick and wounded, and also to use them as concubines. My tension was so constant—both from fear of the guerillas and anger at the nurses under my supervision for whose mistakes I had to take the blame—

that I developed gastric ulcers. In my distress I began listening closer to the words of the "revivalists" because they certainly had a peace and joy in their lives that I didn't have. One verse they quoted from a prophet stuck in my mind—about all our righteousness being only filthy rags in God's sight (Isaiah 64:6). They talked about hatred as being sin, and I was full of it. They spoke of lying and deceit, and I did these to cover up my mistakes. And they mentioned lustful thoughts, which I surely had. Gradually I was getting more interested in what they said. They were very honest.

Then a song we sang in Kikuyu stayed with me: "I said, 'O that's just a little sin,' but it was sending me to hell. . . .'" In the end I saw that hatred was destroying me—hatred for the white settlers who paid my father so poorly for hard work, and hatred for my supervisors who blamed me for everything. I wanted to see them dead.

Then I cried to the Lord Jesus. He took His poured-out blood of the cross and washed away the murderous hate in my heart along with my many other sins. After that He gave me everlasting life with peace and joy and love. Then I remembered the blood of the goat I used to see, which was poured out to appease the angry god of the Kikuyu and which accomplished nothing, while Jesus' blood had changed my whole life. Even better, Jesus stays near at hand to cleanse again and again. Today I know for sure that He is mine and I am His, and I am waiting for His coming again soon.

## "COME KILL ME!"
### A Report about Elizabeth Stefano, Meru

Elizabeth was a strong and faithful Christian. She received a letter from the Mau Mau in the forest directing her to brew a large quantity of liquor called "Kimeru Marwa." This is something Christians never do. She replied to their messenger, "I can't do this."

The Mau Mau threatened her, "If you don't do as we say we will come and kill you."

She replied, "It is better to be killed than to brew this strong drink. I have said I won't do it, so if you want to kill me, be free to come and do that."

She was told which night they would come, saying, "That is when we will come to take your head if you don't make our liquor."

She replied, "That's all right. Come!"

She didn't make their drink, and they didn't come. She is still living and is strong in faith.

## The Power of the Name
### Beth Kimenyi, Kandara, Murang'a

Since my parents were Christians, they took me to church and Sunday School as a child. I followed the rules and was baptized in 1934 when I was fourteen years old. While I was in school at Kijabe, I lived with some missionaries. Then I was sent to teach at Githumu, and very soon after this I was married to the headmaster of the school there, Francis Kimenyi. We began our family and eventually the Lord blessed us with ten children.

I had often taught or preached to girls and women about being Christians and obeying the church, but in 1949 the Lord began to stir my spirit in a different way. At that time I went to a revival fellowship convention in Kabete and was amazed at the joy and freedom of spirit that I saw in the people there. They said they were "saved" and I kept hearing about being "born again." I had many new thoughts when I returned home. I had never before considered the sins in my spirit, like pride and unforgiveness, or wondered what to do about them. One Sunday I heard a message based on Jeremiah 4:3—"Do not plant your seeds among thorns"—and I realized that there were many thorns in me. On September 5th of that year I went as usual to work in my field and suddenly God called my attention to the many weeds in my garden. I prayed, "Now, Lord, my life is also full of weeds. Please save me, because I know that nothing evil or unclean can come to live with You. I get angry and say bad words so often. Father, save me!" I left the field that day a saved person!

I told my husband about it, but he didn't understand. He said, "You? What do you need to be saved from? You haven't done any satanic things."

I said, "Yes, Satan has come out of me now and I am saved. When you did something I didn't like, I got furious and began to beat the children, and didn't even know this was sin." From that time on I had a new peace.

Soon after this change in my life, the war of the Mau Mau came. They were exasperated with those of us who were believers, saying, "These saved ones! We must kill them!" I wasn't surprised or upset. I did nothing about it, but trusted in Jesus and waited. Then one day a fierce battle occurred in our village between the Mau Mau and the government. My husband was teaching school at Githumu, and he had the older children with him there. So I was at home with the smaller children. I had been teaching them from Psalm 56:3 that when we are afraid, we put our trust in Jesus.

One day we saw that the Mau Mau had started burning down the houses of the Christians they called traitors. Because in those days we all had grass roofs, I could see it as a fast-moving fire with great billows of smoke. I quickly took the four children, with the baby on my back, out into our field of tall corn. I was reminding them that we would trust Jesus as we lay down on the ground. We were quite well hidden but we could hear the firing near us, "KA-KA-KA-KA-KA," so we lay very still. All the while we prayed and trusted Jesus.

Suddenly I saw a guerilla fighter, who was wearing a black trench coat, coming toward our house carrying something. I thought he might have seen us among the cornstalks, so I decided to go out to meet him, hoping that he would only kill me and the baby and leave the others. I jumped up and walked straight to him, arms in the air, loudly shouting, "JESUS! JESUS! JESUS!" At this he stopped walking and so did I. Startled, he looked hard at me, but didn't say a word. He didn't hit me or burn our house. He just turned and walked away.

I rushed back to my children, and told them, "You see, the name of Jesus has very great power!" I was overwhelmed with the goodness of God to my family. He had helped me when I most needed Him, and I really had no fear after that. I felt, "Well, if they are allowed to kill me, thank You, Lord, I am coming to You. I am ready." After the Mau Mau had barricaded the road against the British troops, burned down the church and school, taken all the goats and cows of the village and stolen the shopkeeper's truck packed full of all their loot, they went back into the forest.

When the Mau Mau had gone, I took our children, left the farm and walked the four miles to where my husband lived and worked. We lived with them at Githumu and I kept saying over and over, "Jesus is good! He has cared for me and my children!"

In 1970, God took my husband. By this time all of our children were grown, and I was left here with Jesus. I am still praising Him today, because He is still helping me, saying, "I will live in you and you will live in Me." So I love Him very much and am waiting for His coming.

## LAUGHING IN DANGER
### Walter Mwangi Rurie, Murang'a

As a child growing up I wore protective charms and was treated with native medicines. My life was spent herding goats until I was fifteen. Then in 1934 my uncle asked for me to come to help him. My father agreed and my uncle sent me to school, where I got along fine. Two years later both my mother and brother died, leaving only my two sisters and me to help my father. So I needed to go home to be with them. My father was wise enough to let me continue in school near my home, working half time for him. I was baptized in 1937 but this didn't change my lifestyle at all. By then I ran with a rowdy crowd of young people who enjoyed wild dances and lewd songs and loose living.

When I finished my 8th grade education, church people asked me to teach school. I tried it, but I didn't like it much. I felt I ought to take a wife to help care for the family. This was the first church wedding in our congregation, and I was proud of that even though I wasn't living as a Christian.

The same year I went for teacher training to Kigare where a Mr. Simons taught. He liked me and helped me in many ways. He often invited me into his home, where he and his wife gave me some good advice. It was at school that I began to hear the testimonies of the "revived" people, who came to share with us in our school, and also in church. The Spirit of God began to speak to me. One evening in July while I was eating supper with the other students, I heard a Voice say, "Walter, you are full of sins—very many sins." I lost my appetite, left the table and went to my bed and began to cry. Then the Voice said, "You need to repent or you will be lost. When Jesus died on the cross, and people were mocking Him, Walter, He was dying for your sins. Trust Him. He wants to forgive you."

I cried out loud, "Jesus, I accept what You did for me! Please forgive me all my hardness and unwillingness to give You my sins!" At that moment He touched me and changed me. I was full of joy and full of new energy. I ran to see some of my teachers, to tell them, "I've seen Jesus and He has washed me in His blood. I know He is my Saviour now!"

I could hardly wait for our vacation time so that I could hurry home to tell my wife what Jesus had done for me and to beg her forgiveness for not loving and honoring her the way Jesus wanted me to. She forgave me. I also asked forgiveness of the church elders and of my students whom I had treated badly. I was a different person when I finished school and was posted to teach at Maragwa.

Now I loved teaching and happily shared the Scripture lessons. I told them openly how Jesus had saved me from drinking, stealing, witchcraft, and other shameful things. Soon I could see that some of the children were being changed. However, the parents became furious when they saw their children becoming "fanatic" Christians, and they complained to the school supervisor that I was teaching some strange religion. So he moved me to another school at the end of that quarter. This actually proved to be a great blessing for me, because there I found two other "saved" teachers—John Kanguru and Heshbon Mwangi! I had had no one to fellowship with before this, and I learned what a help it is to have even two others near you who are walking in Jesus' way—and I really began to grow spiritually.

Sadly, this caused my wife to be angry, and she attacked me constantly, because she felt I embarrassed her in public. But God helped me and I was able to smile and to just love her more and more until finally, four years later, the Lord spoke to her too and we began a new kind of home life together as believers.

In 1951 we saw signs of the growing, secret Mau Mau movement. One evidence of this was that parents were trying to take over the schools from the mission. As a protest, over 300 children were withdrawn from the Mwunguini school, and so it was empty of both students and teachers. But neither the mission nor the government wanted to turn any school buildings over to become tribal, independent schools. So I was sent to the school where I had been teaching just to take care of the building and equipment. I went every day and faithfully worked at keeping it in order and making repairs, fully expecting that one day parents would come and kill me, as some had promised. All day long I was talking to Jesus about the situation. Then to my surprise, one morning a little boy came to start first grade! I worked steadily with this boy for a term. By then he could read very well indeed. The next term there were nineteen children. I shared my faith with their parents, and one of the mothers came to Jesus. However, at the end of that term I was transferred, and another believer was sent to take my place, Reuben Gitau. Unfortunately, later on he was killed there. (See Chapter 4.)

In the Kaharo school, where I was sent, we had five students and a second teacher, Samuel. The children made great progress. We were protected there, because part of the building had become a temporary police post. At the end of that year, there was uncertainty as to where I would be assigned, but by this time all my fears had gone. I knew that anywhere I was, I would be with Jesus, and that if I were to die I would be in heaven with Him. That was where I was eventually going anyway, so I was full of joy while most of those around me were filled with fear.

I heard that the situation in the Rift Valley was serious, as there were many Mau Mau there and teachers were scarce. I felt the challenge to go to take the Itinga school, which was right inside the Bahati Forest where one section of the Mau Mau were encamped. Even though this appeared very dangerous, I was convinced that to refuse it would be to miss the way of the cross for me. First I went there alone. When the Mau Mau were convinced that I was non-political, taking neither side, just quietly teaching and preaching, they let me know that I was safe. Soon my wife and children joined me and we were happy there. They even stayed on when I had to make short trips by bicycle out to Kijabe or Nakuru. Amazingly, there in the forest I was able to have long, serious talks with all sorts of men. They were concerned about how to achieve unity in our tribe and between tribes, and I told them I had the secret. I told them that it isn't achieved by force and fighting, but in the cross. I had experienced it—unity of people from all tribes and races; it is the work of God. In that unity, no one speaks against a brother or steals his property, no one takes a bribe or gives one, no one considers himself better than another because he has more education or property or a higher position. We are on the same level because we are depending equally on the cross of Jesus for our spiritual life. This is a great secret, but we have it!

We stayed there in the forest until everyone was moved out by the government. Then we went back home to Maragwa in Murang'a District, and were placed in a Home Guard camp so I could teach in the Kawaharura school. There in the camp there was ominous grumbling about me because I couldn't conscientiously take a gun and go out with them to kill the Mau Mau. "Who does this fellow think he is?" they said. Finally I was called into their court for a showdown, and I knew there was murder in their plan. I gave a loving goodbye to my wife, telling her, "They plan to kill me today, so goodbye, dear one, we will meet again in heaven."

When I went and stood before them with their angry faces looking at me, I was fully prepared to die. Finally, I began quietly laughing because nothing was happening. I laughed and laughed. Their leader shouted at me, "You will die today!"

And I replied, "Yes, I know you have a gun and the gun is loaded; why haven't you shot me? What are you waiting for? You know I haven't done any wrong to any of you."

He said forcefully, "You must take this gun!" Then I knew I was not going to die that day.

So very happily I said to them, "Wait, let me tell you how I see it. You are a man of very high rank, and if I fail to take the gun as you have ordered, it will be said that you have not been obeyed, and your soldiers will whisper about it."

At this he lost his temper and shouted, "Get out of here!"

I left singing a song of praise to God. Then I heard that the wives of the Home Guard said to that high-ranking officer, "Why are you attacking our preacher? Don't you know that it is only his words and teaching that have kept us from becoming promiscuous here in this camp?"

Before long I was given the privilege of an identity pass to leave camp and travel on the roads! It was astonishing that all through the dangerous time of the fighting, I was not even beaten up once. But the strains were heavy. I learned to lean hard on my Lord Jesus. He filled me with His joy, and I praise Him for keeping me and my family through it all.

## NARROW ESCAPES
### Nathaniel Wainaina, Murang'a

As a boy I went against my parents' wishes by going to school and following Christian ways. I will always remember how in August of 1947 I went as a young man to the huge gathering of people at Kahuhia to hear the Word of God. There I heard a speaker say, "Jesus is very near you, in fact He is in you and knows what is in your mind and heart." Suddenly, with horror, I realized that Jesus knew I had committed one of the greatest sins of all: hating my mother who bore me and hitting her! I trembled with the bitterness of it and wept many tears.

But then I heard the Lord Jesus saying to me, "Go, and sin no more!" I knew that day that He had forgiven and received me. From then on all sin became very hateful to me.

When the Mau Mau came to our area, I heard how they administered their oath by slaughtering a goat, drinking its blood and eating its meat. I learned that each one taking it had to make terrible promises. Immediately I knew I would far rather be killed than ever to deny Jesus Christ. The Lord strengthened me in this resolve and in sharing His Good News.

One day I was on the road coming home from our fellowship meeting in the house of Joseph Kareji when I met two Mau Mau guerillas, who asked me, "What tribe are you?"

I answered, "I'm a Kikuyu."

"What kind of Kikuyu?"

"A Kikuyu who loves Jesus," I replied.

At this they grabbed me and said, "We're going to beat you up!" So I bowed my head and began praying out loud to God the Father.

Suddenly one of them told the other, "I think we'd better leave this one alone," and he grabbed the upraised arm of the other one. While they scuffled, I was able to get away. This was at the very beginning of 1953. After that the danger increased greatly, especially their attacks on convinced Christians. On Friday of that week I walked with my neighbors Gadson and Rebeka Gachigi, who lived on the opposite hillside, to a weekend revival meeting at Masharage. Saturday afternoon Rebeka walked home to be there for Sunday School the next morning. Then Sunday afternoon, Gadson and I left Masharage about 3 p.m. When we reached my home we parted, saying as usual, "See you tomorrow if the Lord hasn't come."

But early the next morning a cry went up outside the home of Gadson and Rebeka, and I learned that they had both been strangled by Mau Mau during the night! A few years later, when the fighters were surrendering and confessing to British officers, we heard their story of that terrible night. This was their first raid out of the nearby forest and their plan had been to kill this couple, then the Headman of our district, and also my wife and me on the hill across the valley. They did kill the young couple and the Headman with his guard, but as they started to climb the hill on our side, there were definite signs of dawn breaking, and they knew it would be broad daylight by the time they had strangled us, so their leader said, "We'll get them another night," and they went back to the forest.

The following day I went to the funeral and burial at the church of my dear neighbors. It was a wonderful time of singing and praising for heaven. This rejoicing replaced the grief and fear we all had felt. When it was over, Brother Heshbon Mwangi and Rural Dean Obadiah Kariuki told me they didn't want me to go home that night. They asked me to come along with them to Weithaga Mission where others were beginning to set up temporary housekeeping for the duration of the war. I accepted their advice, but my wife, Tabitha Njeri, whom the Lord had saved in 1949, refused to move. She said she wanted to stay at home to look after our livestock: some cows, goats and a pig. One child came with me, the others stayed at home with their mother and grandmother. Later the Mau Mau came, took our cows, slaughtered our goats and the pig, and they forced her to take the oath against her will. After that sad night my family all came to Weithaga and we stayed there until 1956. We were glad because some missionaries, Neville and Vera Langford-Smith, needed someone to help in their house. They hired me because I had worked as a cook and cleaner years before in a white settler's house. In my time off, I was also able to go with others as an evangelist to the Shinga area.

At last we were able to move back home, and the Lord gave us another cow. Our farm plots were still there. Besides farming I have been able to travel all around our district, encouraging the brethren and telling others of Jesus. I am a lay reader in our church, and I have also been part of the team that prepares and cooks for our large conventions. I will keep working for Jesus until He comes again.

## WHAT? A HIPPO?
### Samuel Mukuba, Kirinyaga
### (By Bishop David Gitari)

My father, Samuel Mukuba, was born in Kitui District in 1882, and during the great famine of 1899 he left Kitui, Mutunguri, with his mother, and came to Kirinyaga where there was more food at that time. They settled in a place called Giriambu.

In 1914 he went to Mombasa to look for employment, and while there he came into contact with CMS missionaries. From them he learned the catechism and became a Christian. There were a few other young people in Mombasa at that time who also became Christians, and together they formed their own fellowship.

In about 1919 he heard a voice from heaven telling him to go back home and share the Gospel with the people of Kirinyaga in Giriambu, where his home was. He shared this vision with the other young people from Kirinyaga and they collected money and sent him off to evangelize in that area. When my father arrived home in late 1919 to begin his work, his first strategy was to preach in the big tribal initiation ceremonies. At that time these occasions were attended by hundreds of people and were the big event of the year. He asked them to keep quiet so he could tell them the good news about Jesus Christ, but people would not listen to him. From the coast, he had brought a Gospel of Mark in Kikuyu which he tried to read to them. But they said, "We don't believe you! You may have picked this up in some nearby place and are trying to tell us it is from Mombasa."

Very discouraged, my father wondered why he had failed. It came to him that perhaps he had not read his Bible correctly. So he read the Gospels again and saw that Jesus had not started His ministry by going to big gatherings, but by calling twelve disciples and teaching those few until they understood His message. Then He sent them out. So he changed his strategy and chose twelve disciples. They were all fairly young people. In fact, he had to persuade their parents to allow them to come to his lessons. So every morning these twelve young people met with him. And after the Bible lesson and prayer time, Samuel gave them a lesson in how to read and write. He started by teaching them the alphabet, then he divided them into six groups of two each and each pair went late in the afternoon to a different village nearby to teach what they had learned in the morning. Thus he was teaching many people. When they had learned how to read, he distributed Gospels of Mark. Now the people could learn what God wanted them to be and do. That was the beginning of a number of small churches around Giriambu. By then, in 1910, the CMS missionaries had already arrived at Kabare, but they had not yet reached Giriambu, which was an area about ten miles away. The missionaries heard that someone was there who was preaching Jesus and they came to look for him. One of the missionaries was a Mr. Lampley. He and my father eventually worked together as partners.

My father was a pioneer evangelist and teacher, but he also became a businessman, and a good farmer. In 1923 he married my mother, who is still alive at 91. Her faith has meant a lot to me.

In 1931 my father was persuaded to go to Limuru Bible College to get some theological training. He stayed there for two years and came back to be a trained evangelist for 40 years. He is remembered more than many others because of the impact he made. He was a leader in his community, becoming a county counselor, and an assistant chief for a short time.

During the time of Mau Mau my father was still strong and articulate. He knew these people were fighting for independence, but he also felt the Gospel could not be compromised with the blood of goats. Therefore he never took the Mau Mau oath.

One night when most people were asleep in the village, the people giving the Mau Mau oath came banging on the door of our home, shouting that they were being chased by a huge animal. They spent the night hiding in our granary and the next day they said they had been chased by a hippopotamus. This was astonishing for there are no big rivers in that area where hippos could live. So if it was a hippo, it had to have walked quite a long distance. In the morning they had a good talk with my father and said, "We are not going to give you the oath after all because we saw something last night that made us really scared." After that they decided never again to bother that home, for they they were sure we were under divine protection.

Soon after that we moved to Kiamutugu, a village where there was security during the period of the Mau Mau. This was government policy at that time. My father was also very concerned about the waste of human life, and pleaded for the lives of the Mau Mau who were captured. He pointed out to the government that there was too much torture and killing going on.

His prayer life was tremendous. He had a small chapel in connection with his home and every day he rang a bell at six a.m. and six p.m. for all his neighbors to come to pray with him. He was a good farmer and won several trophies in agricultural shows as the best farmer in the area. He was a good businessman with a shop and a water mill for grinding grain. He spent a lot of his own money for the church. He was also a humanitarian, rescuing twins and babies born or growing in unusual ways from being thrown to the hyenas. He brought these children up as his own. He was very generous, a hard-working man, a good evangelist and a Christian leader.

### A TEACHER LOVED AND HATED
#### Evelyn Wangui Ndung'u, Nyeri

Our father was a Presbyterian church elder and our mother trained her children to be the "Musical Kids." We sang for Jesus in our church and in evangelistic meetings. We were all encouraged in our school work, and I went as far as I could in those days, completing the course of the Teacher Training College at Kahuhia.

It was during school days at Kahuhia that I truly understood the testimonies and message of new life. Someone was speaking one day from John chapter 3. It was Jesus who told Nicodemus that he must be born again—well educated and religious though he was. For the first time, I saw myself as the sinner I truly was, and Jesus received me and made me a new person. From that time I became closely involved with the people of the revival fellowship.

In 1950 I began to teach. All around me there were rumblings of the revolt that became the Emergency. The war was declared late in 1952. Many Christians were frightened, but God gave me courage to stand up in a very large meeting and say, "I have refused to take the Mau Mau oath because Jesus has saved me. Since I have taken the blood of the Lord Jesus, I cannot possibly mingle His blood with that of a goat."

Possibly because of my public stand, we began to experience persecution. Our house was burned down, and my parents' house was burned to the ground also. We lost everything. Others of our fellowship were badly beaten, one wife and mother was killed and thrown into a deep toilet pit. But God put a burden of prayer on us and He led us to rescue some of the fellowship. Even children were in danger. My father was shot several times with a gun and seriously injured. He was taken to the hospital and was there a year and a half. In answer to prayer, God raised him up from the point of death and he is still living today. Through faith in God my husband and I both survived and God has given us a large family. We kept going from village to village to help people and to speak to them of the power of Jesus' name, so we were very much hated by the freedom fighters.

When we went to our old church, the elders said, "We don't want the 'salvation people' here," and they put us out. So we went outside and had our worship service in the shade of a big tree. Before the war was over, however, they changed their minds and invited us back in. In His own ways, God supplied our needs, and our children were blessed by their grandmother.

I was a teacher for 39 years, and just recently retired. Some of our children have earned college degrees. I still have three children living at home, the youngest being in 8th grade. I can tell you that God is very good. He knows how to really save and care for His people.

## TAKE OFF HIS HEAD!
### Ephantus Mbogo, Murang'a

Although I was brought up in a non-Christian family, I was able to go to school as a teenager in 1934. I learned about Christianity and reached the "readers' class." Before I could be baptized, I was drafted, in 1939, to go to war. During my army service I began to wish I had continued learning catechism and been baptized. I was stationed in Uganda in '41 and it was there that I was baptized and took the name of Ephantus. Then I looked for a class to prepare for confirmation, and when I was in Beirut, Lebanon, I was confirmed and took my first communion in 1944. While I was in the Middle East, I managed to take a bus to Jerusalem and spend about two weeks seeing many places that are mentioned in the Bible. During all that time, God kept me. I wasn't killed in the war, and I returned home in November of 1945.

I began looking for a wife and finally got married in 1947. Seven months later I first heard the preaching of Heshbon Mwangi and Elisha Mwangi about being born again. My heart was touched but I argued with them that these were hard words. Before long, however, God opened my heart, and in January 1948 He saved me and washed me clean from my many sins. He reminded me of some things I had which I had stolen, and I returned them. There were many other things I needed to do to right my wrongs, always explaining that it was because Jesus had changed me. I began a whole new life with Jesus, testifying to Him and walking in fellowship with the brethren.

At this time, I worked in the Department of Agriculture, teaching people to make terraces to save the soil and guard against erosion. This was something the Kikuyu hated to do because the British tried so hard to enforce it.

When the Mau Mau oath began to be given, I refused it, and because the people had a particular grudge against the government's agricultural program, they said, "Let's take off the head of Ephantus Mbogo!" I had been sent to see about the water supply in one area and was secretly informed that on a certain day the Mau Mau would come to kill me there. But the Lord helped me and my team, and since we were informed in time, we were able to find a safe place to hide that day.

In 1955 I gave up my work in agriculture and became a free evangelist, continuing in this until 1960 when I became an evangelist for the church. In 1970, my wife, who loved the Lord very much, was taken to heaven in an accident, and I was left with eight children! So for the next seven years my work became caring for the children—and the Lord kept me from temptation and discouragement. In 1971 I was called to be a prison chaplain, and in April 1977 God blessed me with another wife who loves Jesus. Her name is Ruth, and together we are helping the brethren, serving the Lord and praising Him.

## Two Without Fear
### Samuel & Damari Ngeru, Nairobi

Samuel: I was brought up quite near the Weithaga Mission and my parents were Christians, so I was baptized early and learned about the church. I went to school through primary and intermediate and then went to learn a trade at the Kabete Trade and Technical School, where I became a builder. I married Damari and took a job with our local County Council, at Murenjes, building concrete bridges, adobe houses and a hospital. When we ran out of work, I went to Nairobi.

Damari: Although my family lived near Weithaga Mission, they avoided it, and I could not learn to read until I was an older girl. I barely learned to read and write before I was married to Samuel. I was the mother of four children at the time when there were special meetings which we—the children and I—attended. At first I listened to these speakers with no interest, asking, "What's this stuff they are giving us?"

But one day I was startled by their question: "On the day that you die, where will you go? And all of us will certainly die one day." That was a heavy question, and I went home thinking about it and wondering what to do. Some days later I gave up, and said to God, "Even me. Do You think You could save even me?" That was in 1944 when I invited Jesus in, and He did come and change me. Suddenly I was full of joy. It was on that day a lot of things changed for me. For example, I had been mercilessly beating our children when they did something I didn't like. So there was a lot of screaming around our house. I stopped that, but when a child did something that was sin I had a serious talk with him, looking him straight in the eye, saying, "Tomorrow, don't you do that again!" That made a difference.

I began then and am still learning how to walk with Jesus. Over and over I come to Him saying, "Lord, forgive me for what I just said, or for holding a grudge without forgiving, or for my thoughts that hurt You." God is so good, He has forgiven me many many times. Repentance has become a way of life for me, and I spend my time thanking Him for the freshness that comes with cleansing. There is nothing in the world to compare with this—not silver or gold, or land, or children, or a husband (and I love him). When God calls me to heaven, I will go without any of these. So I praise Him in my heart all the time.

Samuel: When I came to Nairobi, I got work with the Ministry of Works and Railways, building the houses for their employees. I worked at this until I was dissatisfied. Then I went home, where I became a drunkard. Soon I ran out of money and didn't know what to do.

My wife told me she had been saved and this depressed me. We stopped talking to each other. When I told her to go buy me some cigarettes, she refused, so we were really estranged. Finally I heard Jesus' voice telling me I was living under the control of Satan. Then I heard a verse read in church: "Come to Me, all you who are tired of carrying heavy loads, and I will give you rest."

I said, "A-laa! I've known that verse since I was a child, but only today do I understand it. What's different about today? What's happening to me?" That verse repeated over and over in my mind without stopping. I asked myself, "Who is saying that? Is it Jesus, or who is it?" Finally I went to the foot of the cross, taking myself and everything else—the cigarettes, liquor and many other things. There I confessed my sinfulness, and when I got up I had so much joy I couldn't explain it.

Damari: It was a wonderful day when Samuel came and told us that Jesus had saved him! Even the children were leaping and laughing for joy. It has made a great difference in our home, and we have been living together in peace until this day.

Samuel: After that happened, I went back and asked to be taken on again at work, telling them that now I was a new man. I asked my boss for forgiveness for all the work I had messed up and told him that now I would be an entirely different worker. I started in with high standards and great expectations at work. After a while I found it very difficult to work with a crew who cheated on time and workmanship.

Finally, I resigned and began work as a private contractor, setting my own standards and carefully hiring my own crew. I contracted with those who wanted to build, and I stuck to the contract, doing good work on time. And I have continued these practices. I pay my workmen first, and if anything is left it is mine; if not, I do without. So I still have plenty of work now when I am 80 years old!

We were all living in Nairobi when the Emergency was declared. I was picked up by the police with all the other Kikuyu and put into the Langata Detention Camp. That was a terrible place. They were screening all of us. An informer sat in a car with a police officer, and we were marched past. The informer identified each of us by saying,

"Yes," meaning he's a Mau Mau, or "No" he is not. When I went by, the informer said, "Yes." Some Kikuyu onlookers shouted, "No, that's a lie!" Nevertheless, I was tagged as a Mau Mau, and I was kept in detention for eight days. Then Archdeacon Bostock of Nairobi, who knew me, heard I was there and came to the camp to sign papers for my release. So on the eighth day I heard on the public address system: "Samuel Ngeru, come to the gate." Police escorted me there and handed me over to the Archdeacon, who welcomed me and took me home in his car. We were living in the Bahati section of town, and he didn't feel comfortable driving any closer than to Kaloleni. So I walked the rest of the way home, and rejoiced when I heard my children shouting, "That's Father! Father's coming home!"

After a while authorities began returning all Kikuyu in Nairobi to their home areas. At that time I was building the new Anglican church in Pumwani, and we were living right there in the caretaker's house. So Archdeacon Langford-Smith told the authorities that I was working for him, which I was, and we were allowed to stay on in Nairobi.

Damari: Since I had been giving my testimony to the rebels for a long time before the Emergency, I wasn't afraid of the Mau Mau at all. I heard that they said, "No use trying to persuade that woman. Leave her alone." They even left my daughters alone though they were not circumcised. No one ever demanded of any of us that we take the oath. Our position was too well known. God protected us so well, I finally had to pray, "Father, forgive me for not being more grateful for all of Your care of us!"

Samuel: God has brought us through the years. When I was working for the government, I was able to sign up for a "self-help" home. This is where we still live to this day. The neighborhood church of St. Barnabas is "mine." I was a founding member of the church, and am one of the lay readers.

### FACING TANKS AND GUNS
Canon Bedan Ireri, Embu

I was brought up in a Christian home, with Sunday School and all. Following my primary education at a mission school, I went to a government African boarding school in Kagumo, Nyeri. There I realized how much of our land white settlers had taken, and I became resentful of them and embittered toward the government. I decided never to read the Bible again or pray. I didn't go to church for four years. When I wasn't chosen to go to high school, Rev. Howard Church, a missionary, told me I should go to Kahuhia Mission to train as a teacher. I refused, because I knew that church-trained teachers were supposed to teach the Bible also. But when my father and uncle put pressure on me, I had to agree to try it.

I went to Kahuhia with a rebellious spirit and was nearly expelled. The Lord reached me by a quiet word from Dr. Joe Church of Ruanda who was visiting his brother Howard in our school. The only thing I remember was his saying quietly, "If you know you are a sinner and do not know the way to be rid of your sins, pray for a mirror in which to see yourself as He sees you." Those words stuck with me, and I thought, "Yes, that is something I have never experienced. I'll pray for a mirror." So that evening I did. But half of me was still muttering that these white people are liars. Nevertheless I prayed this for over a month.

Then one night I was wakened by a bright light shining in our room and I heard a voice saying, "You are a liar." I was cut to the heart. "You have committed fornication." That also was true. "You are a thief."

I cried out, "Enough! Don't speak again!" From that moment I started praying that the Lord would save me, and the light went out. In the morning, I opened my Bible and there was Psalm 51—all about repenting. Eventually on November 21, 1942, when I had asked God to let me die for my sins, I was kneeling by my bed and I heard a still small voice saying, "You *cannot* die for your sins, because Jesus Christ died for them on the cross. You may be forgiven, if you believe this." He repeated it twice. Then I said, "I do believe that Jesus Christ died on the cross for *my* sins. I believe, and I am saved!" Then I got into bed and slept.

A second time that night I was awake and heard the Lord saying, "Your life is now hidden with Christ in God!" Wonderful words. Then I saw a hand writing on the wall: "Luke 7 verse 17." In the morning I took my Bible and it opened to Colossians 3:3—"Your life is hidden with Christ in God." Then I looked up Luke 7:17, and found that it says, "This news about Jesus went out through all the country." From this I knew He wanted me to tell others about Jesus.

I said to my roommate in the college, "Muketha, the Lord saved me last night!"

He said, "Oh no! Anyone else, but not Bedan!" I left him and went around the place telling other people, but at that time there was only one other student there who knew what I was talking about—that was John Mwangi Kanguru. He was delighted when I told him. We had no special praise song then, we just embraced each other and laughed with joy. He said, "I have been alone, but now we are two!" We went about together testifying and preaching and many people got saved. From that moment to the present, I have been telling people about Him and He has kept me.

During the Mau Mau fighting, my wife and I were living in Kigaari where I was teaching in a college. Nearly everyone knew that I could not take the fighters' oath because I had taken the oath of Jesus Christ. After it was all over and Kenya was an independent nation, one of the generals of the guerilla army told me, "We could not kill you, Bedan, because we knew you were praying for us." And indeed my wife and I were praying for them every day, out loud, with all our hearts, that they might be saved even there in the forest. And we were praying for the whole country, for the British army and everyone else.

We were right in the middle of the fighting. Sometimes there were Mau Mau running around our house, and once they were going to leave the body of someone they had killed on my porch, but because they heard us praying for them, they put it somewhere else.

We were in danger for a while because we had a young woman staying with us to help in the care of our children who was a close relative of General Dedan Kimathi, the most famous of all the Mau Mau fighters. We discovered this accidentally one day when our child called her "Miss Kimathi." We knew we could be executed for treason by the government for having her there. But at the end of the term, she left.

At one time, when information reached the British army that General Kimathi was preparing to attack the military base at Kigaari, the British moved all their available tanks and armored vehicles onto our school grounds which were near the forest. I was teaching an evening class that night, and going home I suddenly found myself cut off by tanks with all their guns pointing at me.

So I lifted up my pressure lamp, hoping they would know who I was, and I prayed, committing myself to the Lord and saying, "If this is the time for me to go to heaven, fine! But if not, it is well." My wife could see this, peeping through our front door. After a while their commander told them to stop, and they let me go home.

The thing that kept us going during those days of daily danger was being part of a close, supportive fellowship group meeting frequently. I told the fellowship that I love the Mau Mau and they laughed at first, but I said, "I also love the Home Guards and the whole army and I pray for them. I couldn't pray for them without true love in my heart." Then they understood what I was saying, and we were all praying for the freedom fighters and for the government troops that they might be saved.

My wife, Elizabeth Njura, is a dear sister in the Lord. In my first year of teaching, the Lord pointed her out to me—a small girl in my class—and said, "That's your wife." I said, "No! No!" But six years later we were united in holy matrimony after she had finished her secondary education and had been teaching for two years!

She met the Lord personally when we were in training in the Theological College at Limuru. When Canon Elijah Gachanja spoke about the blood on the doors of the Israelites in Egypt, she asked herself, "When was His blood sprinkled on my heart?" She had no answer and began to weep. That night she received Jesus and His blood into her heart and there was great joy in our home. We have seven children, all grown up. Two now are saved.

### FEARLESS IN FAITH
### James Njogu, Kirinyaga

Though I was born into a non-Christian family in about 1926, I was able to go to school when I was about ten years old. When I was about twenty, I joined the Africa Corps of the British army and rose to be a sergeant major. I worked in the office as pay clerk, paying wages and keeping accounts. Unfortunately this enabled me to steal regularly by falsifying accounts. This went on steadily until July 17, 1950, when I was on a street corner in Mombasa and heard some joyous Christians sharing their faith.

Jesus changed my life that day. I confessed my sins, and immediately began returning the money I had stolen from the soldiers. They were astonished by my testimony and they listened to what I had to say. I stayed there long enough to return every cent I had stolen.

By 1952, when the Mau Mau rebellion was heating up in Kenya, I was working as a clerk and bookkeeper for the Department of Agriculture. Freedom fighters came to me and said, "If you don't take our oath, we will kill you just as we would a white man."

"That's all right," I answered, "If I die I will go straight to heaven. But what about you?—when you die, will you go to heaven?" They left.

My parents came and begged me earnestly to take the oath so that I would not be killed, but I told them, "Don't worry. If I die I will be with Jesus." After that my family let me alone, saying, "Well, whatever God wills."

All through the conflict I kept on sharing about Jesus in my work area and at church, and to my surprise the Lord continued to help me to be fearless and bold to speak His Word anywhere. I was able to go with the preaching teams into detention camps. There we found Mau Mau fighters who had been saved and were overjoyed to see us. On the other hand, as our national Independence Day came near, we were constantly threatened by ex-fighters who said, "As soon as we are free of the British, we will kill those of you who followed the whites and the Bible!"

We said, "So be it. We will then be in heaven." But of course it didn't turn out that way, due to President Jomo Kenyatta announcing mutual forgiveness! The Lord gave us peace in our new nation.

After Independence, I worked in an office of the local authority. Part of my job was to serve the ex-Mau Mau who came out of the forest to receive their plots of land. I was very happy to help them, and they said, "It's because you are saved that you are treating us so kindly and well."

Now it is many years later and we are still spreading the Good News. I love Jesus and count His salvation the most precious possession I have.

### A Five Mile Race
#### Canon Felix Nyoro Muraguri, Murang'a

My father, Muraguri, and my mother, Wanjiku, had only two children, a boy and a girl, so without question I had to herd the cows and goats in our Gathukeini district. But when I was fifteen, I ran away from home and got a job. There I heard a Salvation Army person who preached from a book about heaven and hell. I was disturbed, and decided to go home and go to school. My parents were glad to see me, but my father said, "No! You can't go to school!" and I replied, "Well, father, if you refuse, then I'll run away again and go to Kahuhia or Tumutumu to learn to read. But if you will let me go to school in the morning and herd in the afternoon, I'll stay." At first he said no, but finally agreed.

A Christian family living near the school gave me food and sometimes let me sleep at their house. They taught me much and showed me the Christian life. I kept passing the exams very well and went all the way to Alliance Secondary School.

Until 1939 I was an unmarried man. By then I loved the Word of God, and besides becoming a teacher I felt a call to study for the ministry. I was given a place in Trinity College, Limuru. I was married and became a deacon in 1939. I was fully ordained in 1945. I was dedicated to God's service, but secretly uneasy about my many little deceptions, and by 1947 I kept feeling I was a sinner. This is the year a Gospel team came from Uganda with William Nagenda and Dr. Joe Church from Ruanda. Their message was that no matter who you are, if you do not personally repent and come to Jesus, you will be lost. This gripped my heart and I cried out to God for help. Suddenly everything changed for me, and I became the first one in this area to understand and preach the "revival message."

I began to witness for the Lord Jesus both in faith and power, and spread the Good News everywhere I went. The church elders and some members didn't like it, and they warned me twice. Some people were being saved, so I suggested that I be the pastor of the "revived ones" and the other ordained man in our district be pastor of the rest. This caused a lot of arguments, and finally it was decided by the church officials to lower my monthly allowance to ten shillings ($1.50). Nevertheless I went on cheerfully in faith.

When I was threatened with death over the Mau Mau oath, I replied, "Yes, when God chooses the time for me, I will gladly die and go to be with Him, but until then you will find that you can't kill me!" At this, the church people decided to withdraw the ten shillings, stating that I was disloyal to our tribe's fight for freedom. So my wife and I cheerfully ate sweet potatoes and corn from our own garden. Our missionary, Cyril Hooper, took up a love gift to help the pastors whose allowances had been cut off, so we could buy the clothes we needed. We were grateful for this help and went on preaching Jesus.

In 1953 when the war became fierce, I was high on the list of those the Mau Mau wanted to kill. This was partly because I fellowshiped with white people. One day, with evangelist Ben Karume, I was riding my bicycle to preach in a certain church. Along the way we came upon three Mau Mau fighters. One shouted, "Stop! Where are you from?"

We speeded up and I shouted back, "No! We haven't time!"

We heard behind us a fierce, angry voice, "What! You won't stop?" There was death in that voice and they came after us. We left our bicycles and ran down the hill. Our whole area is steep hills and narrow valleys.

Ben was caught by two fighters and the third continued to chase me. Suddenly he stopped for a moment to make his pistol ready to shoot. I kept running, thinking, "Better a gun than their knives." Then I saw five more Mau Mau ahead on the path, just waiting to catch me. So I changed my direction, ran down through the brush, crossed the river and ran up the other side to where there was a police station. It was at least five miles that I had run. I sat down covered with sweat and gasping for breath. They told me to rest and then they took me to the British officer. I told him what had happened, and that I feared my companion was dead. They drove me to the main police station in our area and we went to the spot where our race had begun. There, sadly, we found Ben Karume's body. The officials took it to Murang'a Hospital, where the brethren came to fetch our brother and buried him with praises. Realizing that the Mau Mau were determined to kill me, I stayed a few days with the Home Guard to rest, and then I joined the other brothers and sisters at Weithaga Mission.

From that time on, I have felt that I have a great debt to the Lord to trust Him and preach His Good News everywhere. Every problem that arises I see as nothing—because I know now what Jesus, who called me, can do.

## A Night in the Fields
### Geoffrey Kamau, Meru

Both my parents were churchgoers, and my mother had a testimony that she was saved, but I wanted nothing to do with that. I became a teacher in 1948. The next year my mother came to stay with me one weekend because she was attending a convention in that area. Of course I didn't go to the meetings or listen to anything that was being said. I went a distance away where I could smoke and try not to think about all my sins.

After the meetings were over and people were gone, I heard an audible voice saying, "You will die, Geoffrey!" I looked around and saw no one near me. "You will die in your sins!" I was really frightened and dropped to my knees and began talking to God and listening to what He said. He changed my life. I was full of joy when I realized Jesus had forgiven all my sins. He helped me tell others of His grace, to return things I had stolen, and to apologize to those I had injured or sinned against.

In 1953 when everyone was terrified of the Mau Mau guerillas, I had peace and even got married on April 11th to the sister in the Lord who is my wife. It was a time of danger, but Brother Felix stood with us in the wedding.

Because of the Mau Mau, most people in our area wouldn't stay indoors at night but slept out in their fields or hid in the bushes. However, my wife and I didn't—we just remained in our home. Then one day at noon I heard a voice telling me, "Tonight, don't sleep in your house."

I went to my wife and said, "The Lord has spoken to me. Tonight you take your bedding and sleep outside in the storeroom, and I will stay in the field."

She said, "Oh, I'd rather go stay with your parents." I agreed, so we had a very early supper and went our different ways.

I was not very far away, and at midnight I heard men pounding on the door of our house. They couldn't get it open, but since it was a mud-block house they cut around the window, lifted it out and put it on the ground. Finding no one there when they entered, they took a burlap bag full of sweet potatoes, and a number of other things. Our books were on the table, and though they took one Bible they left the other one lying open. Nor did they take my bicycle! Perhaps these were neighbors who had joined the guerillas and were sure that I would be taken and killed, because I had been telling them, "I will never take your oath. I would rather die." Perhaps they had come to see if I was still alive.

I reported this to the police station and to the Education Officer, who moved me to the school at Kamarero, where I taught for the rest of 1953 and 1954. After that I was sent to Peresha because so many schools and churches in our area had been destroyed. In that community there was no church or school. The Lord helped us to visit the homes and tell people about Jesus, and a church was begun. We still love Jesus and He has given us six children who are grown. God is very good.

## A REBEL TRANSFORMED
### Rev. Timothy Kamau Njeri, Kijabe

A missionary named Emil Sywulka came to the village of Gatamayo in 1906 and spoke to the people so convincingly about the Lord that a young boy named Njeri made a life-changing decision to follow Jesus. Njeri went to school and learned to read, and then started to teach others—and one of his pupils became his wife, my mother. My father went with Mr. Sywulka all through the Kikuyu hills and valleys preaching the Gospel where there was great spiritual darkness. When Njeri's mother died, he and his wife had to dig the grave and bury her by themselves, because at that time no Kikuyu would come near a corpse. Njeri longed to bring enlightenment and progress to his people.

I was born in 1922, the sixth child of this couple, and was well taught in the Bible both in my home and at the church of the Africa Inland Mission station at Kijabe. But as a child and teenager, I was very angry at what seemed to me the affluence of the missionaries compared to my father, their co-worker, who usually had no shoes to wear; and of course we children had none either. I felt they were taking advantage of him. In 1939 I left Kijabe with my resentment, and went far away to Uasin Gishu District, near Eldoret, to stay with my sister who was married to a Forest Guard. I had learned carpentry at Kijabe from a young missionary named Davis, whom I loved, so for a while I did carpentry. Then I made friends with whom I began a flourishing business enterprise. I also met the girl who became my wife, and we were married by the elder Mr. Barnett—it was the last wedding in which he officiated.

The first time I heard a revival team from Uganda, in 1945, I passed it off, because I had been satiated with Bible teaching. The second time, at a revival convention near Eldoret, in 1946, I realized that these people were giving personal testimonies of a kind I had never heard before and this shook me. But then I realized that if God cleaned me up like that, I couldn't do the business I was in with the partners I had. So I chose the business. Then in October of that year, in church one Sunday the sermon was from Romans 7 and I saw myself in the story about the married woman who is bound by the law to her husband as long as he lives; but if he dies, then she is free to marry another. When the pastor finished, I stood up and said, "I see that I am a sinner like the married woman who loved another. But now that old husband who ruled me in sin has died, and I am free to be joined to the Lord Jesus!" How those people praised the Lord and sang! Without offending my friends, we divided the business. In the end, I was just making charcoal in the forest and selling it to townspeople for their fuel. I also took great joy in going to share about Jesus in Elgeyo College, and in watching some boys be completely changed by Him.

In 1952 I entered Moffatt Bible Institute at Kijabe because I knew I wanted to serve the Lord Jesus all my life. How my father rejoiced to see one of his sons follow his footsteps! There we heard the rumblings of the coming war between the freedom fighters and the government. I declined money offered for tuition by the District Church Council, saying that I wanted to be a free evangelist and a writer rather than a local church pastor.

The Mau Mau war was all around us while we were studying; there were threats, and terrifying things were happening. One night early in 1955, I was working with Miss Ruth Truesdale on translating a booklet called *Calvary Love*. Miss Ruth was a great blessing to me and to many others of our church people. We were in her home which was near my father's home. The Kijabe alarm bell began to ring! We could smell smoke and see flames at the top of our mountain about four miles away. We went outside and saw it was a huge fire. People running down said that the people of Lari were all massacred and the whole village was on fire. Mr. Davis cried, "Maybe some of our Christians are in trouble!" So he took his gun and drove up to the top. After a while he came back and said he had found them and they were safe.

That year I traveled around to most of the detention camps, translating for Pocket Testament League people who were giving out Gospels of John. I still keep meeting people whom God saved through this work in these camps. The next year I was loaned to the Navigators to translate their *Search the Scriptures* correspondence course for these detainees.

Then I found my principal life-work in 1958, when I was called to begin the broadcasting of the Word of God on radio. This ministry has continued for many years, and is still going on. We trust that God's people will pray for this.

My wife and I have eleven children, including one set of twins. One son is studying for the ministry in Trinity Seminary in the U.S.A.

### "SHE IS MAD!"
#### Rebeka Munyange-Phillip, Gaitu, Meru

I was born in 1920 to non-Christians, and I was brought up in all our tribal customs. In 1941, I was married in the old-time Meru way. My husband taught me to read and do a little math. We started going to our nearby Methodist church in 1944.

In 1950 there was a revival convention in our area and I was gripped by a word of Jesus, "Come unto Me, all you who are weary and heavy laden, and I will give you rest" (Matt. 11:28). Without telling anyone, I did come to Him. Then in another meeting, I heard Jesus saying to me, "Whoever disowns Me before men, I will disown him before the angels in heaven" (Luke 12:9). When I understood that, I had to say openly that Jesus had forgiven me. I was joyfully received into the meetings of the fellowship group, and soon was baptized. My husband refused Jesus' invitation. Nevertheless, I was so filled with God's love that I could love and serve him much better than before.

When the Mau Mau war began, I was trusting Jesus. But my husband heard so many people saying that Jesus was a white man and they wouldn't worship a white man, that he refused to go to church and took up drinking.

One night in 1953 some forest warriors with long, twisted hair pounded on our door, and my husband ran away. When I opened the door, they shouted, "Where is Phillip?"

I told them, "He is out."

"What is this book?" they asked.

"It is the Word of God."

Then they threw my Bible into the fire and ordered me to burn any other Christian books I had. I said I couldn't do that because I was saved. One of them raised his long knife to kill me, but their leader said, "Stop that! She's a mad woman!" Going outside, they stole two of our sheep. On the road they found some of their fighters who had deserted from the forest army. Two of these were killed. My husband heard shots and thought I was killed. He was surprised to see me alive when he came home. That day he moved us into a government-protected village. Even there I rejoiced, as some turned to God for His salvation.

One night during special meetings of God's people in a nearby marketplace, the Mau Mau came out of the forest and burned down a store in which some of the brethren were sleeping. Three of them died because they couldn't get out. We knew they were with Jesus, so the next day, while we gathered up the ashes, we sang praises to God and buried them peacefully as we celebrated the joys of heaven.

In 1955 I was severely criticized by many for having a daughter of ours studying in a mission high school. "It will make her into a European!" they said.

I said, "Well, if it does, and you drive all the white people out, they can take her with them!"

This made them very angry, and they shouted, "You just wait and see! When we get independence for our country, all of you traitors who have refused to take our oath will be slaughtered!"

My prayers for my husband were finally answered in 1959 when he came to the Lord.

So in 1963, on Independence Day, we were together waiting for the massacre they had promised. But what actually happened was much different. In his first broadcast to us, Prime Minister Jomo Kenyatta urged all who had been fighting, both black and white, to forgive one another! Some fighters were angry about this. But we had forgiven them long ago, and we rejoiced with many others that there was to be no more bloodshed.

Phillip and I have walked together peacefully in Christ many years. Now all eight of our children are grown up, have finished school and gone to their own homes. One son and one daughter are walking with Jesus. Praise God!

### A SCHOOLGIRL IN DANGER
### Nerea Wathumu-Benjamin, Embu

My parents were strong Christians. My father was a teacher and church evangelist, and he and my mother taught me all the rules and customs of the church. They even took an unpopular stand agreeing with the missionaries' teaching against the tribal circumcision of girls.

I was in primary school, however, when I first remember hearing the message of salvation, but I felt I was such a good girl that I didn't need repentance. As a matter of fact, I looked carefully at my life and saw no sins there except some insignificant things I had "inherited from Adam." After that, however, the Lord Jesus was slowly able to show me that I was so determined to get my own way that I was angry and resentful when I didn't get it. This was making me rebellious and disobedient.

Then a team of young people came from Chuka in 1948 to hold meetings in Kigaari. One young man said, "In the ocean there is a huge mammal called a whale, and he swims slowly, with his enormous mouth open so fish can swim in and out of his mouth quite safely. Then all of a sudden he snaps his mouth shut and all the fish inside are swallowed! There are church young people like that, who like to swim in and out of Satan's mouth and boast, 'See, this doesn't hurt!

I'm O.K.' Then Satan swallows them." For the first time I understood what I was doing. I stood up and told them that I was one of these, and Jesus was showing me myself. That day Jesus washed my sins away, and I began to praise the Lord with the "saved ones" in their fellowship meetings.

Because He really changed me, I apologized to my parents and my teachers. My teachers laughed and advised me, "Don't try to be a grown-up woman while you are still a schoolgirl. It won't last." There were a lot of schoolgirls who made decisions in those meetings, and sadly there were some who gave it up later. I prayed to Jesus to hold me tight, and I kept on praising Him. I said, "For me, there is no turning back."

When danger exploded around us in the Mau Mau war, most of the fellowship brethren moved to Kigaari. At first, our family stayed on our farm, as my parents didn't care for the fellowship meetings. After a while the family moved to a protected camp, and mother said, "Nerea, your fellowship friends have all left you and gone to Kigaari. Why don't you follow them?" So I did, supposing it would just be for a week or two. It turned out to be a long time.

Those of us girls who slept in the mission office had our meals with Brother Francis and his wife. One time I thought we were neglected in the dividing out of the available food and supplies. I became resentful and angry. Then the Lord showed me my sin and took me back to His cross and cleansing blood.

Some time later, I went with an older Christian sister to tell about Jesus in a certain village. On the path, a woman stopped us and said to me, "You will never see your father again. Last night he was attacked and killed by freedom fighters." I couldn't believe it and went right on. We finished our meeting and went back.

The brethren at Kigaari had heard, and when I came as usual to wait on tables that evening, they suggested that I go and rest. They gave me a sister to stay with and comfort me. She reminded me, "Nerea, you have been helping others in trouble, saying, 'Be patient and courageous.' So now when your father has gone to heaven, God will help you to be courageous." She prayed for me and finally the Lord did give me peace.

Months later, against the advice of Sister Jemima, Francis' wife, I decided to go back to our farm to get some fresh food from our field or garden. It was my old stubbornness and determination to have my own way. Near my home I met a woman I knew, who grabbed me and said, "Oh, Nerea, come with me! They are waiting to give you the oath secretly. We won't write it down anywhere, so no one will know!"

I replied, "Go tell them I have already taken the oath of Jesus!"

An old lady heard me say that and pulled me away from the woman, saying, "I will take you back to Kigaari; otherwise you will be killed just as your father was. This is a center of Mau Mau fighters." She went with me as far as the river and saw me cross it. So I arrived back at camp empty-handed but alive.

I first repented to God the Father. Then I apologized to Mama Jemima, saying, "I didn't get a thing for us to eat, but I have come back with Jesus, and now I know that He is the One who is in charge of my life. I won't try to do things without Him again!" How I praised Him for saving me from the Mau Mau, and showing me that only He could keep and guide me successfully in my life.

### HIDDEN IN THE GRANARY
#### Janet Wairimu Weru, Nyeri

Even though my parents did not know Christ, the Lord provided me with a friend who taught me His way when I was very young, and I grew up into my teen years loving Jesus. When the Mau Mau oath came to our area, I quickly realized that I could not take it because the Lord Jesus meant so much to me.

One time I went to visit a woman I knew and was shocked to find out that the house where the fighters were administering the oath was just next door. As soon as my friend saw me, she knew I was in danger and she said, "You must hide!" We ran outside and she gave me a ladder to use to climb into a large tribal-style woven storage bin for corn. It was not too soon. Within minutes, the Mau Mau had a lull in their oath-giving and came outside to look around my friend's yard and house. As they were walking around the granary in which I was hiding, one of them came within two feet of my face. I easily heard him saying that what he didn't like was the people who refused to take the oath. The Christians especially irritated him because they were so peaceful in telling the Mau Mau that they could kill them—as if they were accepting death cheerfully! He had never seen anything like it. Right then inside the granary I knew for sure that the day I was faced with taking the oath would be my day to go to heaven, because I certainly would not take it.

Soon these men moved into my friend's house to continue with oath-giving and I heard a loud voice angrily shouting, "All right! If that's the way you want it, you will get the death you're asking for!" This convinced me that I must stay hidden, so I curled up, shivering on the corncobs, until they were all finished and left. Finally my friend came out and quietly called to me. She helped me—and the Lord had delivered me from fear. Through those years the Lord guarded me and I was never seized by the oath-givers.

In 1960 I had another personal encounter with the Lord Jesus. This time He showed me that my pride and self-righteousness were only dirty rags, and I asked Him to forgive me and take these sins away. Then I began in a new way to rejoice in His life and righteousness that He had given me. Even now the Lord is guarding me, and all I ask of Him is that He will stay with me as long as I live.

## My Wife Was Murdered
### Erasto Mushiri, Embu

My parents were against churches as long as they lived, and I followed them. The Anglican church of Kaithege was the one nearest us, and in the 1930's I said I would never enter it. But then something happened that changed my mind. Some of us had been hired by the Chief to do a job which had turned out badly, so he put us on forced labor. Our Chief was a churchgoer, so I thought, "Maybe if I go to church, he will let me off." This worked as I thought it would, because the rulers assumed that church people were pro-government. Thus, they weren't drafted for forced labor in building roads.

So that is how I got into the church class preparing for baptism and after that for confirmation. I also married a wife in the church.

Then in 1948 we had special meetings. A banner was written and hung up in the front of our church: "Be sure your sin will find you out!" (Numbers 32:23). To my surprise I discovered that I couldn't hide my sins from God. I cried to Him to show me what to do, and the Lord helped me to repent, and repent more, and finally I announced, "Jesus has saved me!" I discovered that I needed to go on being saved, because after that my wife died, leaving me with two children. I went on walking with the Lord and learned what a help it is to be in fellowship with brothers and sisters who love you and are willing to stand with you. After a while I married a sister in the Lord, Josephine, and we learned to live together in Jesus.

When the days of danger in the Mau Mau war began, the fellowship brethren moved from their homes to live together near the church at Kaithege. Our home had been at Mufu. We all agreed that if any of us should be killed, there was really no need for the others to search far for the body, as the brother or sister would be at home in heaven with the Lord. We were living in peace.

Then sadly in 1953, my wife Josephine was killed by the Mau Mau when she went back to our farm to bring some fresh food from the crops we had planted. She left one child with me and had been expecting another soon. That was hard, but I had peace in Jesus.

Later two relatives of mine in the Home Guard requested that I go and sleep in a school building to guard it at night. I declined, as God was giving me other work to do. It was not long before that school was burned to the ground and both men who were stationed there lost their lives.

Another time I went out to Mbere to preach the Word. On that day I met the British District Officer, Mr. Lakin, who gave me a lift to Kadhanjuri where I spent the night. There I heard that our little village of Mufu had been burned and everyone in it killed. At that point, we went to Kyeni where the government was building a fort and we stayed inside the fort for many days.

I was patient for many, many days without a wife and learned that my basic joy was in the Lord Jesus and His salvation. I could live without a wife, but not without Him. Then He graciously gave me another wife and we lived praising the Lord. God took this third wife to heaven also after the end of the Mau Mau fighting. I bowed to His will and during this time there were two brothers who helped me a great deal; they were Epaphras Kariuki and David Kariri. They came to me and we praised God together. They helped me back into the river of grace and the fountain of blood. I was able to see not the loss caused by death but the goodness of Jesus, and I accepted His plan.

The government appointed me Subchief of Mufu area when it was being rebuilt, and they gave me a gun. Thank God, the two brothers Epaphras and David came and sat with me and helped me see the danger I was in of forgetting God. So as soon as I could, I left that job and have been serving the church and the fellowships, and God has given me a fourth wife who is still with me.

### A BRAVE COUPLE
#### Walter and Pauline Njiru, Kirinyaga

As a growing boy I supposed I was going to heaven because my parents were Christians and I usually obeyed the rules. Besides, I saw that the "saved ones" were on too narrow a path and I wanted to do as I liked. But Jesus was pursuing me. I entered the government training school for pharmaceutical assistants in Nairobi in 1949. The life and habits of the city young people shocked me. There were so many prostitutes, such drunkenness! Though I didn't want to be "saved," neither did I want to spend my time in the dance halls and beer parlors. What should I do? I decided to start attending St. Stephen's Church Sunday mornings, and also to join the Christian Students' Association in my training school which met Sunday afternoons. By my being faithful in this, God began to teach me.

Gradually I began to realize and admit my sins of telling lies, lustfulness and stealing. In the training school, we handled many medicines in learning to fill doctors' prescriptions, and I had been stealing these medications to sell, or to give away illegally. Finally I admitted all my sins to Jesus and asked Him to cleanse them in His blood. He did this and I began a new life.

After graduation I was sent to various hospitals and clinics to fill doctors' prescriptions for patients. When the Emergency was declared, I was working in the pharmacy of the Meru Town Hospital and I went right on sharing the joys of salvation in Christ. This became very dangerous, especially when I was sent out to assist in the hospital's out-clinics, but the Lord was with me and protected me, and my wife stood by me.

At that time, some of our brothers and sisters in Christ were falsely accused by Mau Mau prisoners as having taken their oath. So they were put in prison. Many of these were single people and had no one at home to look after their property when they were arrested. My wife, Pauline, and I decided that we would be their family and go to their apartments, pack up their things and put them in a safe place until they were released. This was hard, time-consuming work.

This voluntary work of ours was noticed by the District Commissioner and he phoned me at work one day to ask me to come and take away the stolen property of a prisoner which had been recovered by the police. But carrying so many things was getting difficult because we had no vehicle, and I was feeling sorry for myself. A brother suggested, "Why don't you turn this whole project over to Jesus, and let Him take charge?" When I did this, He provided a vehicle we could use for transporting these things! This amazed the government officials, who were suspicious of everyone. They thought our brothers in prison had taken the oath when this was not true.

The only place we had to store things was in our small house, which became very crowded. Still it seemed to us the safest place. We praised the Lord that He gave us the strength and faith to do this work for Him and for our loved ones.

We also undertook to carry food to our brothers in detention camps where food was scarce. Sometimes when we were there we had a chance to talk to some of the imprisoned Mau Mau in these camps, and this made us forget the long hours and hard travel.

It was even becoming dangerous for us to meet together every day for prayer and fellowship after work in people's homes. There was a rumor going around that we were Mau Mau giving people the oath in these meetings. Fortunately we had a Christian brother who was an English doctor. He spoke for us to the officer in charge of our district, guaranteeing that we were loyal Christians holding prayer meetings and were not at all subversive. We praised God for that.

We are still loving and serving Jesus today.

### EVERYTHING DIFFERENT
### Gideon Irambu, Meru

In 1947 I went to the first meeting where brethren from Kikuyu came to preach in Meru the Good News of salvation. I heard it. At that time I didn't act on it but it stayed in my mind. I was a teacher and supposedly a Christian. Then in 1948 I was asked to preach one Sunday, August 28th. There was a young man in church, Joshua Karurudhu, who spoke at the end of the service telling about the revival meeting in 1947. He said that he had been saved then. Although I had just preached a sermon, the words of this young man touched me deeply. He said a brother named Samuel had read Ephesians 4:17–24 about turning around and leaving the things of the past. Then this young fellow asked the whole congregation, "Have you left your past sins or are you going right on in them today? This is not what Jesus wants," and God gripped me, because just the day before I had beaten my wife and nearly killed her for refusing to prepare my tobacco. Right then I cried out to Jesus and He saved me, and I hurried home to ask my wife to forgive me. When I came back to church for the afternoon meeting, I told everyone, "I have been saved! Here is the snuff I prepared yesterday; I am destroying it, so you needn't come to me for it any more. I am a new man." Some stared in amazement, others rejoiced greatly.

Since then everything is different. My wife, who had also been using snuff, was saved too and we began a whole new life together.

Others joined us, and a fellowship of God's people began.

When the Mau Mau rebellion erupted, I left my job of teaching and went home. Soon a search went out for someone to sell food to the soldiers in their canteen. I knew Kikuyu and Kikamba and a little English, and I decided to take this job to support my family. The captain gave me a case of beer to sell to the soldiers, but I refused to sell it. So he said, "All right, the corporal will sell it, but the other things you will sell." I then moved into the camp, but my wife preferred to stay on our land. Our two older girls came to Kaaga boarding school here in the town of Meru, and the other children stayed with their mother.

My brother and a neighbor of ours were Mau Mau guerillas in the forest. Our farm home was one of the few in our neighborhood where people had not taken the oath. My wife's brother had promised to come on a certain day to help her harvest the food crops. The day he was to come, he met someone on the path who said, "There was a Mau Mau raid here last night, and they took what they could." My brother-in-law was frightened and decided not to go on. That same day the Mau Mau came to our house and asked for Rebecca, my wife, but she wasn't there. It was a narrow escape for both of them.

That night someone came and told me what happened. In the morning the Subchief decided to move my wife and family into the camp. So they gave her a house in the lower camp and brought them in, and also another brother who had not taken the oath. So for the duration we were safe and kept on praising God.

After things quieted down, we returned to our farm. Our children grew up, finished their education and left home. The Lord has truly been with us.

# 6

## LIGHT IN DETENTION CAMPS

*"Who can snatch the prey from the hands of a mighty man? Who can demand that a tyrant let his captives go? But the Lord says, 'Even the captives of the most mighty and most terrible shall all be freed. . . .'"*
Isaiah 49:24–25 (TLB)

*"He pulled me out of a dangerous pit. . . . He set me safely on a rock and made me secure. He taught me to sing a new song, a song of praise to our God."*

Psalm 40:2–3 (TEV)

*". . . the jailer threw them into the inner cell and fastened their feet between heavy blocks of wood. About midnight Paul and Silas were praying and singing hymns to God, and the other prisoners were listening to them."*

Acts 16:24–25 (TEV)

*"He threw Joseph into prison . . . but the Lord was with Joseph there . . . and was kind to him."*

Genesis 39:20–21 (TLB)

### INTRODUCTION

Prison camps everywhere are notorious for suffering, hunger, violence and death. The British detention camps of the 1950's were no different. Even though the official policy aimed at humane treatment, the wardens had big problems. Supplies of food and water were often difficult to obtain. There were epidemics of typhoid and other deadly fevers. Warders in direct contact with prisoners often were full of hate and reacted strongly to noncooperation among the prisoners. Beatings and brutalities were regular occurrences in certain compounds.

Some of the camps were huge, with 80,000 or more prisoners. These camps were divided into sections by barbed or electrified wire fences, so that prisoners could be segregated according to the difficulty they gave in maintaining control. The least cooperative and most violent men were called "the hard core." Prisoners slept in huge barracks or Quonset huts, mostly leftovers from World War II.

Most of these larger camps were a long distance from Central Province where the fighting was going on. Some were in the northern deserts, others along the railroad in the low bush country between Nairobi and the coast. However there were also prisons and smaller camps in the Kikuyu war area, for screening or transit use. These were generally high security compounds. Prisoners here were said to be "in remand."

Official policy allowed Christian ministers to visit the camps to preach and distribute literature. At first these ministers met only anger and antagonism, and guards were fearful for their lives. But when they saw some "incorrigible" prisoners wholly changed for the better in attitude and cooperation, the guards requested and welcomed prison chaplains and gave them special privileges.

Another surprise to the wardens was in observing the Christians who had been arrested and imprisoned with the fighters. These believers had refused to bear arms against the Mau Mau, so the British officers suspected them of being undercover agents. But as you will see in the following accounts, these peaceful, rejoicing prisoners had a healing effect, even in camps where other prisoners hated them most.

### THEY REFUSED WEAPONS
#### Geoffrey Ngare, Nyeri and Nairobi

I was born on the lower slopes of Mt. Kenya in Nyeri District in 1914. I grew up as a herder of flocks and cattle for my father and mother. They did not know Christ, but as a teenager I was allowed to go to Sunday School, where I heard about Jesus and began to learn to read. After a while I could attend adult classes, where I did well. When I was twenty years old I was accepted in a regular school at Kagumo. By then I wanted very much to be a man of God. I managed, with the help of my uncle who paid my fees, to get two years of high school, and by then I was a baptized member of the Presbyterian Church.

When I left school, I got a job in Nairobi as an operator in the Telephone & Telegraph Company. And in 1943 I was able to marry Rachel who is now my "sister," that is, my wife.

In 1945 I felt a call to serve the church and be a preacher. God was with me and I was accepted in the School for Evangelists where I began to study in 1946.

In 1948 I heard the Word of God preached with power by William Nagenda at a convention. It was the preaching of revival, but it didn't touch me because I knew I had been a Christian for some years: I had left a good job for the work of God, so surely I didn't need to be saved. But a verse William read stuck with me: "If we would examine ourselves first, we would not come under God's judgment" (1 Cor. 11:31). I couldn't sleep, and asked the Lord to show me if there was anything wrong in me. He showed me a picture of the times when my wife and I were so angry with each other that we could not speak, and sat with our backs to each other. Then someone would knock on the door, and immediately we would begin to smile and talk pleasantly—so the person coming in would think, "What nice people these are!" But as soon as they were gone, we went right back to our anger. I saw that this was hypocrisy and lying. I also saw that though I didn't beat my wife—for fear people would find out—I did beat her with ugly words. I threw them at her violently until she cried bitterly. The Lord showed me this was the sin of cruelty. God's Spirit also showed me a book I had stolen, and some thieving I had done in school.

When I accepted that I was a sinner and knelt down and asked the Lord to forgive me, He washed me in His blood. I returned the stolen things, and made peace with my wife. From that time, I began to know the power of the Lord and could confidently preach Jesus as my Saviour. My church elders were angry with me for publicly confessing such things, and accused me and two other students of bringing strange doctrines from Uganda into the church. They tried to get us put out of the school, but when we three graduated anyway, they said that no church needed us. We kept on preaching Jesus, but were soon penniless—so we cheerfully lived on the sweet potatoes from our garden.

After a while the Lord called us to Chogoria, on the east side of Mt. Kenya, where a missionary doctor was praying for revival in the church. Two of us went there; the third had already begun teaching again. The Lord blessed the churches southeast of Mt. Kenya with revival and many were saved.

We were there when the Emergency began. The government ordered everyone who hadn't taken the Mau Mau oath to carry a gun or other weapon for protection and for killing the guerillas. I said to the one telling me this, "I have a sword, my Bible. I can't carry another weapon; this is enough. I am ready to preach to the Mau Mau people or to the government army men, because both need Jesus. But if I carry a gun I would appear to have joined one side."

The agent said to me, "You are a pastor. Let us call a meeting of the local people and you tell them it isn't bad to carry weapons for defense."

But I said, "No, I couldn't do that. My conscience doesn't allow me to carry weapons. So were they to ask me, 'Pastor, where is your own weapon?' they would find out that I have none and I would have to explain why to them." So these agents were really angry with me. They had already found some members of the church who had refused to carry weapons, and they came to the conclusion that they were following my teachings.

I got into trouble with our Chief because he tried to stop a large outdoor church meeting after the people had gathered, and found it couldn't be stopped. I was called to Meru to explain this to the District Commissioner, who dismissed the case as tribalism. But another time I came before him because I had been stopped by a white police officer for traveling on a bicycle, for he feared the Mau Mau would see it and kill me and cut up the bicycle frame to make guns. I replied that I couldn't stop preaching the Gospel, and that it was equally good to me to live or die—so I had no fear. He was upset by this, but once again let me go. Another day this same policeman arrested me for not having a special emergency identification card. I hadn't heard about this ruling, so he put me in the police car and took me to Meru to the same District Commissioner again. This time he kept me in a special jailroom for a week and made an investigation of me. The Lord blessed me that week through the love of the brethren who visited me. There was a white brother there in Meru, named Bisley, who loaned me a typewriter to write to the brethren in order to encourage them and tell them that I had no fear, for the Lord was with me. And on Sunday they even allowed me to go out and meet with others and then come back.

At the end of the week, the District Commissioner called me to his office to report on his investigation. He said, "I have found that the leaders of your church do not like you. They say that when you are with them they can't fight the Mau Mau. And we want the Mau Mau to be stopped. For this reason I am sending you out of this area and back to Tumutumu on the Nyeri side of the mountain, so that the people who have rejected you can deal with you."

My family and all our possessions were moved by truck back to Tumutumu, our church headquarters. The church elders said, "Ha! Look at this. We told you he was bad. Now even the government has put him out!" When we asked for a place to stay, they said there was none. I asked to sleep with the other men in the guardroom, but they refused me because I had no weapon. All that was left was a small servant's room at the back of the house of a missionary who was on furlough. My furniture was stored in the missionary's house and we all slept in the small room and were happy. People saw we had no fear, so they assumed it was because we were Mau Mau ourselves. So every night there were government guards hiding where they could watch our house, waiting for the Mau Mau to come and contact us. The Mau Mau never came, but we certainly were well guarded—by God's plan, not theirs! God is amazing.

I began to testify in the leprosy hospital and the school. After a while some of the hospital staff and the children were being saved, and the elders said, "Ai! Ai! This fellow is a real troublemaker; what can we do with him?" So when a request came from the Christian Council of Kenya for our church to assign someone to go to the detention camps for Christian witness, they sent me gladly to get rid of me.

When I first went and tried to speak in a camp, the prisoners absolutely refused to listen, because they believed that all priests and ministers carried guns and were traitors to the freedom cause. When I spoke, they banged on empty tins and basins to make a racket, and yelled as loud as they could until I got tired. Finally I asked the commandant for permission to use his loudspeaker to make an announcement. He said, "Use it!" So I gave my testimony and stated that I had been rejected by my church and by the government and had been in jail because I refused to carry a weapon against the Mau Mau. I told them I had a different kind of sword: the Word of God. The prisoners began to say, "This is a different kind of minister—he refuses to carry a gun against us." They began to listen to what I had to say. They also listened when I went to the locked gate of the camp and preached the same Gospel to the British soldiers there—who got angry and pushed me back to my "Mau Mau friends." When the prisoners saw this was a Gospel for everyone, they thought maybe I had something important to say.

God began to work there and many were beginning to turn. Some who got saved were suffocated at night in bed by others. But others lived and were able to tell yet others, who themselves started preaching as well. Another great help was that in the camps I found some of the saved brethren who had also refused to carry weapons. They were a little nucleus of light in a dark place, and rejoiced greatly to see me. They were a living demonstration of what I was saying and God used them to reach some of the Mau Mau. I visited many different camps all through the war years and beyond.

After the camps were closed, God called me work in prisons and soon I became Senior Chaplain of Prisons in our newly independent Kenya. God did a great work there, changing people's lives. Now, though I am retired, I am still preaching His Word in schools and jails and wherever the door opens. God has done miracles in providing my children with expensive education while my wife and I lived on small incomes or none. Several of them now have degrees and are working as professionals. He is a wonder-working God!

## A PRODIGAL SON
### Joel Mwigaruri, Embu

Although I was born into a Christian family in 1928, and was taught well, I was a troublesome child both at home and at school. I was frequently punished for cruelty and disobedience. Very early I learned to smoke and drink and molest girls.

I took the Mau Mau oath early on, and was picked up by the police in the first raid for activists. I was sent to the detention camp at Mackinnon Road and put in Compound Number 5, in which there were, at one count, 2,550 prisoners! It was miserable!

One day the Lord brought to that camp one of His servants who was sent out by the Christian Council of Kenya, and his name was Kenneth Philips. It was February 18, 1955, when he came, and he preached a message from Romans 9:20–21. It was about the potter and the clay which he was forming into different kinds of pots. The speaker asked, "Does the pot ask the potter, 'Why did you make me like this?'" I knew that I had been asking God, "Why did you make me like this?" He had created me and put me into a loving Christian home—and I had brought my family, my teachers and my wife nothing but grief. Why was this? Gradually I realized that God had intended me for His own use, but I had chosen to rebel and go my own way. These thoughts made my spirit faint. But the Lord is good! Within two weeks—on March 6th—the Lord came to me in that terrible camp in the middle of the day, forgave my sins and changed my life! The first thing I did was to pull out all the cigarettes I had and the other tobacco and throw it all away. An older man said, "This kid has lost his mind!" and I answered, "Oh, no, I haven't. I have found Jesus!"

In that camp there was a group of the joyous Christians who had been imprisoned because they refused to take up weapons against the Mau Mau guerillas. The day I came to the Lord they were as usual sitting on the ground in a circle, a little distance from other inmates, singing praises to God and sharing what Jesus was doing for them there in the camp. I walked over to them while they were singing the Hallelujah song. I sat down in their circle, raised my hands at the end of their song and told them that I had been saved. They burst into exuberant song again, and they all came to embrace me lovingly. It was more joy than I can describe. I stayed for a week in their section of the camp, and they taught me about repentance and walking with Jesus. At the end of that week, their names were called and they were released. Suddenly I was left alone in that huge camp as the only born-again person.

So I began to testify to the men there. They threatened to kill me, but I wasn't afraid to die. I kept on telling them about Jesus until we left. That camp was closed that year, and in August we were moved to Manyani Camp. There I was in Compound Number 25, still telling about Jesus, and some of the prisoners finally began to listen and turn to Him. In the next year and a half I was moved to other camps—Karaba, Kathihiriri, and Kanja, and in each camp I told fellow inmates what Jesus could do for them, and some came to Him to be saved. I was released to go home in 1957.

My wife and parents rejoiced greatly at the change in my life. My old drinking buddies came to welcome me with liquor and jokes, but these disappeared after I told them how God had turned me around. From then on I saw very little of them.

Three of the fellowship brothers became spiritual fathers to me: Francis Ndwiga, Junius Mbugu, and David Karigi. For them it seemed like teaching a baby to walk his first steps. There were many,

many things I needed to make right, and many apologies I needed to make to my parents, to my wife, to my teachers and to those with whom I had sinned.

It is absolutely true that the Lord Jesus is capable of saving a person no matter how wicked he or she has been!

### A CHIEF TURNED AROUND
### Peterson Kariuki, Murang'a

My father died before I was born, so as a child I cared for the family cattle and goats, and also helped my mother because I had no sisters to do it. Our home was in Kiriaini Village. When I was about fourteen, in 1928, a friend came to our home and said I could go with him to school, so I went. My mother said nothing and I continued to help her before and after school. Our school was Presbyterian and I was baptized in 1931. After teacher training I taught school, both teaching and preaching. I was talking about a Jesus I did not know personally, but I was a good speaker. In 1936 I was married to a girl brought up in a Christian home.

After fourteen years of teaching I became a businessman and then a politician, serving as Counselor in two locations. At the end of 1946, the District Commissioner appointed me to be a Chief. After that I stayed in the church only two years. At that time church members were not allowed to drink beer, which at first was no problem because I hated the taste of it. But gradually I was persuaded by the other Chiefs to drink with them, so I left the church and before long began to marry other wives.

After the Mau Mau war broke out, the District Commissioner called me to his office twice and falsely accused me of having taken the Mau Mau oath. This made me angry, and then a friend of mine told me, "You are going to be killed if you don't take the Mau Mau oath." So one day I was ambushed along my path. A Mau Mau fighter jumped out of hiding and pointed a pistol at me. I was frightened, having nothing with which to defend myself. He was a man of my constituency, and I asked him, "What are you going to do with me?"

He answered, "I am going to kill you."

"Why?"

"I have been told to kill you because you refused to take the Mau Mau oath."

"Bring it!" I gasped. "I'll take it."

He said, "Wait—wait—wait . . . I don't have it here. Go home and tomorrow we will bring it." I agreed but asked him to come along with me then to my home to protect me from other Mau Mau. He said there was no one else charged with killing me, so I was safe. That night he came to my home and said I had to wait for three days to take the oath.

When I went to the place where they were administering oaths, I took it and then said to them, "I am a public servant and now you have given me your oath and I am on your side. But one thing I want to tell you: Don't force any Christian here in my district who does not want it to take the oath. If I hear you have beaten or killed someone like that, I will get you imprisoned."

Again the District Commissioner called me and asserted I had taken the oath, and I replied, "Well, twice before you said I had when I hadn't, so I learned that this is what you expect, and now it is true, I have taken the oath. It is you who caused me to do it."

He said okay and gave me guns to fight the Mau Mau. I said, "I can't kill anyone. My duty is to prevent killing." He didn't like that, and some of the Home Guards told me, "If you are not willing to kill, you won't stay in your position long."

In December of 1953 I was arrested and taken to a detention camp far up north, at Maralal. I was happy to get away from my dangerous situation where the Home Guards didn't like me and the Mau Mau didn't like me either! In this camp I learned all about the "freedom" the Mau Mau were fighting for, which I had not really understood. I was taught well by Phillip Kibuthu, a prisoner who had been a Mau Mau Administrator and knew much about it; also by others who were senior in the rebellion. So I said to the Christian preachers who were sent to us, "I don't want to listen to you because the British with their Jesus have taken our land from us."

Then in 1955 there were some people who came to our compound who not only preached but gave their personal testimonies. This was new to me and exciting. Also at that time I thought I was going to die because I had a disease in my feet and couldn't walk, so I thought I had better make my peace with Jesus. When I was younger I had preached about Him, and later had hated Him because I thought He was one of those who had taken our land. But now I said, "I am going to accept Him as my Saviour." I was seeking Him for two days; then during the night of March 15 I decided to pray in the name of Jesus. (The Mau Mau never prayed in the name of Jesus. They prayed only to Ngai, the god on Mt. Kenya. In the camps if anyone named Jesus, he would not be given his rations and could be beaten or killed by other detainees.) That night I accepted Him, repented and was freed from guilt. I began to praise Jesus, that He had forgiven me all my sins!

Then I was moved to Manyani Camp. When I declared there that I had taken Jesus, the other prisoners kept me from getting any food. But another man quietly went for his food and mine and brought it to me. When someone noticed that I was getting food, they began to intercept it and I stayed some days without food. But I went around preaching about Jesus whether I was hungry or not. There were many who heard and who also received Jesus in that camp. Even now when I go to a town like Nyeri or Nairobi, I find people coming to thank me for bringing them to Jesus in the detention camp. I stayed in that camp until 1958 when I was released.

When I came home, I called the girls whom I had married and told them, "Now I have been saved and this is what I am going to do. I loved my wife when we were married, and now I shall not have another wife. But I married you, so I give you a choice. If you prefer, I will give you a sum of money and you can go find someone else to marry you. Or you may stay in this area and I will give you land." Most preferred the land that they could cultivate, but two took the money and went away to another marriage. Since that day I have been living with my first wife who finally became saved in 1978, and is with me today. I am praising Jesus, and wherever He is preached, I love to go there.

## SAVED BY HUNGER
### Alvan Nyaga Njuguna, Runyenjes, Embu

I was a shopkeeper with a lot of friends with whom I enjoyed a life of loose living. Then my wife got "saved" in 1948, and I made life very hard for her after that. I commanded her not to testify to my friends and rob me of them. I told her, "This way you have of saying openly that you have been saved from certain sins is embarrassing me, and I don't want you to talk to my visitors like that." I threatened her, and told her that if she did that I would lose all my customers. Actually it was because I knew it would offend my partners in sin.

When the Emergency was declared I had already taken the Mau Mau oath, and so I became an agent for the fighters in the forest. As a businessman I was able to purchase guns to help them, and bullets also. When I was arrested I was found with a consignment of bullets, so I was put into the detention camp called Mashiara. We suffered quite a bit in this camp and often went hungry.

In our camp were some other detainees who had been locked up because they had refused to carry weapons to fight against the Mau Mau—they belonged to the Presbyterian Church. They had told the government officers that they were saved and couldn't carry any sort of weapons. They said their weapon was prayer. They claimed they were praying that the war between the government and the Mau Mau might stop and that there would be reconciliation between these warring groups.

Even when we were going hungry, these prisoners were always at least able to cook porridge for themselves, because their Christian brothers and sisters kept bringing them things they needed. Seeing this, a few of us went secretly at night to the camp of the saved ones to beg a little porridge. They welcomed us and fed us and then spoke to us of salvation. They said, "Even though you are in prison, your spirits are not locked up. And the sins you have in your lives, the Lord is able to save you from them and forgive you completely. Then when you leave the camp and return home, you will be saved people."

That was when I got this precious gift from the Lord, for I confessed my sins and was saved. I really saw Jesus for myself and was rejoicing in Him even in detention—from 1955 until I was released to go home in 1958.

When I reached home, my wife received me gladly for now she was my "sister in the Lord." I had a lot of things to confess and ask her forgiveness for. Not only was there my fighting against my wife, there were adulteries and stealing and drunkenness, and all these I had to try to make right. There was also the matter of a soldier who had robbed me of a large sum of money during the Emergency. When I returned home, I wrote him a letter saying, "I want you to know I have forgiven you. Jesus has forgiven me a huge debt of sins: theft, immorality, fighting and more. He has forgiven me completely and holds none of this against me. So I want you to know you are free. Have no doubt or misgivings to make you fear me, if you should meet me on the street. I have forgiven you and hold nothing against you."

On our journey since then we have much to praise the Lord for. I have seen His power. He has helped me in business and blessed me. We have been able to build our own shop because of Jesus; also a nice home of stone-block. A greater blessing is the restfulness and peace of spirit we have at home. In Him we have so much, and I rejoice in Him tremendously. My church is here in Kigaari, a part of Runyenjes Town. I am still a businessman, and also a lay leader in my church. Praise God!

## A TRACT IN TIME
### Arthur Kihumba, Othaya, Nyeri

I was born in Nyeri, but grew up on a farm in the Rift Valley where my father was working. As I went on in school, I returned to the family home in Othaya, Nyeri, and was later baptized (1937) in the Anglican church of Weithaga where I studied for a year. Eventually I went to Alliance High School for two years.

Then World War II started, and I had to join the army. In January 1943 we were sent to Ethiopia to fight the Italians. Returning to Kenya the following year, I was being given the battle course in Lanet, getting prepared to go to the Far East. It was a terrible course for teaching killing, but I went through it. Then the World War ended and we were taken to a rehabilitation center to cool down, because we were becoming vicious.

After taking a teaching course in the Jeanes School, I taught first in Kabete Girls' School for two years. But in the middle of 1951 I left and came to Othaya to teach in the Kikuyu Independent School which was related to the underground freedom movement. So I was in very serious trouble when the Mau Mau oath came. By 1953 the State of Emergency was declared and the school I was teaching in was closed by the government. While teaching there I had refused the Mau Mau oath as a "Christian" but they forcibly gave it to me, nearly killing me to do it. It was only God's miracle that I didn't die. I didn't really want to serve the movement, and went back to teach in a mission school.

In 1954 I was arrested and taken to a detention camp, first to Othaya Camp, then to Aloth Work Camp, and from there to Manyani, and that is where the Lord found me. We had church ministers who came around preaching to us. But we closed our ears because we were so wild. However, they persisted and gave us tracts. Finally I took one of them to read and started thinking deeply on Matthew 16:26, "What will a man gain if he wins the whole world but loses his own soul?" Those words were very appropriate for me. It took 93 days—until sometime during the night of December 17, 1955, I gave myself to the Lord Jesus.

In the morning I started to tell the other prisoners what the Lord had done for me. That was dangerous because the men were very tough and didn't believe the Word of God. But I said to them I had decided to serve the Lord, and even if they killed me, I knew where I would go. I didn't fear anything. I knew that any night they could get blankets to suffocate me and I would die. But I took courage and started to testify there in the detention camp. I was unafraid in my witness to the detainees, the policemen, the wardens and the white men in charge.

Later when the authorities saw I had changed, I was moved all the way to Mwea in Kirinyaga District. There we started digging the fields for rice growing. Finally, when I was able to return home, I found to my joy that my wife was also saved. I began to testify in all the villages, joining our brothers Silas Muchina and Solomon Maina. Since then we have been going on in fellowship, praising God.

### TERROR IN A JAILROOM
### Solomon Maina, Nyeri

It was really true for me that day, when I gave everything to Jesus, that I was saved anew. I loved Him more than ever—because I knew I would soon be with Him in heaven. The door was already open!

I heard Jesus saying to me, "I want you now to give yourself wholly to Me to serve Me in any way that I choose." I agreed and said I was ready to give up tailoring, and if He sent me to a difficult place, I would go.

Soon I was arrested by our local Chief for not giving him the bribe he expected, and was put in the prison cell where the fiercest Mau Mau fighters were kept. This was a difficult place.

We were all in one room with no window. Our cell had just one door with the latrine bucket in the corner. We slept in very close quarters. All conversation was about the forest, the oaths and murder. When I looked at my cellmates, I was sure I would be killed if I said a word about Jesus. I was quiet the first day and the second day.

Early the third morning, the Lord said to me, "I brought you here for one special purpose—to testify to these people, that's why." I got up early that day and called out, "I want us to pray!" I had no idea whether or not they would agree, so I went on, "I didn't take the Mau Mau oath, because Jesus has saved me. I am satisfied with Him. I'm not concerned whether I live or die, because I am looking forward to heaven and life everlasting." Then I prayed and ended "in the name of

Jesus Christ." I heard a few of them say quietly, "Amen." Oho, I thought, so this is the reason God brought me here, because even these fierce guerillas want to pray and hear a testimony. He has His reasons. For three weeks I stayed with them, telling them all about Jesus. Then God released me by His strong arm.

## A HARD WORKER
### Jediel Ngaara, Chuka, Meru

The Lord saved me in August 1945, when William Nagenda and a team came from Uganda to tell what Jesus had done for them. The first thing I did after that was to return things I'd stolen and ask forgiveness of people I had injured. For one thing, I had been hunting colobus monkeys in the forest with my bow and arrow, and selling their valuable skins on the black market. I confessed to the District Commissioner and asked forgiveness. He replied, "It is a good thing that you got saved. If all the illegal hunters got saved, we wouldn't have to keep police patrols in the forests!"

When the Emergency began, I refused to take the oath and also refused a government order to carry a weapon to kill the Mau Mau. So I was caught between two forces: on the one hand, the Mau Mau wanted to kill me as a traitor, and on the other hand, the government was angry and suspected me. Both were wrong!

I was arrested, together with Rev. Geoffrey Ngare, and taken to Meru. I was church treasurer, so the soldiers who searched my house found the church money I kept there, and reported that I collected money for the Mau Mau! So I was sent with George Moria, Erastus Mukira and other brethren to the detention camp at MacKinnon Road, not far from Mombasa.

In camp our work was to break large stones into gravel. Even there the hard-core Mau Mau prisoners kept trying to force everyone to take their oath in goat's blood. Those of us who were really God's people told them that we had taken Jesus' oath and that His blood was all we ever needed.

It helped us a lot when Rev. Geoffrey Ngare could come to preach in the camp. This angered some of the Mau Mau and they would take the offered tracts and defile them by using them for toilet paper. But there were others who listened and were saved in the camps; one of these was Joel Twibori. I spoke for Jesus whenever I could and taught Bible classes in the evening for new believers.

Finally there was a time of "screening" when they sorted out the

ones who were not guerillas, and I was moved to Mwea, which was
nearer home. In this camp I met Alvan Nyaga, who had been saved in
detention. I saw that when unruly Mau Mau were being disciplined
for disobedience by short rations and were stealing from them,
Alvan and his Christian friends used no force and stayed peaceful,
praising Jesus. Alvan is even now going on witnessing for Jesus.

I was moved to a work camp near Meru Town in 1956 and given
work with those who were digging a canal to bring water down from
the snows on Mt. Kenya. Finally I was moved back to Chogoria and
given government work hauling sand for building. In that year
William Nagenda came back again and spoke to us!

At the very end of '56, I was released to come home! Again I could
take care of my farm, plant tea bushes, and be free to preach and
serve Jesus whom I love, and wait for His coming. (In 1991, we found
Jediel an old man—but very strong and working hard on his tea
plantation. *Compiler*.)

### A MAN WHO CARED
Erastus Ethang'atha, Meru
(Told by some who knew him well.)

Although he was born into a non-Christian family near Meru
Town, his parents sent Erastus to school when he was seven years
old. He learned fast, did well, and was baptized into the Methodist
Church. He was trained as a medical assistant in Meru and was then
sent for further training to the large King George Hospital in Nairobi
(now the Kenyatta Hospital). When he graduated there, he married
Ruth Mukomune in a Christian wedding in 1938. He was a good
nominal Christian, but like so many others took the Mau Mau oath
under strong pressure.

In August 1954, while he was at work in the Meru Town Hospital,
he was arrested and detained for having taken the oath and joined
the rebellion. He was kept in the Manyani Detention Camp for seven
years where he became well known for his skill and dedication in
serving fellow prisoners who needed medical attention. The Director
of Medical Services, who had taught Erastus in Nairobi, found him
there and appealed to the Governor to release him. He wasn't able to
do that, but did order that he be put in charge of medical services in
that huge camp. Both the prisoners and guards already knew his
skill. Now he was given some extra camp uniforms so he could keep
clean, and was permitted to go to the hospital with the camp vehicle

to get medicines.

Some brethren of the fellowship visited him in 1956 and spoke to him of the power of Jesus' blood to forgive all sins and transform his life. The Lord showed him his sins, he repented and went to Jesus for cleansing. Joy and peace made him a new man from that time on.

Erastus was released in 1961 and returned to Meru Town where he found that all his possessions had been stolen except one table, and his coffee trees had been cut down. The District Officer had heard of Ethang'atha from the Director of Medical Services and wanted to give him work in the Meru Town Hospital, but the County Council opposed this and sent him to Tharaka, a backward lowland town on the malaria-ridden plain east of Mt. Kenya.

The people of Tharaka had no school or church and knew nothing about preventing illnesses. Erastus went right to work both as doctor and missionary to Tharaka. He opened a clinic, preached the Good News, taught the people to dig pit latrines, and saw to it that a school was started. Before long the people of Tharaka loved him very much and saw that he had a great treasure in his walk with God. Many newborn babies were named for him.

One year when drought and famine hit that area, most other government employees found reasons for leaving. But Erastus and his family stayed, organized food shipments, and kept the people alive—suffering with them—until rains came again. The Governor of the Colony recognized his labors as being far beyond his call of duty as medical officer and gave him a Certificate of Commendation. Later, when he was to be moved, the whole population objected, saying they still needed him there.

Nevertheless, he was moved to Timau, another backward desert community north of Mt. Kenya. He went and undertook the same community-wide projects that he had in Tharaka, establishing a medical center, a church, a school, and a disease prevention program. He worked hard and the people loved him.

With his grown sons, he also sparked a project of building a large new Methodist church in Meru Town. He taught its members the joy and blessing of generous giving, and demonstrated it himself. His children loved and appreciated their father and twice during the building they put on fund-raising drives. Over and over he said to the people, "My great desire is to finish this building without a debt, and see it packed with people filled with the Holy Spirit." God used him in a spiritual awakening, and in encouraging young people to go out with the Gospel and to serve God in many ways.

When he died, December 14th, 1988, there was an enormous funeral, with revival brethren coming from all over Kenya. His sons told about his hope to finish the building without debt, and as a memorial to him this was accomplished.

## VICTIM OF TRIBALISM
### David Mutembei, Meru

My father and my grandmother were both witch doctors, and almost every day they were busy surrounding our home area with spells to keep the evil spirits from me. My mother had given birth to seven children. All had died except my sister and me, so they were constantly doing everything they knew to keep me alive. I was well insulated against the mission and Christian teaching.

But in 1945 I was allowed to go to school. The most significant thing I remember about my first year was the coming of a witnessing team from Kikuyu. The group included three men and a boy named Paulo Nguruduma, who said that when Jesus saved him He helped him to return all the things he had stolen! I thought about this for years. Then in 1949 a Rev. Murio came to our school and talked to us about being born again, and we asked him questions. Then he said, "Now I will ask you questions. He started reading in Mark seven from verse twenty, where Jesus lists the sins that make a person unclean. He said, "Hold out the fingers of your hands. Good! Now when I read a sin you have done, fold down one of your fingers." We said we couldn't do that in public. So he told us to put our hands underneath our desks, and that was better. He mentioned sexual sins and I had to put a finger down; then stealing—oh my! I closed my eyes and God showed me all the schoolbooks I had stolen when my teachers had trusted me and had made me a prefect (a monitor). Then I thought of all the honey I had stolen from my father and eaten with my friends. I was so miserable I couldn't hear the rest. That evening when I went home, I gathered up all the stolen books that were still in my possession and next morning I took them to my teacher. I told him all I had done and that I knew I deserved to be expelled from school. To my great surprise, my teacher hugged me and sang the Hallelujah song of the "saved people." He took me to the principal, Hezekiah Mkiri, who also praised God with us and hugged me! From then on I had the joy of being forgiven, and of meeting with the brethren who taught me to "walk in the light," listening to Jesus and quickly repenting of any sin He showed me.

After I finished school, I answered what I felt was God's call in a letter from Tiras Kariuki. I went all the way to Kiambu to serve as a helper in the home of Tiras and Madlin, two of the leaders among the brethren. They needed someone to take charge of things when they were gone on their evangelistic journeys. Part of this was giving hospitality to all who came. So I met brethren from everywhere in East Africa and overseas, including William Nagenda and Festo Kivengere from Uganda, Silas Muchina, Heshbon Mwangi and many others from Kenya.

When I arrived at Tiras's home, the Emergency had already been declared, not only in the Kikuyu tribe, but also in the "cousin tribes," the Meru and the Embu. The Kikuyu Subchief in Kiambu area hated my Meru tribe and wanted to get rid of me, even though I lived with Tiras whom he admired.

When Tiras was gone, the Subchief's men pulled me out of bed one night, undressed me, and dragged me up a ladder with six exposed nails, which cut me deeply. Surprisingly my injuries didn't bleed! They took me to the local court, and I waited there from 3 a.m. until the magistrate arrived. At daybreak the brethren all gathered outside singing, and the guards beat them. However when Judge Njonjo came, he recognized me as Tiras's messenger boy and demanded, "Who brought this boy here?" When the Subchief was brought in, the judge said, "You have made a big mistake! You take care of him and return him unharmed to the home where you got him!" When I reached home, I found Heshbon and Silas there and was comforted. But this was not the end of the persecution. When Njonjo was no longer the judge, the Subchief arrested me again and threw me into a jailroom with Mau Mau prisoners.

For forty days we were crowded into a small room. We endured terrible hardship such as lice and the misery of sleeping standing up. Our food came in the evening, and I suggested, "When the food comes, let's pray."

Some agreed, but one prisoner asked, "Pray what?"

I answered, "We'll thank God." It was agreed, but when I prayed in the name of Jesus, there was an uproar.

One shouted, "Who is this fellow? Let's put him to sleep." I feared for my life because I knew they could easily smother me under a blanket.

But a more authoritative voice was raised in the crowd, "Listen!

Since the time we were put in here, has anyone prayed for us except this young man? Let him pray. Who knows, we might get out of here to a better place." That settled it, and from then on I gave thanks for our food.

At night also someone would yell, "Where's the young man? Pray to that God of yours." So I would pray for the Mau Mau fighters, for the government, and for each of us there in the prison—for our release. Amazingly, no one harmed me.

Finally the Chief was told that there was a young man from Tiras's home in the jail. He was amazed and had me brought to his office. I begged for water to wash my body and I asked for my clothes which had been taken away. He granted this and then told his soldier to take me back to Tiras's home in Kanyerere.

Tiras and I used to go together to preach Jesus to the Mau Mau in detention camps and we were never attacked by them. For me that was a wonderful seven years.

When I returned to Meru I owned nothing but my pants and shirt, because all through the Emergency no one could earn any money. I had only four shillings and thirty pence in my bankbook, and I slowly used that up for food. But I found my brothers Kamau, David and Simeon, and we had fellowship together.

When I went to see my father, he indignantly said I was lost to him and there was no way at all that he would help me with a dowry to get a wife. I told him, "My God will give me a wife when the time is right." At that time I had no money at all, and no idea how, without my parents' help, I could possibly marry. I only knew I loved and trusted Jesus. I was living then with our young English brother in the Agriculture Department, Ian Wallace.

One day I prayed, "Dear Lord, You know me—that I am Your servant. At this time I have no house, no work and no wife. Today I am putting all three of these into Your hands, because I have no idea what to do. You have told me to cast all my cares on You and You will care for me. I trust You."

The next day a boy brought me a note from our District Commissioner, Mr. Hodge. I wondered what I had done wrong. But the note said, "Dear David, if you would like to work as my driver, please write an application in your own handwriting." I couldn't imagine how he knew me, but the next day I wrote my application and took it to the guard at his office. That day in 1959 I began to work as his chauffeur. How I praised God that one of my prayers had been answered.

A week later, I received a letter and in it I found 500 shillings (which was like 50,000 shillings now!). The anonymous letter said, "David, take this money and start building yourself a house for us. Go cut the trees in the forest and build. Yours in Jesus." So I cut trees and made boards and put up the walls of a house. Then I received another anonymous letter in different handwriting with 480 shillings in it "for corrugated iron roofing for our house." So I finished the house—and to this day I do not know who sent those gifts, but I knew my second prayer had been answered!

At the end of that month, the brethren who were going to a large Central Province fellowship took me along to Chogoria where we linked up with Sister Burt and Dr. Irvine. When we reached Chogoria, I had a very severe headache. When we greeted two sisters in the Lord there, my friend said to them, "This young man has a headache. Please take him and give him some water and some aspirin if you have any, because we want him to go with us to the meeting."

One of these girls asked me, "Have you eaten anything today?"

"No," I replied.

"Well, next time," she said, "don't start on a journey without food." She gave me some medicine from her pocket, then told me to go to the home of Brother Simon who would give me some food and a place to lie down for an hour. "By 3 p.m. you'll be feeling fine," she said.

I was, and I knew right away that I loved her, although I hadn't even asked her name! Of course, I soon found out she was named Judith. Before long she became my wife! (God is wonderful!) Now we have a happy home with six children.

I am a living testimony that it pays to trust in God!

HARD QUESTIONS BY DETAINEES
Reported by Solomon Maina

Three of us went to speak for the Lord in the "hard-core Mau Mau" camp at Karatina. The guards were afraid to have us go in, so we signed papers taking full personal responsibility in case of injury or death to any of us.

The Mau Mau prisoners refused to listen to us or to pray. They said, "When we prayed before and shut our eyes, the white people took our land! But we do want to ask you questions."

We answered, "All right. We are three, so you may ask us three questions."

They said, "Fine!"

"First," we said, "you must let us preach, and then you may ask your questions." They agreed. So after we had told them about God's salvation, they were ready. We had been praying and claiming the promise of Jesus in Luke 21:14–15: "Don't worry about how you will defend yourselves, because I will give you such words and wisdom that none of your enemies will be able to refute or contradict what you say."

The first question was: "Why did you change our Kikuyu custom of circumcising girls as well as boys?"

Rev. Paulo answered, asking the prisoners, "Is there any one of you who knows me?" One said he did. "Do you know where I live?" Yes. "Do you know my children?" Yes. "Are they good-looking or ugly?" Very good-looking. "Well," he continued, "my wife and I were the first to become Christians after the missionaries arrived. When we heard about their rule not to circumcise girl children, my wife and I had many doubts, saying, 'If we bear daughters, no one will marry them and what will we do with them?' But we accepted the ruling because we were Christians. We watched our beautiful daughters growing up and your sons liked to talk to them. So we said, 'Why worry about their being uncircumcised? These boys like them. They'll marry them.'"

Then he asked the man who knew his family, "Did my daughters get married?" Yes. "By circumcised or uncircumcised boys?" Circumcised, of course. And he replied, "All right, then you are the ones who changed our custom."

They laughed and clapped at that, and said, "That's true we did."

Then they asked their second question: "Before the white people came, we had not a single prostitute in our tribe. Where did all these harlots come from?"

Rev. Paulo answered again. "You are right. In all our land there was not one single whore. When the white men came without wives, they hired Kikuyu men to cook and wash and do other things. After a while they would give these house-workers money to go and find a girl for them. The employee knew there were no white girls around, so he would bring a Kikuyu girl. Now she lived for a while with a white man, then he left her. Would she go back to the tribe and marry in the ordinary way? No, she was accustomed to a different style of life. You were the ones who caused this bad thing among us! You were the ones who worked in the houses of the white men and brought them girls."

Again they agreed and laughed, saying, "That's true!"

Then they asked their third question: "For countless generations our people have worshiped one God (Ngai). We didn't worship Satan, and we knew that God is One, not two or three. How come you worship three gods? You call one the Father and another the Son and another you call the Holy Spirit—why all these gods?"

Rev. Paulo answered like this: "Truly God is One. As you believe, so we also believe. Please bring me a burning piece of wood from that cook-fire." They brought it and he held it up and asked, "What is this white stuff rising from it?" Smoke. "What is this black part that is hot?" It's charcoal. "And the rest of it?" The firewood. "Are these three one thing?" Yes. "God is like that. You have a hand, you have a foot, you have an eye, but you are one person. There are not two or three gods, just One."

They accepted this answer also and clapped in appreciation. They said, "You have won in our contest!" They became friendly, even though at first they had been hostile and dangerous.

## IMPRISONED BY ACCIDENT
### Kuria Wa Mathaga

My parents were not Christian, but they were baptized by a Catholic priest they once heard speak when they were visiting in a distant village. I was baptized while studying in a government high school in 1940. I stayed for three years with a Christian named Shelta Kamuriwa and learned many things from him. And through reading Genesis I was impressed by the way in which God led Isaac to Rebekah, the right girl for him to marry.

When I finished school, first I was a clerk, then I entered Kenya's first school for seamen in 1943. While I was in the Navy, I prayed to God, "Please, Lord, give me a girl who will not divorce me, and with whom I am not going to fight. Please give me a sign: the one who comes to shake hands with me when I reach home from Mombasa, let her be the one." I had many girls in mind who I thought were beautiful. The time came in December 1946 when I went home. Three sisters, who were our neighbors, came to greet me and they were all good-looking, but I did not like Mary's color too much. She, however, was the only one who shook hands with me!

So one day I casually asked my neighbor, their father, if Mary had a special boyfriend, and he said, "No, not now." So I courted her, and we married in 1947, and God blessed me very much with this girl that at first I thought I did not love.

That same year I started working in the Meteorological Service in Nairobi. Then on September 9, 1950, the Lord saved me, and two or three months later He saved my wife, Mary. So in 1952 when the government declared war on the Mau Mau and every man in Nairobi with a Kikuyu name was detained, I was picked up too. Even though I gave them my testimony, they sent me to the huge camp at Manyani and later to Mackinnon Road, both in desolate, wild animal country. We slept in hangars. There was never enough food or water, so most of the time we were hungry, and every day three or four died. You could be beaten when you were questioned about taking the Mau Mau oath. Some said they had taken it when they hadn't, just to stop the beating.

The wonderful thing for me was that there were other brothers in the Lord who were also detained by accident. We found each other by listening to hear who was telling others about Jesus—what a joy! Then we could read the Word of God together. We could pray for our fellow prisoners, for the British who were fighting us, and for the Mau Mau in the forests. We were all together in the huge hangars and we had no fear of death, so we were like Chiefs. We could freely tell others that if they were saved, they too would go to heaven when they died, and could even be happy in the camp.

In the camps I gave my life completely to serve Jesus the rest of my life, so when I was released I didn't look for a job to earn money, I went to join the Church Army and went into Bible training. While I was studying John's Gospel, I learned to love and forgive those who used to beat us. I knew the wrong was caused by Satan and that Jesus loves my enemies. I became a fisher of men first in the Church Army under Captain John Ball, and then for twenty-four years as hospital chaplain in Nairobi's great Jomo Kenyatta Hospital. God gave me love for patients of all tribes and nationalities. I pray for the sick. I have seen God heal some miraculously, and many have given their lives to Him.

My home has been a joy to me. We have eight children who are doing well. I love and trust my wife. She loves and advises me. We give each other freedom to obey the Lord. My wife raises coffee and has her own bank account, so she can give to the Lord's work and help people as she sees fit. We both can sing from the heart: "The joy of the Lord is my strength!"

# 7

# THEIR SECRET POWER AND JOY

*"'Father,' the son said, 'I have sinned against God and against you. I am no longer fit to be called your son.' But the father called to his servants, 'Hurry! . . . let us celebrate with a feast! For this son of mine was dead, but now he is alive; he was lost, but now he is found.'"*

Luke 15:21–24 (TEV)

*"God is Light and in him is no darkness at all. . . . If we are living in the light of God's presence, just as Christ does, then we have wonderful fellowship and joy with each other, and the blood of Jesus his Son cleanses us from every sin."*

1 John 1:5–7 (TLB)

*"Let us be concerned for one another, to help one another to show love and do good. Let us not give up the habit of meeting together, as some are doing. Instead let us encourage one another all the more, since you see that the Day of the Lord is coming nearer."*

Hebrews 10:24–25 (TEV)

## INTRODUCTION

The Kikuyu freedom fighters, who had known from childhood only the *terror* of death, simply could not understand the peaceful readiness-to-die they found in that small minority of Christians they encountered. It was even more puzzling to find a fellow-Kikuyu, either man or woman, who could *love* the ones inflicting pain. And for someone to ask God to forgive those killing him or her was *incredible!*

Also, how could these tribespeople have fast friendships with white people?—it was disloyal to the freedom movement. How could they laugh and sing joyously, walk freely in the marketplaces

251

and on the highways, talking about this "foreigner"—Jesus—wherever they got a chance, even though they knew perfectly well the danger that threatened them every day? Why didn't killing one of them scare the rest of them? How could they make such a joyous celebration of burying him or her? This joy was infectious, making the undecided go and join them, and even fighters were defecting from the forest to be with them! It was intolerable! It was all impossible from the Kikuyu point of view. What was their secret?

If you have read some of the accounts in this book, you know that each one of the joyous ones had had a personal encounter with the living God. Some had been actively seeking Him, others were totally surprised by His invasion. Some had begun to admit their sins, others saw Him first and then realized that He wanted to rid them of their filthiness. However it came about—by a sudden light or vision, or by their own cry for help—there was no doubt in their minds: they had met Jesus and He had changed their lives. All realized they were forgiven and made clean, and that was their *joy*. They made their restitutions not to *get* joy, but because they already *had* joy and were walking in a new power and under a new Commander.

Then when this happened, except for the very first ones, they found themselves being folded into a loving family of fellowship: men, women and young people affirming them, hugging them, warning them, and steadily walking with them through the years. This was a family ready to help them in any way needed to the end of their lives, and then bury them praising God!

What was the secret of steadily going on with Jesus and growing spiritually? They would have told you it is by walking in the Light. This phrase is from 1 John 1:7: "If we walk in the light as He is in the light, we have fellowship one with another, and the blood of Jesus keeps on cleansing us from all sin."

Each one knew that any day it was possible for him or for a brother or sister to slide into "a shadow of darkness." So, individually and together, they daily kept listening to God's words in the Bible, always asking, "What do You want me to do?" They learned to recognize the gentle promptings and guidance of the Holy Spirit, and to distinguish it from the voice of the Evil One.

Unless severe coldness had set in, the troubled one in the "shadow of darkness" always remembered that the cross was very near, with the blood of its cleansing fountain. So they hurried there with the intruding sin, no matter how small or large, and plunged it in.

Instantly the joy and peace of forgiveness returned! So how could they help but run with this good news to the brethren of the fellowship who would affirm God's forgiveness by singing His praise? Usually they would also hug the one renewed, affirming that the family also forgives and forgets. The sin forgiven was never again brought up against him or her by the family.

No one, not even a world-class preacher or a bishop, ever got beyond needing this frequent cleansing of the blood, and the loving affirmation of the fellowship. So naturally they all wanted to share with the people they met the joy of having a once-for-all Saviour who is a *daily Saviour* as well, who brings you into a warm new family of His people. The Good News that spread was *happy* news. When they held big meetings, many people came to look and listen because of the total change in lifestyle they had seen in people they knew.

Obviously there must be some real power involved. Those who knew Maitai, for instance, said, "He can't stop drinking!" But they were surprised. It seemed that his thirst had been quenched by what he called "living water."

Another total surprise to every African was the new way husbands treated their wives. A wife was no longer a slave to be beaten and ignored. First he humbly asked her forgiveness for mistreating her. Then she became someone to be honored and consulted, like a man's sisters, whether or not she had been saved. He now called his wife "my sister" to make clear to the tribe her change of status.

In the home, from then on, each could ask the other for forgiveness and receive it. Both parents could ask the children's forgiveness when it was needed. Family singing, prayers and sharing began usually very early every morning.

At work, employers and businessmen recognized the new integrity in the fellowship folk, and some were promoted and given responsible jobs. So there were those who prospered in the marketplace, the church, or on big farms. Others were just as happy, fruitful, and obedient in subsistence farming or menial jobs.

Prayers of all sorts were answered, sometimes by miracles. This was accepted matter-of-factly, and only outsiders were surprised that they never advertised signs or wonders except Jesus' saving power to transform a bad person into a good one, which was to them by far the greatest miracle.

Evangelism for them was not only preaching God's Word, but also sharing freely what He had done to change their lives. They preferred to preach in teams: men, women and young people all sharing, one after another, what Jesus had done for them. This answered people's doubts and broke down barriers by a demonstration of the intergenerational oneness of the family of God, which is also an intertribal, cross-cultural, loving, and durable fellowship. This evangelism was very effective and their numbers doubled and tripled in the years after the Mau Mau war.

✝    ✝    ✝

## HE CHOSE TO GO
### Obadiah Gakunju Nthukire, Embu

My parents and home were tribal and anti-Christian. My entire youth was spent working as a herd boy and cultivator on my parents' section of land. My ears were pierced and stretched for ornaments in honor of my parents' gods. I took part in all heathen rituals and witchcraft, singing and dancing with my young friends. I especially loved to sing lewd songs. When I married in 1933 it was entirely by tribal custom, though I had some twinges of conscience because God was beginning to seek me. I ignored His voice and went on. There were two churches in our area, but I didn't go near them.

As we were working in the fields one day, some people who knew God came to talk to us. The amazing thing about them was that they had washed their clothes with soap and they were really clean. They had stripped off every one of the charms and amulets we wore to protect us from evil spirits! Also they could sing their words about God in songs! But I still loved my pagan songs, so inside my mind I kicked away these new ones, realizing that their message would endanger the way of life and songs that I was used to.

In the early evening they came again and began to preach and sing near our place. I couldn't help hearing young people my age repeat the words of one song, declaring, "When God comes and calls His people to come to Him, my name will be there!" Then the preacher said, "When Jesus comes, those whose names are not written in the Book of Life will be thrown into the fire."

I thought, "Oh-oh—those singers are my age so this might apply to me, and I might be thrown into the fire!" For the first time my heart began to tremble inside me. Soon I enrolled in the learning class at church. I was soon in trouble, because my parents put me out of their village when I followed these church ways and stopped sacrificing with them to their gods. My wife also left me and ran home with our child to her parents, telling them all the bad things I was doing. So I was left alone with my God.

Then the members of our church banded together and decided to move a distance away from this very pagan area and establish a new farming community and church there. In those days, land was still free for anyone who wanted to settle in it and cultivate it. So we moved, and in 1938 I was baptized and made an elder of the church and a preacher. Finally my wife and child came back to me.

In 1942, Pastor Moses invited an evangelistic team from Murang'a to come and tell us the new things God was doing for them, reviving the church. The Bible verses that stuck in my mind were in Mark 7:20–23. There Jesus said a man is unclean because of the things that come out of his mind and heart, like lustful thoughts, anger, jealousy, and lies. I realized then that I was full of these and more, and unless I became pure in heart I wouldn't see the Lord, even though I was baptized and an elder in the church! I repented deeply and knew the joy and assurance of forgiveness, and began a new way of life with the Lord and His children.

The Mau Mau war reached us in 1952. While we were all at a meeting at Kiruma, our church at Kyamuringa was burned down. Mau Mau had moved into our area and wanted nothing to do with the Christians who were always telling people of salvation. "We are taking over," they said, "so where will you go?"

"We'll go out preaching Jesus, and if we die we will go to heaven!"

One day the Mau Mau captured twelve people (some of them weren't Christians) and marched them up the mountain. All twelve refused to take the oath and were killed and buried together in one large pit. One survived because he wasn't quite dead when he was thrown into the pit. The other bodies were on top of him, so he had a hard time getting out. But he finally managed to climb out and run away to report to the authorities!

In those days the people who had taken the Mau Mau oath but had not joined the guerillas in the forest were gathered up with their families to live in guarded villages—where they could still cultivate land, but were kept from sending supplies into the forest for the guerillas.

One Sunday, a missionary named Smith came with our Canon Moses to visit our church. They declined to preach so I went ahead with the service as usual. Afterward they took me aside into a private room and told me why they had come. "We have been praying to God," they said, "for those whom He wants us to send to be chaplain-evangelists in the guarded villages. Someone suggested you, and we feel that God may be calling you to be God's spokesman to some of these villages." I agreed with them.

After they left, however, some people frightened me by their predictions: "They are sending you to those Kikuyu villages just to get killed!" My job at that time was that of cook in our coffee shop; so on the day that I had said I would go, I didn't. I gave the excuse that I needed to find someone to take over my work—but it was just cowardice on my part.

That night I began thinking about Jonah who refused to go to Nineveh, and I couldn't sleep. I kept hearing the question, Are you refusing to go as Jonah did? I had no answer. Then I had a dream in which I saw a man preaching, who said, "Two men were called to be soldiers. One went into battle and was killed. The other stayed at home and was killed. What do you think about them?"

I answered that the one who stayed at home was looking after his own business and pleasures. But the preacher said, "No, they were both killed. But the one who went out and fought against the invading army and was killed there will receive the medals of honor and the embrace of his Lord when he arrives in heaven." This helped make it clear for me. I saw that if the Mau Mau killed me while I was hiding, I would lose the prize. But if they killed me while I was risking my life to preach in the villages, I would be received into heaven with joy.

The next day I was ready to die for Jesus. So I closed the coffee shop and went to the villages of Githimu and Karurumo in Embu District and Murinduko in Kirinyaga District, to which I had been called. Daily I testified and experienced that Jesus is able to save and keep. And I am still preaching this same Good News in 1991! Praise God!

## A PROPHET'S WIFE
### Hagar John Kangoro, Murang'a

I was blessed by having Christian parents who taught me Christian ways and sent me to school so that I was able to begin teaching school in 1944. A young teacher named John Kangoro was also teaching in that school. He had gone with another young man to a convention in 1937, where they had heard the testimonies of some people from Uganda and Ruanda about a new kind of Christian life called "salvation." This changed his life in many good ways. When he told me about it, I told him that truly this salvation was a wonderful thing. After a while we fell in love with each other, and because of my Christian training I was able to understand a good bit and follow along and claim to be one with him in it, but I somehow didn't have the same power of God's Spirit in me that he had. John did love me very much, and we were married in 1945.

I enjoyed being John's wife, and entertaining his guests who came to talk about revival. But as time went on people were coming in crowds and I was exhausted. I started asking myself, "Why is it you don't really love these 'brethren' of John's?" If John had told me a lot were coming on a certain day and then they didn't come, I was secretly delighted. My critical spirit made me realize that I was not really "saved" in the same way he was.

Our first child was born, and then we went together to the first revival convention, held at Kahuhia in 1947. I met one sister there who had a chance to observe me and said to me very honestly and lovingly, "Hagar, you are rejoicing in Jesus' salvation, but you don't really have Him in your heart." She came along home with us and I was grieving because I saw that though I had been working hard for the Lord, yet in my heart I had no freedom; I was bound. That was the day I opened my heart by faith to Jesus to come in, and He took over and I became free and strong. That began a new life of partnership with John, for I was full of the joy of Lord and was gladly able to do my part in welcoming guests to our home.

In 1952 when the Emergency was declared, there was no question for us, we could not take the Mau Mau oath, and before long it became clear that we should take our family and move to Weithaga Mission for the duration of the war. Our children were small, so Obadiah Kariuki and Heshbon Mwangi were able to borrow Chief Evan's bus to take us and some others to Weithaga. During those years, we had many opportunities to help and encourage others.

When it became possible, we moved home; and we lived by the grace of God, traveling with the Good News—either together or John alone—especially to the conventions, large and small, near and far.

We had ten children, who are now all grown and in their own homes. John was found to have diabetes, with other complications, and the Lord called His servant home in 1983. I couldn't really grieve for him, because I knew he was with Jesus, but there were difficulties with the children, and I wished I hadn't been left behind alone. Then the Lord showed me my sin of a grumbling spirit and washed it in

His blood and gave me rest of heart. He also helped the children. So far one has been saved, and I have peace.

### A CARE-TAKING BROTHER
### Francis Ndwiga, Embu

Because my parents were committed to tribal customs, I was not able to go to school or church until 1937 when I was seventeen years old. I studied until 1941, when I was delighted to be baptized and given the new name "Francis." But Satan followed me closely and I couldn't stop my evil habits of loose living, and I was suspended from church membership for six months because a girl reported me to the church elders. After that I was ashamed and determined to live a clean life, but found it hard.

In 1942 I finished grade six in primary school, and that year some preachers came from Kiambu sharing the joy of salvation in special meetings at Kigaari. I had never heard testimonies like that before. I was especially touched by the words of a blind man, Samuel Mugaru, because he was free in spirit while I was full of self-pity. The Spirit of God convicted me of that sin and all the others. As King David said, I saw my sins right in front of my face (Psalm 51:3). I stood up in the meeting and cried out, "Lord save me! I am a sinner!" From that time on I knew I was saved and could walk with Jesus.

My wife, who was a young girl then, was also saved, and our home life has been good. In 1945 we wanted our marriage to be blessed by God's people, so we renewed our marriage vows in church with brethren witnessing it. For a while I continued my work as a tailor and dressmaker, then became a full-time evangelist.

A few years later we heard about the forced Mau Mau oath in which one had to deny Jesus, and we began to panic. A woman of our church told us, "Night before last the Mau Mau came and forced us to take the oath—see how they cut my hair off!" So we knew the oath had reached us.

We talked it over in our fellowship meeting here at Kibogi. We knew we could not take it, but what should we do? We had heard of those in Murang'a District who had been killed for refusing the oath. We knew that most of the brethren had left their homes and gone to live at the Weithaga Mission together. We talked of doing something like that. So I went with Brother Ephantus Waweru to the missionary in charge at Kigaari Mission and told him, "The Mau Mau oath is being forced on people in our area and we would like to move here."

He said, "Let's go together to the Chief and see what he says."

We said, "No, some of them there may have taken the oath secretly. We would like to stay at the mission. We would rather be under the protection of God." He finally agreed.

So after the church service the following Sunday, many of us moved to Kigaari Mission, planning to camp there as long as necessary. The missionary asked, "Where will you sleep?" Some of us temporarily slept in the bookshop, some in servants' quarters, etc., but we quickly built ourselves little houses of poles and grass. Brethren from all around moved in. It was splendid to have prayers and fellowship all together both morning and evening!

In 1955 I was sent as an evangelist to the detention camps, and began at Mashiara where some of the Mau Mau detainees had already repented and come to Jesus, including Alvan Nyaga and Josiah Njiru. I also went to speak for God in the camps of Mwea Kandongu, Thiba, and Kathigiriri.

In 1958 I went with Ephantus Mbogo to the huge Manyani Camp and found the prisoners furious and threatening, unwilling to listen at all. Even those in the infirmary beat us twice with canes. We went outside and praised Jesus heartily. After some time I returned home, but Ephantus continued.

Back at home, I found people now moving back to their small farms and busy visiting those Christians who had taken the oath. Many of them were willing to repent and come back to church, so soon it was flourishing again. We are still praising God.

## OUT OF PAGANISM
### Sara Igandu-Thomas, Embu

I grew up a very heathen girl, and was married to a man named Thomas. Then the living God broke into my life. In 1945 when I went to a meeting held by "Revival" people, I heard Jesus call me personally. He said, "Come to Me, all of you who are tired from carrying heavy loads, and I will give you rest." As I went home I wondered what the heavy loads were that I had been carrying which made me so tired. I supposed it related to not being baptized. But in the middle of the night the Lord appeared to me and began to show me the loads I had been carrying: my thieving, loose living, making false accusations, fighting, using alcohol and tobacco, hatred, disobedience, vanity, selfishness, on and on. These I had taken on myself. I cried out to Jesus, "Lord, I come to You and give You every one of my loads!

Please take them away, and give me that rest." Somehow I knew He had saved me from my sins.

The next day I went back to the meetings and told the team of preachers about it. When people looked at my face they asked, "What's happened to her?" At the meeting they rejoiced and hugged me, but back at home people hated me. A government soldier beat me because I told his wife what Jesus had done for me.

A neighbor became angry because I had been telling his children about Jesus. He cut slender branches of a certain tree to make whips, and stood them outside, leaning them against the woven granary, ready to whip me. His little son came after dark and called me outside to tell me about the whips and what his angry father had been saying he would do to me. He took me to see the whips, but I wasn't afraid. Early the next morning I went to this neighbor's house and asked his wife if I could speak to her husband.

She said, "Why so early? Why aren't you at home making tea for Thomas?"

"I won't have tea until I've been beaten by your husband."

Laughing, she asked, "What will you be beaten for?"

"Because I was teaching your children. He has the whips ready. See, they are over there leaning on the granary."

As her husband came out, I went to greet him and said, "Here I am, sir, for you to whip me."

His head dropped, and his wife said, "Oo—oo, you're going to beat Sara because she preached to the children? Are you afraid you might get saved yourself?"

"Well, I might if God appeared to me," he answered. "Enough! Go bring the tea so Mrs. Sara can have some."

"I can't drink tea before you beat me," I replied.

"Bring the tea!" he shouted.

She brought a tray with tea and asked, "Why did you prepare those whips?"

He said, "Bring them here." She brought two. "Cut them up!"

I asked, "Are you going to break them up before beating me?"

He replied, "Drink the tea and then go back and cook for Thomas!" I returned home with my heart full of praise to God.

When the Mau Mau troubles began in our area, our neighbor, a brother in Christ, Ezekiel Njiru, was seized and dragged by the neck through the Ena River to Kirimiri in the forest. His wife Rebeka was there with a small daughter. They had to watch helplessly as the Mau

Mau jeered at Ezekiel and beat and cut him mercilessly. She heard him pray for them while the Mau Mau sneered. Then someone shouted, "Government men are coming!" and the guerillas all disappeared into the forest. Ezekiel was rescued and God remarkably restored his strength, even enabling him to walk to Runyenjes Town!

The school there in town soon became the camp of refuge for many of us who had chosen God's way. I moved there too. Because I had been a teacher in the school, one man in the camp, who thought I might have some money, offered to sell me some stolen goats and cows very cheap. I refused, telling him, "No, I would never buy anything in an illegal way." Nevertheless he went ahead and filled with goats the little house where he and his children slept.

Then one night we were all awakened by a loud whistle and trumpet blasts to find that all our houses with grass roofs were on fire! None of us had time to change into our daytime clothes when we ran out, but we went and slept outside the District Officer's house. The very next morning work was begun to build us new houses, using prison labor. They also dug a trench around the compound: a deep ditch with spikes planted in it to keep intruders out. We were cared for there until the fighting decreased. Then we were moved to a government village called Mbiruri. Finally we could go back to our own land. My house had been burned down, but the land was there.

There has been no letup in the battle against Satan, but I have learned not to put my heart on anything here on earth, not even on my children. I love the Lord Jesus and am waiting for His coming.

## REPENTANCE AND FAITH: A LIFESTYLE
### Jemima & Francis Ndwiga, Embu

Praise the Lord! He saved me in 1942 when I was just a girl. My name then was Jemima Nguru. I had been saying, "I don't need to be 'saved' because I am a daughter of Christians." Then the time came when there was a convention in Kigaari where they were preaching the Word of God. I attended, and among the preachers were some young people my age.

I asked myself, "Would I be able to give a testimony like that?" and I knew I couldn't because I would be too scared. I was full of fears and cowardice. Then a speaker read from Revelation 21:8 where cowards are first in the list of those who will go to hell. Immediately I knew that I was on my way there. I knew that I was a sinner, and cried to the Lord to save me from my sin of cowardice! No sooner did

I know He had forgiven that sin than I saw all the rest of my sins—lies, stealing, hating, deception and telling dirty jokes. Jesus washed them all away in His blood, and right away I had a testimony to share. I went to tell my parents that Jesus had saved me. I told all my young friends about it and everyone else I knew, urging them to find this same joy.

The Lord continued to help me and I went regularly to the meetings of the brothers and sisters in Christ. In one of these meetings I saw that I had been careless in my relationships with boys and was a fornicator. I took this to the cross and told the fellowship that Jesus had saved me from this sin too. I really hadn't realized that I had been in sin, but now I trusted Him to hold my hand and keep me clean.

About that time there was an uproar in the church. People said, "These saved ones are saying terrible things in church that we never heard there before. Even some ministers are being 'saved!'" I went to the Lord, asking Him to give me wisdom and strength, but then I went on saying openly that Jesus is my Saviour.

In 1945 I was married in the church to a brother in the Lord, Francis Ndwiga, and both of us were telling others about Jesus. As we went on, Satan brought some hard things between us in our home. But the Lord helped me to repent and He healed us. We went on with Him and He gave us some children.

When the Emergency came and I heard that people were being forced to take the Mau Mau oath, I felt we should move to Kigaari. We were among many families who moved into the community around the mission. We couldn't go back to our homes because of the war going on. We could only go to the marketplace of Manyatta to buy food, escorted by the Home Guards. All of us were living close together, at peace with the Lord and constantly praising Him and praying together. A man of the Mau Mau told us to stop praising Jesus and take their oath, and one of us was killed. But we said we would keep on praising the Lord till the end of our lives. He went away, and we kept on telling about Jesus as before.

During that time we often wondered if we dared go back to our homes just to get some food from our farms. A few of us dared to go back one day. While we were filling our baskets with old corn and sweet potatoes, a man of the Mau Mau challenged us and asked, "What are you doing here?" We said we hadn't been coming to our homes because of the Mau Mau, but our children needed food. After he had listened to us awhile, he escorted us safely back to the public road, walking in front of us with his big knife. Then he gave us his knife and left us. This is how we escaped being attacked! Later we found out that the fighters had an agreement that if they found women outside their "safe" villages for good reasons, a fighter who knew them should escort them to safety. If he walked in front of them, he protected them. But if he walked behind them, he left them open to attack! We didn't try that again.

In 1955, we felt we could move back to our homes. We hoped that our children would be obedient to the Lord as we were learning to be. And while they were small they did obey, but when they grew up they were rebellious and went into whatever sin they fancied. I became very upset about this. Then the Lord showed me that I could be washed from my own sins, but not theirs. So I went on repenting of my own sins and praying for our children.

### DETOUR ON A BYWAY
### Eunice Kagio, Weri, Murang'a

My parents would have nothing to do with church or Jesus, and by watching them I came to know some evil ways, and to use words I wouldn't say now. I was a grown woman when I first entered a church and heard the Word of God spoken. I was attracted to it and wanted to learn to read the Bible. So even though I was much bigger than the others, I went to school, and without help from my parents managed to finish the sixth grade.

During this time I came to realize that I had grown up into a sinful life which was a stinking thing to God. I began to long to be delivered. Satan said to me, "You're all right; stay with me and I will make you beautiful and attractive." But God showed me that my rages and cursing and false accusations were hateful to Him. Finally I repented of all my sins and and Jesus washed me in His blood, made me clean and truly set me free!

Then I couldn't help sharing in the neighborhood the joy of His salvation. In those days this was a new and despised Way. Because people were living in great darkness, they would spit on me and beat me with sticks, but I didn't mind because God was with me. I loved the fellowship of brothers and sisters and I went right on sharing Jesus wherever I could. One day when we went to church we found someone had written on the blackboard: "Kagio [me] thinks she is the Holy Spirit, and that this brother is God and another brother is Jesus." They named these brothers. We erased the words and said, "Praise the Lord," and went on with our worship.

There was a time in 1946 when some people came and told us that unless we could do miracles and speak in tongues, we weren't saved. I was very zealous for God and thought this must be from Him. So I left the fellowship and began meeting with these people, preaching with them and speaking in tongues for about three years. During that time, in 1949, I met and married one of their men. Then in 1950 they made a new rule that the men and women in their group could sleep together whenever they liked and it wasn't sin. I rebelled and spoke up because I knew this was not God's way or according to His law. So they made a rule that if anyone does not agree with their decisions, he or she will be banned and is no longer married to the partner in the cult. I was scared, realizing that this was not the way to go to heaven, yet I didn't know what to do if and when my husband threw me out. In 1951 I gave birth to a baby girl. I was in great distress about the way this group was going, fearing they were on the road to hell.

By now they had decided that a man could marry two wives. I knew this was not according to the Gospel, but they said they were taught this by the Spirit, so it was right. I was living in misery. Finally, in 1952, they told me I had to make my decision, to stay and be obedient to them or be driven off by my husband. I prayed long and hard to know what to do, and because I was pregnant again and I felt too that divorce was such a bad testimony, I was prepared to accept their rulings. But when they came and confronted me, my mouth said, "I cannot agree with your way." When I heard what I had said, I knew that it was the Lord who had taken over my mouth and kept me from saying a lie.

Then my husband shouted, "Go! Take your things out of the house and leave!" After I did, he locked the door of the house behind me. My baby girl and I and our things were outside.

I decided to go back to my mother. My father had died, and I explained to her that my husband had sent me away. She said I could stay with her if I had some way to support myself. That was July of 1952.

I remembered the story in *Pilgrim's Progress* of Christian when he missed the way and wandered off onto a bypath. He heard a Voice saying, "What are you doing here? Go back to the place where you got off the road." So I went back to the fellowship I had left, and told the brothers and sisters that I had gotten off the Way, but the Lord had brought me back. I asked them to forgive me, and they received me lovingly. I began again to study the Bible with them and to go out with them to tell of Jesus. I was at peace.

In September the Mau Mau war began and it was terrible. My baby boy was born. Someone warned me that if I was seen openly carrying my Bible I would be marked as an enemy to be killed. I replied, "Well then, that day I will go to heaven to live with my Lord!" I gladly continued under this threat of death during those years, and kept on deeply repenting of the sins I had gotten into in the cult. Word reached us that my husband had been killed in his schoolroom. A Mau Mau gang running from government soldiers had rushed into his schoolroom to hide. The soldiers had machine-gunned everyone in the room including my husband, the teacher.

I cried to the Lord because I was poor and had no way to pay the school fees for my children as they grew. I thought He might give me another husband, but He Himself has cared for us. When we all moved to Weithaga to wait for the end of hostilities, I was given a job to work with the Red Cross because I knew how to read and write and keep accounts. Later, I was called to be matron of a dormitory in a girls' school. So with God's help, my daughter finished high school and married a teacher in a church wedding. My son earned a college degree and became an engineer—all perfectly amazing, and due only to the tender mercies of our Lord and Saviour!

## A PATIENT ENCOURAGER
### Felix Imaita, Kithirune, Meru

My father was a medicine man, making charms to protect our household. My mother did the farming and I herded the goats and cows. My father died when I was about fourteen. Then I was able to go to school and eventually I finished standard seven. I was baptized in 1942.

In 1947, a team came from Murang'a preaching salvation—they were Samuel Nguru, Virginia Nchoki, and Mbobwa. I thought their message was strange and I felt antagonistic. However, a few people here were saved, and I liked what happened to them. But I still had my doubts. When I went to teachers' college I heard more, but thought this new teaching wasn't for me.

I started teaching school in 1948, and in 1950 the Lord Jesus finally reached my heart and saved me. I gladly became a part of the fellowship of the brethren, and this was the best preparation I could have had for the Emergency that engulfed us. Though I was a teacher,

I felt that my main job was traveling around to the other six fellow-ship groups in our area to encourage and strengthen the brothers and sisters. I did this outside of school hours, at first on foot. Later I had a bicycle.

Those were difficult days because the Mau Mau fighters were coming out of the forest from time to time to kill those who would not join them. The three who died in a burning building were right here in our Kithirune area. And the joyous celebration of their going to heaven helped many. But it was not always easy. We were constantly harassed by people who said, "Look, we are fighting and we are going to get independence for our country. Then you will see how we will deal with you traitors! What will you do then?"

A man said to us, "You people despise your land as if it were just a fly to be brushed off." This was hard for us to take. We knew we couldn't take the oath, but we loved our land and wanted freedom as much as anyone. We prayed for it, and together went on through the years of fighting and danger.

By 1954 we were pressed on both sides. The government and its soldiers were after us because we refused to take up arms to fight against the Mau Mau, and the freedom fighters were killing us because we would not take their oath.

One day after school I found several government soldiers waiting for me. One of them asked me, "Are you Felix?"

I answered, "That's me."

"Are you the one refusing to carry a weapon to fight?"

"Yes, that's me. It's because Jesus has saved me. My work is to preach the Good News, and I want you to be saved too."

Then they set a trap for me, saying, "Do you mean that because we have been killing the Mau Mau, we have sinned?"

I said, "You've been given permission to do that, but I haven't. God has only permitted me to preach."

They said, "Go away!"

I went and found a committee waiting for me, so I sat with them. They asked, "Are you ready to take weapons and go to fight with us?"

I said, "Yes, but I will go with the Word of God as my weapon."

"So! You go with the Bible, and then the fighters come out of the forest against you. What will you do?"

I said, "So who told them to come out right where I was? God! So when they come, He will tell me what to say." At that we parted;

they had no more questions.

As it turned out, the next year was the beginning of the end of the fighting. When the government proclaimed amnesty, many of the fighters came out of the forest and surrendered. We were finally released from living in government-restricted areas and could go back home to our farms and villages. It was very important to help and encourage the brethren to be strong in faith at that time. That was especially because when they returned to their farms and homes they found there had been much destruction and looting, and they had to start again from the beginning.

Also it was our job to go to those who were still being kept in detention camps. Most of those who were there were loyal to their Mau Mau oath, but we found many had turned to the Lord and were saved! This is God's greatest miracle . . . when someone turns from his old life, believes in Jesus, and becomes a new person who walks with Him!

## Durable Forgiveness
### Mary Wambui-Samuel, Murang'a

God broke into my spiritual complacency one day after I had been married for three years and had my arms full of small children. I had felt quite comfortable that I would go to heaven because my Christian parents had me baptized as a child, and I had been confirmed at the proper age, and had a church wedding. Then on that early November day, in 1949, I heard a message that said every single person will have to bend the knee before God and give a full account of what he or she had done in life. Suddenly, I saw all the lies I had told since I was a child, my hatreds and fighting, my disobedience and fornications, and I cried to the Lord for forgiveness. Marvelously, He washed me clean in the blood of His cross, and received me as His child. What joy and peace! But my husband was disgusted with me.

When 1952 came and the oath of the Mau Mau fighters was being pressed on every person, my husband took the oath and ordered me to take it too. When he saw I was unwilling, he said, "Either you take this oath with me, or I will leave you and these children and never help you again!"

I told him, "I could never betray Jesus, my Lord, because only those will go to heaven who have turned away from their evil ways and been saved." He gave me some more time to decide whether I would live with Jesus or live with him. I chose to stay with Jesus, even though from then on my husband never helped me or our five children again.

I had to turn to farming for all our needs, as I had only been able to go to school through fifth grade. The brothers and sisters of the fellowship helped me much, and with the blessing of the Lord my children went to school, helping me as they could. They grew up and each has found work to do.

When one of our grown daughters died of severe malaria, the social worker insisted that the father as well as the mother must come to claim the government burial assistance. I saw my husband again at that time. Though I had cared for her all by myself, he collected the money and kept it. I repented of my anger about that and forgave him. Then I trusted the Lord—as I had for everything in our lives—and with the help of the brethren, she was properly buried.

I am now getting old, and I still love my husband and pray for him every day, asking the Lord to touch his heart and bless him with repentance.

## RETURN TO PEACE
### Penina & Paul Kibe, Kiambu

My parents were not Christians, but I had been going to church for three years before the Emergency was declared. I was a church member, but not a good girl. Then something happened on Sunday October 11, 1953. Someone read the story about the Samaritan woman who met Jesus at a well. Jesus told her all about her sinful life, and He offered her the water of eternal life (John 4). Suddenly I knew I was full of sin just like the Samaritan woman. I was guilty of prostitution, hatred, lying, hypocrisy and more. But the grace of God reached me as a sinner that day, as it had reached her. I wept bitterly, but then I knew I was forgiven.

I went to my mother and father and asked them to forgive me because for a long time I had been sneaking out of the house at night and going to boys' houses. From then on I began walking with Jesus and with those in the fellowship, and making restitution as much as I could.

Then Kibe came out of the forest, having seen the Lord. Everyone was amazed that the grace of God could reach a Mau Mau fighter so full of hate as he was and completely change him. He took the name of Paul because, like the Paul in the Bible, he too had been a killer and persecutor of Christians.

I was glad and proud when he wanted to marry me, and we began our new life together with Jesus. But after a few years, Satan got into me again. My husband didn't want to do anything but preach about Jesus. He didn't earn a salary, and we had to live on very little. I began to lust after the nice things I saw other women had. I became very discontented, even though the fellowship brethren loved us and took care of us. Our home life became miserable and I blamed Paul for it. It seemed to me we were always poor and he seemed to like it that way, even though we had eight children, two boys and six girls.

It wasn't until 1973 that Jesus was able to break through all my resentment and bitterness. He showed me *His* pain. He brought me back again to the foot of His cross where I saw His sorrow and His suffering for my sins. There He cleansed me and I began to learn again to rejoice in Jesus alone, not in children or possessions or a good house. I asked my husband, my children, and the fellowship to forgive me.

Now Paul and I have peace and joy together again, and Jesus satisfies us.

## HOLDING TIGHTLY TOGETHER
### Gershon Karubara, Kirinyaga

My parents were not Christians so they brought me up in all the customs and ways of the Kikuyu and the traditions and remedies of the shaman. I was a herd boy, as was the custom.

When I was grown up, and before I got married, I went to church for the first time. I learned to read the Bible and chose to join the church, leaving many of the customs of my parents. I was baptized and confirmed while still unmarried. My intended wife was not with me in this, but in 1933 we were married in the church. I was considerably older than she was. I tried to follow Christian customs but my wife clung to her Kikuyu ways. In 1936 I went to Nairobi to begin work in the postal system, in which I continued until I was retired.

While I was in Nairobi, William Nagenda, Festo Kivengere and E. Matovu came from Uganda to preach the Gospel of salvation. That year, 1942, I was truly saved and began to be a part of the fellowship of the brothers and sisters in Nairobi. I was both strengthened and guided by the fellowship. First, I needed to tell others what the Lord had done for me. Next, Jesus began showing me things that grieved Him. For instance, one thing Jesus changed was my attitude of pride and dictatorship in my home. When I asked my wife to forgive me, she did, and also began listening to the Good News. Not long after that she also was saved.

Later when the Mau Mau Emergency was declared, there was great confusion in the land. It seemed to me that the Mau Mau were following the ways of Russia in throwing out Christianity. They said that Jesus was a white man, and white men came here to deceive us and take our land. Everything was being upset, but I found refuge in the fellowship with brethren. I didn't take the Mau Mau oath because God strengthened me.

In the end, our nation was granted its independence and we had our own president. But more important to me was that Jesus, the Prince of Peace, was ruler in my life and home, saving and keeping me. I knew that He was all I needed.

I have gone on in fellowship with those who walk with Jesus from 1942 until now, 1991, and He is my life. The enemy has tried to divide the fellowship into different camps, but we have held tightly together. Though we are of different churches and different tribes—Jaluo, Kikuyu, Abaluhya, Baganda, even English and Americans—we are all one in the Lord. Now I am waiting for Jesus to come again, having this sure hope that I will be with Him forever in heaven.

## A LONELY SEEKER
### Abraham Wamutitu Kibanya, Nyeri

My childhood was difficult because I was the only child of a wealthy witch doctor. My father had large herds and flocks that needed to be cared for. We were living on the land of a white settler near Rumuruti, so our animals had to be kept off his farm. When I was young I developed a passion to go to school and learn to read. But with all this work of herding animals, how could I? I tried going to school part-time, but my parents cried that I was disobedient and deserting them.

As a compromise, I started going to Sunday School. There I read the leaflets that we were given, and I practiced writing on smooth rocks. The more I learned about Jesus, the more I loved Him, but I couldn't find anyone, even at church, who could tell me how to belong to Him. The church there was the African Independent Pentecostal Church, and in all the time I was there I didn't hear anyone give a testimony. I did learn a few things though about the triune God, Father, Son and Holy Spirit, and I heard about the creation and how sin came in. So I knew I was a sinner, but I didn't know what to do about it. By the time I was 15 I was able to buy a Bible, and when I read that Jesus got up very early in the morning to go out and pray, I started doing that. When I heard the crow of the first cock before daylight, I would get up to pray.

One morning in 1945, before the cockcrow, I was lying awake in my little hut, separate from my parents' house, listening. Suddenly I heard a voice say, "You—Abraham!" and my blanket was pulled off. I lifted my head to look and saw that the hut was full of bright light, and standing at the door was a man all in white holding a sword. Oh, how I trembled. I covered my head with my arms in fear. The man said nothing more, and I said nothing—and soon it was dark again. But something had happened in my spirit. I was changed and strengthened, and I began to tell others about Jesus. Later in 1947 when I was in Rumuruti Town, a woman asked me where I had learned to preach. All I could reply was that I read the Bible. I was still preaching as much as I could until the Mau Mau uprising began.

My "Independent" church was very much involved in the politics of the fighters. Our church leaders told us all to take the Mau Mau oath, and one person kept after me until I took it too. But as I tasted the blood of the goat I knew instantly that this was wrong, and I was miserable in spirit. I cried to the Lord to help me find out how to be saved. I prayed, "O Jesus, You suffered for me, but I have refused to suffer for You!" The church leaders who were now Mau Mau told me that Jesus was not the Son of God and I must drop my "white" baptism name. But I wouldn't do that and insisted that He was God's Son. They warned me, "Anyone who has taken the oath with us and then changes his mind, we strangle him. You'd better watch out!"

I went away and cried again to the Lord: "You hear what they say. Help me!"

In September of 1952, I left Rumuruti and went to stay with an aunt in Kiganjo, Nyeri District. There I diligently read the Bible. More and more I became convicted that I was a sinner, and I longed to be saved. On July 3, 1953, I knelt down and prayed, "Lord, please forgive my sins!" Right away I had wonderful peace inside. Very soon Brother Christopher Gichuhi, who later was a pastor in Nairobi, came and asked how I was. I answered, "I have accepted Jesus as my Lord and Saviour!" We began to praise the Lord together and then with a sister named Susan and another sister—it was wonderful! This is how, after years of loneliness, I was introduced into the exceeding great joy of fellowship with brothers and sisters of the fellowship.

I was helped by Silas Muchina who praised the Lord that I had been saved and then asked, "Have you paid your debts yet?"

The Lord helped me to make some things right. I wrote a letter to confess to a white man that I had ruined some of his tools when I was younger. I asked forgiveness, telling him why I was writing, and if he put me in jail for it, that would be fair. I confessed to the white farmer that I had stolen a sheep, killed and eaten it with my friends. Also to an old man, a neighbor, whose hen had laid some eggs near our house, and I ate them. Later, after the war, I met him and paid for the eggs.

The brethren helped me in many ways to grow spiritually. There were some girls with whom I had committed sin, and one day I met two of them, and said, "Jesus has saved me, and has set me free from the kind of things we did, and He can do the same for you." I was pretty sure that I would never marry, but in 1967 when I was 43 years old, the brethren helped me and I was able to marry. We have had seven children! I became an evangelist-teacher in the Presbyterian Church, and then a pastor. Jesus is my Lord and Saviour daily, teaching me to be humble and quickly repent of the sins that creep in, and to quickly apologize. The greatest help I have is the constant fellowship of the brethren. Praise God for it!

# 8

## SURPRISING ENEMIES TODAY

*"Jesus Christ is the same yesterday, today, and forever."*
Hebrews 13:8 (TEV)

### INTRODUCTION

Thus far the stories in this book are set in the period of the Mau Mau Emergency of the 1950's. The narrators naturally are senior citizens now. Sometimes the question is raised: "Have the lessons these people learned then been useful to them in recent days?" and "Have they passed on to the next generation their faith and the lessons they learned?" Or, "Is their kind of walk with God able to make an impact in, for instance, the modern business world?" So we now include a testimony coming out of the business world, with its powerful temptations to greed. This is but one of many instances.

People also ask: "Since today there is no Mau Mau threat in Kenya, are there no dangers to be faced?" Here are some testimonies that shed light on this. The first is by the old-timers Heshbon and Elisheba Mwangi, whom you met before (in Chapter 3). They live in a rural area, but lust and greed produce criminals everywhere. And God's love and joy are still stronger than hate.

"But what about the cities and large towns where gangs are more sophisticated?" and "How do the children of the Revival meet the life-threatening dangers they face in the new materialistic godlessness of today? Is there any evidence that Jesus' command to 'love your enemies' has been heard by the younger generation in this area of Kenya?" Here are the stories of two of these children of "Revival Fellowship parents." They are well-educated, very modern, living in a city with up-to-date conveniences. Their homes were broken into

273

by gangs of thieves from the underworld. Such gangs in Kenya have become a serious problem. Their presence can be explained by unemployment, poverty, American movies, and other things. The fact is that they have murdered homeowners who resist them and have seriously hurt others who were simply frightened and uncooperative. Apparently the police are not eager to challenge these gangs face-to-face. Both of those who report here are young adults, with children at home. In these instances, the gangs that broke in were nonplussed by the calm and friendly attitude of the householders, and their genuine concern for them as persons having problems. You will see as you read that this made it hard for the robbers to know how to proceed.

Some have also asked this question: "Has the 'Revival Fellowship' movement faded away now?" Well, there is still an All East Africa Revival team meeting annually, representing Uganda, Tanzania and Kenya fellowships, and sponsoring the same kind of conventions they have had from the beginning. There is, I should mention, a different situation in each of these countries. In general, however, the attacks on the faith and lifestyle you found in this book have been many and serious. Erosion has occurred, so that in some areas only a few small, besieged groups can be found.

However, in Kenya's Central Province, as in many other places, the same revival fellowships are thriving. Young people have been catching the vision and there is a new generation of those who are committed to following the Lord at any cost. They are putting on their own rallies and in due course, perhaps, they will tell their story too.

There are currently in the '90's revival conferences, greatly influenced by East Africa, being held annually in Switzerland, Great Britain, Canada and the United States.

"How did it spread?" First through the East Africans themselves and under the ministry of Dr. Joe Church and other Ruanda missionaries. Then through the ministry and books of Roy Hession, Stanley Voke, the De Benoit family, Donald Jacobs and many others in England, Europe and America—so that the message has spread through many cultures and various denominations. Apparently the message of the power of God's amazing grace and the effectiveness of groups for spiritual fellowship, with both accountability and encouragement, applies universally.

† † †

## A BANKER'S INVESTMENT
### Moses Mahugu, Nyeri

I was brought up by Christian parents, but by the time I had finished school and teachers' college, I was doing all the sorts of things that other young men were doing. I was very fond of strong drink and chasing women. Even after my marriage I went right on with these things. Eventually I was fired from teaching because I had violated a schoolgirl. My wife and I had one child, but I was such a drunkard that we had no savings at all. One time when I was called for an interview, I knew I couldn't appear in my ragged, old clothes. I remembered that my wife had carefully put away her wedding dress in a box, so I took it and had a tailor make me a shirt out of part of it. The Lord is amazing! In His mercy He gave me work in a bank, which was an honorable position.

There came a time when I was disturbed by all of the filth in my life and my helplessness to change. I lived in a town where some saved brethren met every Thursday evening. They used to visit a different home each week, read the Bible, testify, sing and pray. I was present when they visited a neighbor of mine, and the Lord Jesus revealed Himself to me. On June 18, 1964, Jesus became my Saviour and transformed my life. After two days my wife also was saved and since that time we have lived together in peace and joy, united in Him.

My work in the bank changed from that day. I was able to tell all the rich, clever and educated people who came into the bank that Jesus had saved me. And the Lord blessed me in my work. From then on, I kept being promoted and finally became one of the officers of the bank. At that point I began to have more severe temptations—how should I deal with requests from my relatives and friends when they asked something that looked wrong in the light in which I was walking? The Lord helped me to refuse things that were dishonest or questionable, and this was a real victory in the Lord. He continued to bless me and eventually I was made Manager of a branch bank.

Now I was pressed even harder than ever with requests I could not grant. But the Lord took over for me in His lovingkindness. A person in that position always has a great many "friends" and bribes were offered me in many ways. I was offered a portion of a loan as a "commission," or people would try to prepay my bill at the service station or in a restaurant, but I always insisted on paying it anyway. What they did with the other person's money was their business. It was my job to live straight before the Lord. Some people brought presents to our home, such as a goat, in order to get a job at the bank for a son or daughter. Some tests were really hard, but every time the Lord told me "This is a bribe," I refused it without anger.

After twenty years of serving at the bank, a great celebration was planned in my honor because of "Twenty Years Service with No Fault." The head of our province, the District Commissioner, and other notable and good people were invited. When I heard about it, I said, "All right, go ahead, but I don't want even a drop of liquor to be served." This was because of my testimony that alcohol had ruined my early life, and I didn't want to touch it again. So the celebration went off with plenty of soft drinks served.

At their request, I went on working after the celebration for another seven years. Finally I knew I had reached the time when I should retire. My testimony was that I would continue to depend on the Lord all my life. I am praising the Lord who helped me to stand firm in His strength and to hope in Him. He is my refuge as I cry to Him. What I know for sure is that Jesus Himself knows how weak I am and all about me. And what He promises me is that in all my weakness He has been and will be my strength. I believe that strength and victory can be gotten nowhere else except in Jesus.

### HESHBON AND THE FIFTEEN
#### Heshbon & Elisheba Mwangi, Murang'a

On June 3, 1987, about 3 a.m., a gang of fifteen young men came to our house when we were asleep and beat on the door. When I heard them, I called out, "Who are you, beating the door?" No answer. Then I shouted, "Stop! I'll open it for you! Don't hit it again, I'm coming to open it!"

I got up immediately and unlocked the door for them. Then I found that they had broken a window and unlocked the kitchen door and all fifteen had come in. So my wife, Elisheba, and I sat down peacefully in our living room to watch and talk with them. They were hurriedly inspecting all our things. They took my watch first.

Shining their big flashlight in our eyes, they said, "Now don't you raise a hue and cry to call neighbors!"

With a smile, I answered, "In this house we don't raise a hue and cry, we pray to God! Besides that, when people raise a cry they are calling for the young men to come to help; but all our young men are already here in the house, so who could we call?" Amazingly I found I was full of love and concern for these boys, and this helped us to talk to them quietly without fear.

"Bring us your money!" they shouted. So we gave them all we had on hand. I had been to the bank to get the money to pay for repairs on the church—365 shillings (about $50). They took that money and some clothes, my camera, tape recorder and portable clock.

When I saw these, I said, "Say, young men, this recorder has never spoken anything but God's Word, so you probably don't want that. Would you like to leave it here?"

They said, "Yes," and gave it back.

"And say! How about the small watch? I'm a person who likes to be on time everywhere. Would you like to give that back, too?"

One of them handed it to Elisheba and said, "Mama, here! Give it to him."

Then they asked for the keys to my car, and I handed them over. Then I noticed those were not the right keys and I called, "Oh forgive me, I've given you the wrong keys. Bring those and take these." They did that.

After a little while they came back in and said, "Mzee, come here! Show us how to turn on the headlights!"

So I went, reached in and said, "Take hold of this knob and turn it this way and the lights come on. To turn them off, turn the knob back. O.K.?" So he did that and the lights came on. They locked us into our bedroom and then all fifteen and their loot were piled into our small five-passenger car! We could hear them take off at great speed down our very pot-holed dirt road, so it was not surprising that the car soon broke down and stopped. They left it there and took someone else's pickup truck.

Neighbors began to come over, and unlocked our bedroom door. I said, "Let's pray for them that no one gets killed." We went outside and joined hands in prayer for them with great compassion.

We truly loved our enemies that night.

### ALONE WITH THE THUGS
Grace K. Muguongo, Nyeri

I love Jesus. He is the Saviour of my life. He saved me when I was a young schoolgirl, and He has been with me until today. He gives me strength and leads me in His victory. I am working now in the

Kimathi Institute of Technology as a secretary. I am married, and my husband and I have five children.

One Friday night in April of 1984, at 2 a.m., my home was attacked by thieves. I was asleep, and so were my two small children. The older child was away in boarding school, and my husband was head teacher of a distant school. So that night we were alone.

The thieves came into our house after breaking the front door with a heavy stone. I didn't hear that, but my mother had taught me to listen for the voice of Jesus, and I heard Him speaking to me before they reached my bedroom door. I have lived with Him for years, and I knew it was His voice calling me, saying, "Grace, thieves have come, and they will leave."

I woke up and said, "Thank You, Lord."

I reached for my flashlight as they were coming into my bedroom. The thieves had knives, clubs, and a flashlight. They said, "Turn on the light."

As I turned on the room light, I told them, "I won't watch you. You go ahead with your stealing, and I will go on praying." I was asking Jesus to change my appearance, as His was changed on the mountain when He was transfigured—so the thieves wouldn't see me as a helpless and desirable lady, but as a strong person of God, whom they must fear. He did this, and I had no fear. From then on, I saw these men as ordinary sons of Adam who could not overcome me. I knew I was on God's victorious side.

They gathered up many of our things and put them in a pile. After they carried these items into the sitting room, I got up. I was in my nightdress. They told me they were taking the TV. I thanked them, and asked if they wanted me to get them some food. They said no, they would look for food themselves and sit on the floor to eat, which they did. I sat on a chair and asked God to bring me the watchmen, but Jesus told me that they wouldn't come at all. Then I told Him, "All right. I am sitting here like Jacob looking at the angels of God on the ladder, and I know that I am seated at the foot of the Throne of Grace."

When they were finished eating the food, they told me to stand up. I asked permission to put on my clothes, but they refused, so I picked up a sweater that was there, and we went outside. They said, "Ma'am, take these things back into the house." And they returned many items, including some good clothes. They were trying to take both of my big sewing machines: the one I use for braiding and the one for sewing. They also wanted a large box with my wedding clothes, and some double bed sheets. It was too much. Finally they said, "This is the machine we will take, but you must carry one end."

I said, "All right, but let me get the cover for it." I brought the cover that fit over the machine and helped them by carrying one end of it. One of them carried the other end.

On the way, one of them said, "What is it with you? Are you a saved person? Aren't you afraid to die?"

I said, "Why should I fear death? It is just the beginning of ever-lasting life. Just now you think that whether I live or die is in your hands, but it isn't. God will make that decision." We walked on and they didn't ask any more questions. We walked up into the forest. It was a long way, about two and a half miles, and I knew that they could kill me there with no one seeing or knowing it. But there was light in the dark forest. We reached a grass clearing surrounded by bushes where we put the loads down. Some of them went to collect property they had stolen from others.

During that time, the Spirit of the Lord filled me. I looked at them and pitied them. I said, "Now God bless you all greatly! This work you are doing is very hard, and it is very cold. May the Lord change your work to daytime work. This job has great difficulties."

They were very surprised, and one said, "Let the woman go!"

I said, "The Lord bless you and give you riches so you can stop doing work like this."

They said, "Mama, pray for us!" And they released me to go home.

I didn't even think about the dangers of walking alone at night, I just hurried to reach home. On the way I noticed for the first time that I had no shoes on. But no thorns had hurt my feet! I was amazed that the thieves really had seen me not as a weak woman but as a strong person to respect. Not one of them had touched me. I laughed for joy as I thought of my captors who had tried to frighten me. When I got home, my children were still asleep!

Then I began to get nervous and wondered about calling my child in boarding school. But it was night, and I realized that Jesus had been with me all through this, so why was I bothered now? I did call my principal and he was astounded. He called the police, but it took them a long time to come.

I saw the power of the Lord in all this, and realized that to Him there is no day or night, they are both alike to Him. And if God wants to use His child, He makes the way. A few years after this, the

principal was saved, and there were others also. I had never thought
that the Lord could use me for the salvation of others. I have lived
with Jesus since I was in fourth grade, and actually before that too,
because my parents were Christians and taught me from the beginning to walk with Jesus.

### THIEVES MEET THE CHILDREN
### Wilfred Nderitu Gichuki, Nyeri
### (Principal, Kimathi Institute of Technology)

My parents were saved, and my mother, who was a very committed
Christian, died in September of 1988. I had been principal of Kimathi
Institute of Technology for ten years. I held offices in the church;
however this didn't stop me from drinking and doing all sorts of evil
things.

One Sunday morning in November of 1988, I was standing before
the students when I felt a great Power come down over me. I was
crying and told the students, "I have decided to join the Lord's side
from this day." The Christian students were jubilant. I went to church
and although it was a rather formal service where people don't
usually get a chance to testify, I couldn't calm down until I told the
congregation what Jesus had done. Since then I have found the hand
of the Lord helping me in everything.

Now let me tell you what happened at my home on the 28th of
August, 1990. It was late at night when my wife woke me up because
she had heard a bang on a downstairs door. Our children, ages 15, 12
and 6, woke up and came into our bedroom. I opened our front
window and looked out. I was hit hard by a stone thrown by the
people who were outside. Obviously a gang of robbers was breaking
into the house. I locked that window and opened others at the back
of the apartment.

When they broke into the downstairs apartment, the woman tenant
there and her children started screaming. Four of the robbers went in
and told them to shut up. They beat the lady enough to make her
keep quiet. Then they took what they wanted and put it outside.

By this time we realized that we had no lights. They had removed
the fuse from the main electric transformer which was outside the
house. They also had cut the telephone wire and used it to tie up the
night watchman. I found out later that they had locked the doors of
all the workers who live around us, about thirty of them, so there
was no help to be had from them. We realized there was nothing else

we could do, so we started praying. We prayed hard.

As they finished looting the downstairs apartment, I heard them say they wanted the principal's house. They started pounding on our outside door with big rocks. They must have done that for about 15 or 20 minutes. Finally, they used axes to hack it down and came through. Once they were in our sitting room, they started hacking at the second door.

By now we had seriously committed ourselves as a family to the Lord in forty minutes of prayer, holding hands and each one saying to Him, "Lord, if this is the day for me to die, then let it be. I am ready. Please receive me."

Finally the men were in the corridor coming up to our bedroom, so I opened the two other doors that were upstairs and told them, "Welcome, gentlemen, to our bedroom." They came in. They had axes and long knives and they threatened my wife, demanding that I give them money. I told them I didn't keep money in the house. All this time my wife and I were praying quietly and the children were praying out loud. In between the children's prayers, they kept asking for money, and I kept saying I didn't have any here. Surprisingly we discovered that even thieves have some fear of God, for they would wait for a prayer to finish before asking again for money.

Discouraged with this, they went back to the sitting room, telling us to prepare to leave. I said, "No, there is nothing that can harm you in this house, and besides God is giving us a chance to pray for your welfare." We prayed that the Lord would give them money enough to feed their families and supply their needs without having to do such dangerous work. We also prayed that they would be able to leave our house without being caught. I knew these weren't our words, it was God who put them in our mouths. There they were, armed, but they acted as if they were scared! We realized that the Lord and His angels were there and that the atmosphere was so charged with spiritual power that our attackers couldn't do a thing, and we were kept from harm.

Some of them kept searching for money; however, before long they started to move out, taking only my wife's leather handbag! We waited five or ten minutes, thinking they would come back. But they were gone. God gave us courage through this ordeal. But after they left, we were scared just thinking what might have happened. We looked around to see what they had taken and to our surprise the TV and radios were there and everything else was intact. We even found my wife's handbag lying on the ground outside with a hundred-shilling note inside. The only things they took from it were a coin purse with 18 shillings, a watch needing repair, and the two booklets she had carried: *How to Focus on Christ*, and *How to Walk with the Lord*. We thought they had taken our house keys, but we found them a few days later after I had already had all the locks changed.

So we saw the hand of the Lord. The police came after a few days and took our statements. They commented on the general lawlessness in the country. Nevertheless, I have no gun in the house or any weapons, nothing—just Jesus. The experience left us better Christians. We are more committed to the Lord because we have personally discovered that it is only the Lord who can save you; you cannot save yourself.

We have heard that in all the other houses that were attacked that night, the people tried to fight and got hurt. And many things of value were taken. So now even non-Christians are seeing the power of prayer.

That is not the end of my story. Almost four months later, that gang, or another, came again. It was before bedtime, and only my wife and children were at home. As was our custom, and as we always do now, my family had prayed that evening: "Lord, we are covering all the doors, all the windows, the whole of this house with the blood of Jesus Christ. And we are praying for the watchman and everybody here, that each of us will be protected with the blood of Jesus Christ. And as we sleep, Lord, take over. We know that to stay awake is useless. It is only You who can take care of this home."

So when the eight robbers came, they didn't touch any of the doors. They did fight with the watchman about three or four yards from our house, but he managed to beat them off! Soon other people came, and praise be to the Lord, the thieves ran away. They hadn't cut the wires or touched the lights or the doors. In this we saw the hand of the Lord on us once again. This has nothing to do with my wife's or my faithfulness, it was only the grace of God. We recommend Him to others, because He can save, He can protect, and He can do all the things we cannot do.

# APPENDIX

HISTORICAL SIDELIGHTS
By Joel Murega, Ngobia

## How the Independent Schools and Churches Began
### (The Protestant Ban on Female Circumcision)

An old custom of the Kikuyu was to circumcise girls as well as boys (by excising the clitoris). But in February 1928, the Anglican, Presbyterian and Africa Inland Mission missionaries took a stand against it. Their medical people pointed out that a great number of girls died because of the practice, and that it caused difficulties in childbirth for the others. Together with a few church elders, the decision was made to outlaw female circumcision in church families. This caused a division in the churches and a majority of Kikuyu people withdrew, calling themselves the "Independent Church." Jomo Kenyatta and his followers allied themselves with these Independents and began to promulgate an oath that they would follow the old customs of their fathers. They then established their own independent schools, hoping to maintain higher education.

When the Emergency was declared, the colonial government closed all of these schools because the teachers were loyal to Kenyatta and had taken this oath. This caused an angry division among the people, and most of those involved in the Independent schools automatically became freedom fighters, either in the forest or in their villages. There was much hatred, and a number of white settlers were killed as well as some of the tribal people who did not take the oath. We Kenyans were in great danger, because there was no way of knowing which of our neighbors was truly friendly and which was about to kill us. Those were terrible days.

## How "Development" Continued During the Fighting

The government wanted to continue with plans for development even though the Mau Mau war was going on. They moved most Kikuyu people off their farms and into "protected villages." The appointed Chiefs were told to encourage the people to continue cultivating the land. The authorities also wanted schools to stay open. They informed the people that if they sent their children to school this would be a sign that they were not fighting the government. And a way for them to earn government subsidies would be to plant coffee. (The Mau Mau had forbidden, under penalty of death, the growing of coffee, as it was a white man's crop.) So of course the government kept a watch on the Chiefs to see if they and their people sent their children to school and planted coffee. As a result, in some areas the schools were full and much coffee was planted. The government tried to keep a close watch also to prevent bribery, and were concerned that women's self-help meetings continue with activities for the advancement of women. Children were taught about health and the importance of cleanliness. These projects all continued to some degree during the war.

## Mzee Jomo Kenyatta

When he began to rule the new nation, Kenyatta suprised his people by announcing that there must be no revenge taken. He said, "If a father is killed, his children want revenge and there is no end to the killing. So what we need to do now is to forgive one another." He was able to enforce this only because he was so honored and admired that his every word was obeyed. Dr. Kiano who had been in prison with Kenyatta was also listened to. He reinforced Kenyatta's stand on forgiveness, so the nation was founded very peacefully. Schools and hospitals could be built. The coffee industry thrived, and enmity was laid aside. There was friendship among church people of all denominations. Now they were able to work together on community projects. Aid for those in special need was a concern shared by all.

Our God is greatly to be praised!